UNDERSTANDING
CHILD ABUSE
AND
NEGLECT
IN CONTEMPORARY CARIBBEAN SOCIETY

A Recipe For Change

BEATRICE E. KIRTON

AuthorHouse™
1663 Liberty Drive
Bloomington, IN 47403
www.authorhouse.com
Phone: 1-800-839-8640

First published by AuthorHouse   10/12/2011

ISBN: 978-1-4670-3832-4 (sc)
ISBN: 978-1-4670-3833-1 (ebk)

Library of Congress Control Number: 2011916878

Printed in the United States of America

ABOUT THE AUTHOR

Mrs Kirton has been working as a clinical social worker in the child protection team at the Barbados Child Care Board for eleven years. She served as the child abuse coordinator of the team for ten of those years. As a full time team leader, she gained widespread experience in the detection, prevention and treatment of child abuse and neglect while working with children and families. This resulted in her frequent appearances in court as a material and expert witness. She has lectured extensively on the subject and was a representative at conferences on child abuse and neglect both nationally and internationally.

Originally from Barbados, she completed her formal training in the United Kingdom graduating with a Diploma in child psychology and a Certificate and Diploma in social work from the University of Kingston-Upon—Thames. U.K.

Since working in the field of child abuse she has received many requests and enquiries on the subject. Her knowledge and experience in this field prompted her decision to author this Book.

Contents

ACKNOWLEDGEMENTS

I would like to thank the many people who helped me in the preparation of this Book.

To Jean Sadbobjr who was my case work supervisor in the Department of Social Services UK, where I was employed and to whom I owe special gratitude for her influence in my professional development. My appreciation to the Administration at the Barbados Child Care Board who gave me the opportunity to follow through and enhance my expertise in child abuse and neglect management. This was achieved through knowledge and skills from my participation in seminars, workshops, symposia and conferences nationally and throughout the Caribbean region. This exposure enabled me to work efficiently and effectively. To my many students of adult learning from across the Caribbean and other individuals who shared their experiences and observations of Caribbean family life with me. To my son Michael, who formatted the draft and provided literary advice. To my husband for his patience and understanding, while I researched and typed the manuscript. I give praise and thanks to the Almighty who has given me the wisdom, inspiration and courage to carry out the research in writing this Book.

FOREWORD

The Islands of the Caribbean also known as the West Indies are an archipelago or chain of Islands between North and South America from Florida to the coast of Venezuela and separating the Caribbean Sea and the Gulf of Mexico from the Atlantic Ocean.

In his publication 'The West Indies illustrated" Mc Millan, A. described in great detail the discovery of the Caribbean, including its history, commerce and industry.

According to extracts from Macmillan's writings, "The Caribbean" is named after the Caribs, which were one of the dominant Amerindian groups in the region at the time of European contact during the late 15th century.

The name "West Indies" originated from Christopher Columbus's idea that he had landed in the West Indies when he had actually reached the Americas. The great explorer as he was known thought he had actually succeeded in reaching the East Indies by a western route which was always his aim and ambition to do. As it were, he was discoverer of nearly all the Islands, the first being San Salvador in the Bahamas in 1492. On his second voyage, he discovered British Guyana, Trinidad and Tobago, Grenada and St. Vincent. It was not until 1502 that St. Lucia was raised from her obscurity. However, for many years after the discovery of these Islands by Christopher Columbus, they remained in possession of Spain.

The only Island of importance which Columbus did not seem to have visited was Barbados which was first discovered by the Portuguese in 1536. The earliest British settlements were made in this Island.

However, St. Kitts is entitled to be called the mother colony of the West Indies, for although Barbados was visited in1605 by the crew of the sailing vessel the "Olive Blossom" it was not definitely settled until 1626 while St. Kitts was colonised in 1623 by Sir Thomas Warner.

Natives of the English speaking Caribbean are usually referred to as West Indians and the use of the terms are used interchangeably.

The nations of Belize and Guyana although on the mainland of Central America respectively are former British Colonies and maintain many cultural ties to the Caribbean.

The present population of the Caribbean is of a decidedly cosmopolitan character which includes Negroes, East Indians, and Red-leg whites as they are culturally referred to, Chinese, French, Spanish, Portuguese, Syrians, Americans and Europeans. The bulk of Caribbean inhabitants are Negroes who are the descendants of the slaves who were imported from West Africa. In British Guyana and Trinidad and Tobago, East Indians form a large proportion of their population while in Barbados there is an abundance of this population for its size.

In recognition of the Caribbean generally, it would be almost remiss not to make some reference to its climate and scenery which may be counted among the most valuable assets. The extreme heat of the tropical sun tempered with the north-east trade winds and their unspoilt landscape and beautiful beaches make the Islands of the Caribbean a favourite destination for vacationers and the envy of many travellers from North America and Europe.

In the Caribbean, there are no sharp marked changes between winter and summer. The main difference between seasons is the amount of rainfall due to the hurricane season from June to November which plays a large role in bringing rainfall to the Islands and can be very devastating to homes and crops.

Between 1958 and 1962, most of the British controlled Islands became a West Indian Federation and struggled to survive on their own or under the control of colonial power before they separated into many separate nations having slowly emerged from a state of hopeless depression.

During the 19th Century, some nations gained independence from European powers while some smaller Islands are still dependencies today. All things considered, there is much to be said in favour of the realization of the prophesy that while the 18th century was the greatness of the West Indies under colonial rule, and the 19th century that of their depression, the entry of the 20th century saw the restoration to prosperity where many of the Islands declared political independence as a means to providing a better way of life for its people and bring about an end to the indignity of colonial rule."

Although some of the Islands are still dependent upon agriculture for their sustainability, with a growing commercial and industrial potential for diversity, other Islands saw increasing national wealth and income through a steady growth in commercial trade and a flourishing Tourism industry.

Because the English speaking Caribbean is so extensive and embraces so many countries, the author found it almost impossible to include all of them in this work. However, an effort is made to portray the social and economic conditions which impact negatively on the livelihood of children and their families in the English speaking Caribbean including Guyana and Belize because of their resembling colonial histories.

In reality, the Islands of the Caribbean are more than a geographical expression, but also a distinctive socio-economic order manifested in social stratification, economic disadvantages, social structures and cultural contradictions that will persist with little or no change.

Social Stratification in Caribbean Culture

Smith, M.G. 1984, a leading Caribbean scholar described the Caribbean as a cluster of countries with great cultural complexities where regional differences can be explained in terms of a class and caste system. In this respect we can see how social class and ethnicity can create variations in family life and economic viability. Understanding these variations can give us a more sophisticated understanding of contemporary family life styles as they operate in the Caribbean region, and how these variations impact the well-off and the not so well-off citizens. For example, the upper class emphasize lineage and the maintenance of family position which also affects their behaviour where they do not see themselves as simply a member of the nuclear family but rather that of a larger family tradition where there is much concern about family tradition and the status quo. Lower class families on the other hand do not often have the worry about family status, but are more concerned about them and their children's survival such as being able to manage their finances and other crises creating special challenges in their child rearing practices and other basic needs normally associated with life in poverty. While the gap between the rich and the poor within Caribbean society remains wide so too is the gap between its rich and poor citizens which can be attributed to their weak and dependent position in the global economy characterized by poverty and the caste system of stratification. However, the range and rigidity of Caribbean classes are not separated mainly by differences of colour, status, power and wealth alone; they also exhibit diverse cultural patterns and social frameworks. These differences reflect in, and help to validate class stereotypes where both of these classes at opposite ends of the nations hierarchy reflects the importance of ascribed status and achieved status. Research has shown how the ascribed status of this group is particularly vulnerable to many socio-economic disadvantages such as unemployment, poorly paid employment and in many cases end up on the lower end of the occupational ladder. Richard Jenkins 1991.

Carl Stone 1973 in his research puts forward a rather different economic model of social stratification in the capitol and stressed its difference from society alternatives including an illuminating study of the relations of political attitudes and behaviour in Kingston, Jamaica to social class. His major thesis is that:

"Material affluence and income are the main determinants of social status in contemporary urban Jamaica, although race, education, training and class acculturation clearly affect the economic life chances of the individual. This is not to suggest, however, that other factors such as race, colour and occupational prestige do not influence social status. It merely implies that in the weighting of these categories, income level is the principle determinant of status."

It is equally clear that over and beyond the dimensions of status, power and economic controls among the upper classes, the definition, conditions and types of imperative control does not include every mode of exercising power or influence over the lower classes. Weber, M.1971.

For many years, the nature and basis of Caribbean societies have been concerned and sought to clarify the roles and relations of class and culture and how these influence social structure and sound critical understanding of relevant evidence of economic status and social position and the restricted mobility between these groups. Smith, M.G. 1984 contends that the social and economic order of the lower classes, are not the same because they live under adverse economic conditions of existence. These include a lack of monopolization of ideas, material goods and opportunities and a disproportionately small share of the national income all of which separates their way of life and their culture from other classes. These families face the problem of being unable to perform in accordance with their society's dominant values because they lack the necessary resources to offset the pressure of environmental conditions and social integration. It is here that distinct and individual behaviour patterns and family systems emerge, and where changing social structures, family types, trends and needs can give rise to appalling and tragic situations that can have a profound effect on Caribbean family life.

Political Behaviour in the Caribbean—Participation and Apathy

Mintz and Price 1985 describe the Caribbean region as the only areas in the third world where politics based on free elections and liberal democratic freedom are still prominent. The guiding principle here is that since the Caribbean islands share a common way of life they should together achieve a total result in their economic and political development. In theory a representative democracy will function most effectively and fairly if government leaders familiar themselves with the process of political socialization. It is against this background that the issue of Caribbean integration has emerged under the recommendation of the West Indian Commission. However, on the wider economic and political scene the reality of small Island States is that integration does not guarantee economic prosperity without the pooling of resources and the unification in making important decisions, because an economic system cannot exist in a vacuum. In their study of politics and government, political scientists are concerned with social interactions among political groups and their impact on the larger political and economic order. Lasswell, Harold, D.1936. It could be argued then that if the need for power is the guiding light in the Caribbean political arena, this could account for the wavering commitment to integration by some regional authorities.

PREFACE

Child abuse and neglect has been a feature of societies for centuries. However, until within recent times it had received little attention in Caribbean society because of a lack of public awareness of the scope of the problem, its complexities and the lack of understanding that families who live in adverse social and economic situations need to be supported and protected. Because of this lack of perception, various forms of abuse within these vulnerable families have been identified. Many psychologists in their theoretical research and practical experiences hold the view that sources of stress within families at times have a negative impact on a child's health, development and wellbeing either directly or because they affect the capacity of parents to respond to their children's needs. In a Caribbean context, families that fail in meeting the needs of their children paint an agonising picture of families predominantly from low socio-economic backgrounds resulting from poverty related conditions impact on the lives of children in Caribbean society. It is essential that we recognize further that not all abuse and neglect is a consequence of poverty to the exclusion of other environmental or intra-familial factors such as family structure, homelessness and unemployment in particular.

Overtime, there has been considerable public concern about the changing structure of the family, particularly in the effect that these changes may have on Caribbean child rearing habits. Although research is limited in this area there is still some value in providing a brief overview of the available research into the relationship between child maltreatment in the context of family functioning in Caribbean society. Today, with the seriousness of the problem growing a multifaceted approach is needed to reflect the desires of every one to break the cycle of this dreadful disease by placing emphasis on education and prevention efforts. It is therefore in the best interest of children and families that communities and Governments make a concerted effort to combat this problem. Other contributing factors are associated with cultural values and attitudes of families who do not understand the fundamentals of effective child rearing where it is accepted that parents are expected to perpetuate abusive behaviour particular as methods of discipline.

The focus of this book is an attempt to add substantively to the existing literature on what is currently known about deprived families and their influence on child abuse and neglect in the English speaking Caribbean, and to share with others the complexity of deprivation, hardship and distress which afflicts the lives of individuals and families primarily from the rural and urban areas who are described as unskilled and economically vulnerable, and those whose roles and relations are influences by cultural practices and economic conditions. Given the overwhelming nature of these psychological consequences it is therefore not surprising the impact these deprivations have on the way children are raised within diverse cultures and the lack of child care needs and objectives. One primary concern is to determine the precise significance for social relations of each of these factors in differing historical and contemporary contexts, and the existential reality of family life together with their specific implications and cultural traditions

Many psychologists in their theoretical research and practical experiences hold the view that sources of stress within families at times have a negative impact on a child's health, development and wellbeing either directly or because they affect the capacity of parents to respond to their children's needs. As citizens of Caribbean society it is their responsibility to nurture, protect from social ills and create a safe environment for Caribbean children to survive and grow up, and to ensure that services are provided to allow their parents to take on the responsibility for their own and their family's needs. From a Caribbean perspective, families that fail in meeting the needs of their children, paint an agonizing picture of families predominantly with low socio-economic backgrounds resulting from poverty related conditions and the way these adverse conditions impact on the lives of their children. It is necessary to recognize further that not all abuse and neglect are a consequence of poverty to the exclusion of other environmental or intra-familial factors such as family structure, homelessness, drug and alcohol misuse, low income and unemployment.

In all situations, members of a common society are internally distinguished by fundamental differences in their institutional practices and at all levels of the social structure within which child abuse and neglect occurs drawing on the analytical tools of such disciplines as its history, its economic challenges, sociology, psychology and social anthropology.

To further advance our understanding of the dynamics of these structures there must be an understanding of cultural realities of existing practices within the dynamics of Caribbean family life while recognising the result of multiple forces that impact the family

The Book attempts to draw an association between socio-economic deprivation and child abuse and neglect and considers the implications for community wide prevention strategies. The Author opined that the size and gravity of the problem as it relates to poverty, deprivation and child maltreatment is crucially dependent upon the effectiveness of the Caribbean research community to better recognise and confront measures to alleviate these environmental and socio-economic pressures especially among the disadvantaged and the working poor within Caribbean communities which can seriously impair parenting capacity.

In keeping with the theme of this Book are strategies for improving the chronic conditions where parents facing issues of instability are not able to provide basic nurturance and care for their children. For example, if social and economic disadvantage which produce stressful living conditions contribute to the abuse and neglect, decreasing the likelihood of future abuse would be through attempting to improve their living conditions which are marked by family life style, chronic poverty, unemployment, mental health disorders, substance abuse, homelessness, substandard housing, and community violence therefore reducing overwhelming stress factors thus eliminating the need for maltreatment of their children.

In order to advance understanding of the dynamics of family structures and how parenting is conducted in most Caribbean families in contemporary society, there must likewise be an understanding of the psycho-social realities of existing practices where parents with abusing histories need to have some insight into what stress factors contribute to their children being at risk psychologically and socially. Many factors have been proposed to explain why adults abuse and neglect children, however, there is no one factor that can explain why an adult has abused or neglected a child in each and every case as it is likely that multiple factors are at work in each situation

At a broader societal level, Chapter 1 focuses on the evolution of childhood through the historical records where children were treated very poorly by parents or caregivers from as recent as 1962 through the period of rapid change. It addresses the need to examine the characteristics of parents or caregivers who are deemed to be abusive to children when stress levels are very high. These stresses can also be caused by, or lead to substance abuse or alcohol; and the characteristics of children who are vulnerable to be abused or at risk of abuse especially for certain forms of abuse. Chapter 2 explains how child abuse and neglect are usually defined in terms of the condition of the child or the action of the parent or caregiver. It also features the principle idea that for a situation to be defined as child abuse and neglect there must be certain definable and avoidable parental behaviour in relation to the child. Chapter 3 features discussion regarding learning to recognize the signs of child abuse and neglect which is the first step in helping to protect children from harm and has significant implications for their health and development. Further discussion in this chapter is to take a closer look at the family situation to determine suspicion especially when these signs appear repeatedly or in combination. Chapter 4 emphasises that all child care professionals are expected to recognize and respond to child abuse and neglect because recognizing and reporting is important to promote child safety, health and welfare through the provision of supportive, protective or therapeutic intervention. It incorporates the need for mandated reporters and other interested persons to understand their reporting responsibilities through ongoing training programmes. Chapter 5 discussed the obstacles which confront the ability to adequately gauge the amount of child abuse and neglect in

Caribbean society. Nevertheless, a comparison was made between available statistics from within the Caribbean and those from North America and Great Britain. When viewed together they suggest the commonality and scope of child abuse and neglect as a major problem Chapter 6 focuses on the structure, functions and expectations of the family within Caribbean society where there is gradual erosion of the extended family, where gender roles are less rigid due to the changing role of women in the family, and the changing traditional role of men where fathers are gaining connection with their children, and where co-dependence develop among members living in overcrowded situations. This chapter also discusses these changes which may be positive or negative, functional or prohibitive with the trend toward teenage pregnancy, single parents families, the stress of role change, gender issues in performing prescribed roles and the lack of parental skills where stresses occur in the flow of transactions that influence the probability of the occurrence of child abuse and neglect. Chapter 7 suggests that child rearing in Caribbean society is emerging from an era in which many widely held beliefs, values, attitudes and practices have been out of harmony with the genetically influenced nature and needs of the developing child. Throughout history, parents have sought to produce orderly behaviour in their children. Their degree of reliance upon disciplinary measures as a form of chastisement to instil values and behaviour should be based on expectations that are appropriate for the age of the child acknowledging that they do not have the knowledge, skills, abilities or resources to pro-actively manage the myriad of conditions and circumstances to which they are vulnerable. Neither can they personally assure that their needs are met. This chapter draws reference to the building of a positive relationship between the parent and child that require a lot of effort to make that relationship strong and successful because it is understood that children who experience a warm and loving relationship with their parent or parent figure tend to feel good about themselves and perform better whether at home, at school or with their friends. This self-assurance can provide them with a solid foundation that will facilitate their pro-social development. This chapter further explores the qualities in the socializing process of the child which is dependent upon whether and how parents communicate their love to the child and which helps to ensure that both parent and child stay connected. Parental correction and guidance can and does take different forms. However, while discipline is necessary to teach a child how to live comfortably in a society, it should not be confused with punishment. Chapter 8 defines the standard definition and indicators of child abuse and neglect, and identifies the many factors that may contribute to the occurrence. It addresses such issues as acts of omission and commission by parents or other adults. This behaviour can be either physical or emotional and is associated with physical injury, delayed growth and development and the child's vulnerability to sexual abuse. The chapter further discusses some of the many factors that contribute to the occurrence of child abuse and neglect in Caribbean society and emphasizes the fact that while there is no standard definition the term encompasses a broad range of harmful acts perpetrated against children due to parents inability to cope with the stresses resulting from their socio-economic conditions and other environmental factors, and the effect these harmful acts can have on the psycho-social development of the child. Chapter 9 gives an explanation of the term incest which encompasses sexual behaviours with a variety of patterns, variations, causes, relationships and effects stressing the dysfunctional nature of the family and their vulnerability to the trauma with all its horrific and long lasting consequences affecting all the relationships caused by the intra-familial abuse. The chapter looks at the general behaviour changes that may occur in children who are victims of incest which is often the result of some form of seduction. It also examines the difficulty in accurately estimating the incidence or its prevalence because it is not well documented. Also the rigidity of boundaries with regards to outsiders rendering them socially, psychologically and physically isolated. The chapter finally tries to incorporate all of the theoretical frameworks used in the formulation of a safety plan to prevent future offences through treatments such as individual and family therapy. Chapter 10 features research information which indicates that child sexual abuse is a serious problem within Caribbean society and occurs more frequently than people realise. The aim of this chapter is to put in perspective the problem of child sexual abuse and the association between what behaviours and social conditions contribute to it. Also described are the different types of sexual activity which range from acts that are not necessarily of a violent or forceful nature, and offences that do not include intimacy yet leave psychological scars. The chapter further focused on society's attitude and cultural beliefs about holding the victims responsible for the transgressions committed against them which lead to a sense that the child victim must have provoked a sexual relationship. Chapter11 attempts to cover all the stages of the court process from the preliminary protection hearing to the prevention of unnecessary removal of children from their homes and making appropriate arrangements for those who are unable to be reunited with their families.

Chapter 12 addresses the attitudes and customs relating to the age of consent for sexual activity within Caribbean multi-cultural society where the law is slightly different among certain groups and where child marriages are customary. The chapter also discusses issues within the cultural milieu where children cannot validly consent to sexual activity yet are considered to have reached physical or psychological maturity at different times even though they are not sufficiently mature to make an informed decision. Chapter 13 aims to give an overview of the standards and approaches to prevention goals and treatment strategies through an evaluation of essential resources recognizing that these interventions are seen as keys to successful prevention services and protective factors that can increase the health and wellbeing of children and families. This chapter also looks at how comprehensive treatment services are dedicated to helping abused children and their family overcome and heal the trauma of abuse while attempting to break the cycle of abuse in all its forms. Included in the chapter is the essential role of the therapist in recognising children who have been the subject of abuse and intervening effectively by breaking into these complex and destructive patterns of family dynamics.

The following Appendices amplify the inter-agency management procedures by outlining how agencies and professionals should work effectively and cooperatively to protect children from abuse and neglect; also to safeguard and promote their welfare through the availability of preventive services required for effective work in the case where there is a risk that children might need to be removed from their home into protective care. They examine aspects of the child abuse and neglect management system code of practice for all levels of professionals involved in tackling child abuse and neglect.

The Appendices also describe the level of activities needed to provide services to children at risk of abuse and their families starting with the screening of referrals to the social service agency intake team which includes the initial investigation, the inter-agency case conference, the criteria for registration, the monitoring of parent/child relationships and the need for ongoing intervention and closure.

Consistent with the agency's standard for training and qualification in good social work practice requires designated individuals with the careful exercise of professional skills and judgement to offer specialist advice or expertise in order to manage complex child abuse cases.

CHAPTER 1

INTRODUCTION

Despite the promotion of development within Caribbean Society, there is the need to examine current trends, problems and needs where there is a preponderance of child maltreatment among to Caribbean children due to socio-economic conditions among the poor and disadvantaged groups.

For years child abuse prevention programmes have been expanding from purely child survival concerns to include components which foster the healthy psychological and social development of children. This is in recognition of the fact that physical survival and early psycho-social development are interdependent in intricate ways, and that the intellectual and emotional aspects of a child's life should not be separated from his physical wellbeing. It would seem that the identification of children who are at risk psychological must take into account existing child rearing practices, the society's express goals in raising children and its belief about the potential and nature of children. Parents who need help in adapting to the new modern situation need to feel that some traditional practices in how they raise their children have positive values and that their attempts to integrate change into their child rearing practices are based on essential sound instincts. In the Caribbean, in both rural and urban communities. Parents who are failing to cope with such rapid change undoubtedly still have the best interest of their children at heart but in many ways are overwhelmed by the consequences of this change and find that accepting child rearing habits and previously held values are no longer operational. Therefore, any attempt to intervene on behalf of the children being raised in these contexts must focus on helping parents in their adapting skills. The starting point of such an effort will be based on what the parents already know and practice in raising their children.

The following case study intends to give an illustration in a practical way the reality that child abuse and neglect is a social ill not only related to social and economic deprivation or cultural norms, but to negative parent/child relationships, abusive child rearing practices and attitudes to children on the whole It demonstrates most emphatically that violence within Caribbean cultures is a major public health problem worthy of serious research. It demonstrates the lack of general systems theory and practice in the management of child abuse and neglect and the way it should be applied to child development and child care objectives, goal planning, prevention and treatment, permanency planning and termination in child protection.

Case Study

Amanda was brought to the attention of the Child Care Agency after a neighbour reported that she was being maltreated by her guardian who is the father's girl friend with whom she lived.

Investigation by a caseworker revealed the following information.

Amanda is a very attractive six year old child with a pleasant and outgoing personality. She has naturally straight hair and a light complexion. At school she was described by her class teacher as an above average student.

After the death of her mother, Amanda lives with her father, his girl friend and her biological children ages seven, nine and eleven.

When she was five years old Amanda was treated at the local hospital for a broken arm which the girl friend explained was the result of a fall while playing outdoors with the her children. At the age of six Amanda was allegedly sexually assaulted on her way home from school. Her guardian did not report the allegation because according to her Amanda is in the habit of telling lies to gain attention. She further informed the caseworker that Amanda's father is currently out of the Island and there was no certainty when he would be returning.

On a subsequent visit by the caseworker, it was observed that Amanda had sustained a black eye. She presented as dirty and unkempt, and appeared tense and withdrawn, occasionally appearing to seek the approval of her guardian to questions posed by the caseworker. The guardian, in a very hostile and aggressive manner explained that Amanda is a boisterous child who is always injuring herself. She was also described as a very "hard ears child" and presents a lot of behaviour problems while describing her own children as independent and cooperative and lamented that Amanda was not that way inclined. Amanda was removed from the home and placed in foster care while attempts were made toward reunification between Amanda and her guardian through a therapeutic intervention programme to bring about a positive and meaningful relationship. It became quite evident that the guardian was adverse to any form of treatment plan with Amanda and she remained in foster care. A routine medical examination revealed that Amanda had a slight hearing impairment. On her father's return to the Island he maintained regular contact with Amanda while she remained in Foster Care. Amanda settled well in that environment and her grades at the new school started to show some improvement. At the request of her father Amanda was removed from Foster Care to live with paternal relatives. She and they developed a warm and caring relationship and with Amanda there were signs of a healthy self-esteem.

For thousands of years, the birth of a child has usually been a cause for joy and celebration. Its existence and power is so great that it enables both parents to make the necessary sacrifices for its proper nurturance and protection from danger. There is also evidence to suggest that the quality of the parent-child attachment is related to the development of social competence and later cognitive development Ainsworth & Bell, 1974. Up until the last century or thereabouts, both the process of birth and the health of small children have also been the source of great and realistic anxieties because the survival of both mother and child was assured. Since then, medical advances have helped to minimise such risks. In the past, a large number of children in a family was more often found to be desirable than it was found burdensome. Today children usually survive to their adulthood only after prolonged and expensive dependency on the family and society. Unfortunately, medical accomplishments to enhance life expectancy have not always been comparable to the quality of maternal and child health that is necessary for their optimal development.

19

One of the truths held to be universal by specialists in child development is that the first two years of a child's life are as crucial for mental development as they are for physical development. Since at such an early age it is not as easy to assess psycho-social development and deprivation as it is to assess physical development. However, when traditional child-rearing practices no longer efficiently or effectively correspond to conventional child rearing and nurturance, or when there is a breakdown in the social structure of the family or the community, the best instincts and normal practices are not intrinsic to proper child care where the child is deprived of conditions for healthy growth and development during the early childhood period.

Interventions to strengthen the parenting process at this early stage will no doubt identify families who may need help in their childrearing. Accordingly, the child who is at risk physically is probably at risk psychologically and socially. These prolonged and persistent threats to his physical development can lead to deficits which, as they accumulate become more difficult to overcome. Studies of the attitudes and expectations of natural parents to their children are agreed that the child care values they hold are similar to the rest of the population, however, their capacity to care for their children as they intended may be a final reaction to environmental pressures which are aggravated and indeed caused by family dysfunction resulting from overwhelming environmental and social pressures.

It is not the theme of this book that child abuse and neglect or even the lack of capacity stem only from environmental factors. Research has shown that child abuse and neglect can also be associated with a broad array of less visible negative outcomes that may emerge at different stages of children's lives and which can result from specific injuries and aggressive actions between parents and their children, and a lack of response to a child's basic physical and emotional needs. Personality traits and behaviour patterns will depend upon genetic endowment, early childhood experiences and the influence of external conditions.

The view is that a section of the population is so restricted by social deprivation that the capacity and desire to care for its children are not allowed to develop or operate because child care embraces certain inadequacies in the way childrearing is practiced within disadvantaged communities. Although society proclaims that all children should have equal care and opportunity, the phenomenon of child abuse and neglect remains ominous and undocumentable.

In following a human ecological perspective that examines the family life of Caribbean people within the context of multiple factors that affect them directly one only has to engage attention to research particularly from developed countries such as Europe and North America over the past thirty years where there was great increase in interest with regards to the number of children who were harmed by the very people who are expected to protect them. On the other hand, during that period much less attention has been given to the less developed countries. As a consequence, fields of study have shown that a large population of children throughout the world still experience deprivation in that they and their families lack access to certain resources which are available to the majority. This discrimination being experienced by families living in dire conditions in the Caribbean prevent them from enjoying equal access to fundamental economic and social rights for the benefit of their children's needs and desires.

The United Nation Convention on the Rights of the Child 1959 has outlined basic assumptions that children have certain essential rights and upholds that each state worldwide must identify certain objectives for children focusing on promoting, implementing and monitoring their protection. These essential rights are set in the context of recognising that children must be treated as children and should be responsible for their wellbeing by intervening on their behalf if parents and care givers are found not to be providing proper care in their best interest. These essential rights include: access to free education, freedom from discrimination and exploitation, the provision of material security and the provision of health and social services.

But what is considered proper in terms of how parents go about fulfilling their primary responsibility with regards to the child care needs which are necessary for their ultimate development and protection from the challenges of child abuse and neglect? In considering the actions of parents that are detrimental to the needs of children it is necessary to identify what parental responsibilities are, and what needs are necessary for children's proper wellbeing when these parents cannot and will not meet their responsibilities therefore causing harm to a child which could otherwise be avoided. To put this statement in the context of contemporary Caribbean society means that the concept of child care embraces certain inadequacies in the way children are being raised. There is considerable evidence to show that not all parents have an ability to recognize the needs of their children due to emotional and social maturation. Tanner, J.M. 1961. Other studies have shown that the parent who is both warm and nurturing have an ability to recognise the needs of their children and can respond without much or any conscious thought or formal knowledge but can respond to the needs of their children. Becker, W.C. 1964.

In order to understand the fundamentals of effective child rearing within Caribbean culture and sub-culture and the responsibility of parenthood one must have some insight into the basic needs of children. To put it in its proper perspective, all children need the same things they have always needed for survival. It is recognized that there are certain needs of children which should be guaranteed for their optimal development. These are: love and security, praise and recognition, the need for responsibility and the need for new experiences. Pringle, K.H. 1974. The degree to which children's needs are not met is clearly important in determining what constitutes child abuse and neglect allowing for professional and social opinion or legal judgement. Most importantly, when the needs of these children are fulfilled they can provide hope for the future, standards of right and wrong and guidance to develop and promote personalities which can contribute to the development of positive tendencies.

Even though there are varying opinions about what constitutes children's needs and rights in practice, there must be clear understanding that there are factors or circumstances in the general discussion which are likely to prevent the acquisition of specific child care needs and the recognition of their rights and although differences do occur in this respect, studies continue to show that the relationship between the child, his family and the role parents must play in this exercise play a major role in the general conclusion.

In considering the actions of parents which are detrimental to the needs of children, it is necessary for parents to identify what their responsibilities are and the needs of children that must be met. Naturally, it falls upon parents as a right to feed, to clothe, to provide basic education, the right to see that they are in good health and to provide the necessary care for their children. Katz, S.1971. In addition they are expected to ensure that this care allows them to develop to their full potential thus the accepted objectives of quality child care for all children is for the ability of child care practitioners to ensure these child care needs are met which can do credit to any nation.

Here attention must be focused on other features of family life which may impair the reaching of these child care needs, Studies have found that a child is considered to be abused or at risk of abuse by parents or permanent care givers through either intentional or unintentional acts by such factors which have an impact on the capacity for parents to maltreat their children. A parent's lack of knowledge about child development may result in unrealistic expectations. These unmet expectations can accumulate in inappropriate punishment. Other parents may become frustrated with not knowing how to manage a child's behaviour and may lash out at the child. Still others may have attitudes that devalue children or treat them as property. Children need to be regarded as valuable national assets because the future welfare of any nation depends on how its children grow and develop. In this context, child abuse inflicted on children by either a parent or guardian is defined in different ways. Some authorities limit the term to physical maltreatment of a child resulting in visible injuries. Others extend the definition to include neglect or sexual abuse. An even broader definition includes psychological maltreatment that threatens the child's emotional development.

Child abuse and neglect has been a feature of society for centuries. However until recently it had received little attention in Caribbean societies because of a lack of public awareness of its problem and its complexity.

Unlike physical abuse, psychological abuse and neglect which have become part and parcel of the different forms of maltreatment to children, child sexual abuse, an even more distasteful form of child victimization has been highlighted. This form of abuse which was once a hidden type of abuse is an especially complicated form of abuse where its layers of shame and guilt was long believed to be extremely rare among western society, and was being recognised as occurring only in primitive cultures or lower classes in society However, research has established that the sexual abuse of children under the legal age is now recognised as far more prevalent than once imagined. Hard data on the subject are scarce but many signs including increased public awareness and reporting indicate that it is a problem which is more widespread, more serious and more difficult to discuss than many other similar sensitive social issues. Disturbing as the actual experience of sexual abuse victimization may be for both girls and boys, the long term effects may hold the greatest significance for the child, and while every new story presents a dilemma once the evidence begins to be recognized, it is an even more frightening thought that sexual abuse usually occurs at the hands of someone the child knows and trusts.

Factors Associated with Child Abuse and Neglect in the Caribbean

Child abuse and neglect has been a feature of society worldwide beyond the nineteenth century, yet it had received little attention in Caribbean society because of a lack of public awareness and its complexity. However, it is only within the last two decades that it was recognized that many children within Caribbean Societies were experiencing various forms of child abuse and neglect.

Despite public attention directed toward the definition there is little agreement among researchers regarding what specific acts constitute various forms of child maltreatment because the terms abuse, maltreatment and neglect are difficult to define objectively and are used to describe different behaviours depending on the different purposes for the definitions.

Since it has been identified as a major problem within the Caribbean region, there have been a number of efforts among interest groups to understand and address the problem through growing emphasis on the rights of children and the need to protect their interest against present and future harm. However, these actions have often been uncoordinated with a lack of disciplinary feedback on the usefulness and effectiveness of different approaches in tackling the problem. It is against this background that an attempt is made to look at the issues of child abuse and neglect in a holistic way across many disciplines. Primary concern is with those children in particular who suffer at the hands of adult caregivers who are unable themselves to take any action to avoid such suffering because of their own deficiencies.

In Caribbean culture, child abuse and neglect are described as maltreatment to children by parents or guardians. Some authorities limit the term to physical abuse, neglect and exploitation that is outside the norms of conduct and entails substantial risk of causing physical or emotional harm to the child's health, development and dignity.

Others extend the definition to include sexual abuse which was once a hidden type of abuse and which, unlike physical abuse and neglect is considered an especially complicated form of abuse where its layers of guilt and shame have presented a new dilemma.

As the evidence began to be recognized child care professionals became more alerted to its incidence and their investigations alerted them to the fact that the problem of sexual abuse is not associated only with the poor and disadvantaged but among all classes, creeds and societal status presenting many complications in its prevention and treatment strategies because of the difficulties of bringing about prosecution of perpetrators. An even broader definition includes psychological maltreatment which threatens the child's emotional development. Research efforts suggest various causes of these childhood experiences that include characteristics of the abuser, the child's characteristics, the family, the community and the larger culture. Belsky 1980.

Rates of child abuse and neglect within the Caribbean are controversial and continue to challenge the capacity of current survey methods due to its immense multi-cultural, multi-ethnic and multi-religious populations creating problems of socially marginalized and economically disadvantaged groups. Children within families and environments in which these groups exist are likely to have a high probability of experiencing child abuse and neglect, therefore it must be emphasized that while certain factors often are present among families where child abuse and neglect occurs does not mean that the present of these factors will always result in the occurrence of child abuse and neglect. However, fields of study have indicated that a large population of children within this group still experience deprivation in that they and their families lack access to certain resources which are available to the majority.

Practitioners in the field of child care and development within the Caribbean region are aware that the whole area of child rearing is in itself a complex venture with which most families today are having great difficulty. This is evident where problems of poverty and deprivation in the Caribbean are disturbingly widespread and afflict the lives of a cross section of communities especially the black indigenous families within rural and urban areas where basic amenities and socio-economic resources do not allow them to maintain an adequate standard of living for themselves or their children. This means that these families continue to live at the brink of subsistence where such professionals as psychologists, sociologists and social workers continue to search for solutions. Some of these challenges include children's rights to be protected against the different forms of abuse neglect and exploitation which are being gradually realised. Undoubtedly, some of these parents will not cope whatever their social condition because personality traits and behaviour patterns will depend upon genetic endowment, early childhood experiences and the influence of external condition.

Anyone who seeks seriously to understand how a deprived community live will quickly come to appreciate that the different strands of life in deprived areas of the Caribbean has become entangled to form a cluster of great complexity. This discrimination experienced by families living in dire conditions prevent them from enjoying equal access to fundamental economic and social rights for the benefit of their children's needs and desires. Further research into Caribbean family life has found that what began as a straightforward curiosity about the extent of material poverty rapidly developed into a much clearer understanding of the complex dimensions of the many different deprivations which are experienced in the urban slums.

By looking at such factors which may increase the risk of abuse in high risk Caribbean families, it is worth examining two important factors which contribute to the gravity of the problem:

1. The breakdown of the institution of the family with its changing functions and its dysfunctional characteristics, and

2. The deterioration of the communities where dangerous trends including a rise in violent crimes involving younger children and a resurgence of drug abuse and addiction which has left a bad image of communities throughout the country creating an alarming increase in the amount and intensity of serious child abuse and neglect.

This argument used to justify the means of identifying this social change is based on reality rather than idealism and has evidenced a detachment from the accepted value systems. For example, there are difficulties in obtaining decent housing, a density in the population, individual families are more isolated, alcohol is more widespread, drug trafficking is high, there is much overcrowding and the lack of privacy affects many who live in those environments.

As the family data illustrates, within these communities stable marriages are being replaced by single parent families characterized by frequent changes of partners leading to more confusion and more stress for the entire family. Also within these communities and neighbourhoods there is likely to be an increase in the number of generation of children with lower levels of education and intelligence and poor success in school which leads to rising rates of drug addiction, criminal activity, welfare dependence and out of wedlock teen births. The reality is that families who have to endure these types of economic stress through its impact on their emotional state, education achievement, their parenting practices and the home environment they create is associated with a wide array of health, cognitive and emotional outcomes in children. Brooks-Gunn, J. & Duncan, G.J. 1997.

Much research on low income and disadvantaged families have realised that if it is accepted that this life pattern creates pressures which endangers family relationships therefore inhibiting the attainment of child care objectives, then it is to be expected that such children will be particularly vulnerable to separation from their natural homes and families to alternative care arrangements despite the interests, hopes and affections of the parents.

To understand how these disadvantaged families and their children are caught in the mire of poverty, disillusionment and lack of incentives, there is the need for more valid concepts and methods for studying the familiar structure of the black Caribbean family by those who know and have experienced black culture first hand since from studies carried out not all poverty is found within socially deprived areas.

Poverty and its link to Child Abuse and Neglect

Problems of poverty and deprivation are disturbingly widespread and afflict the lives of a cross section of communities especially the black indigenous families within rural and urban communities from the slums and low income areas where they tend to endure basic amenities and socio-economic resources which can impact on methods of childrearing giving rise to child abuse and neglect.

While there is a vast amount of research on poverty and its effect on child abuse and neglect, there are no large scale studies that specifically examine the nature of the relationship between poverty and child abuse in the Caribbean However, it has been found that stress factors associated with social deprivation and poverty are risk factors that are compounded by substance abusing parents who divert money that is needed for basic necessities are used up in buying drugs and alcohol which may interfere with their ability to hold down a job or through mental illness. Although it is evident that most parents who live in poverty parent their children effectively some research show that children who grow up in poverty can be more vulnerable to neglect and emotional abuse.

On the other hand, during that same period much less attention had been given to the less developed countries where reported cases were usually tend to be found mostly in certain areas and neighbourhoods that are marked by other signs of poverty such as delinquency, violence, drug use and community decay.

Research into Caribbean Family Life has found that what began as a straightforward curiosity about the extent of material poverty rapidly developed into a much clearer understanding of the complex dimensions of the many different deprivations which are experienced in the urban communities such as difficulties in obtaining decent housing, population density, overcrowding and the lack of privacy which affects many who live in those environments. These families with a myriad of life circumstances which are reflected in a basic sense of hopelessness and powerlessness cause them to accept their situation where the overwhelming majority fail to have any broad social expectations almost as though they have learnt that such expectations are beyond their reach or control. Because of these calamities these disadvantaged families are forced to stay in the arena of these daily situations will find themselves in the precarious situation of unproductive and unrewarding behaviour patterns that can lead to a lifetime of trouble with no hope of getting out of these positions or winning approval within their community or environment.

What is needed is research to be supplemented by studies which take samples from geographical areas of social deprivation with extensive poverty in order to ascertain how they differ from the population at large. It would seem that societies are strongly in favour of placing the responsibility for child abuse and neglect problems on the families themselves while ignoring the challenges that social conditions have on human behaviour without taking into account the remaining fact that it is harder for socially disadvantaged families to disguise incidents of child abuse and neglect. It is therefore virtually impossible to ignore the probability that the main reason for the high incidence of identified abuse is that child rearing is a greater problem for those living with the stresses of poverty. These stresses can include the existence of unemployment over which individuals have no control, low income levels, lack of financial support, damaged relationships, health issues, the continuance of long term deprivation, long term habits and behaviours and inadequate housing which all contribute to the stress. It is not to suggest that poor housing alone causes child abuse but that poverty and associated problems reduces one's ability to escape stress.

Issues of Diverse Culture

To have a better understanding of the way in which culture can influence how children are raised in Caribbean culture and sub-culture, it is important to consider their cultural experiences and values that determine how family life is shaped and the variability of diverse practices and beliefs of human behaviour. As one begin to explore the considerable variation in the way these parents interact with their children it has become clear that there is not a universal standard for child rearing or for child abuse and neglect. This concept of cultural boundaries present a dilemma for child care practitioners for if they fail to allow for a cultural perspective in defining how parents raise their children they may find themselves in a position where their own set of cultural beliefs and practices can be considered preferable and in fact perpetuate one prevalent view. For example, what behaviours should be labelled as abusive or neglectful, how professionals should go about intervening, how the causes of the problems are understood and what can be done to alleviate the stresses within the families' milieu. This depends to a large extent on an attempt to translate the meaning of social functioning into some more tangible term which have much to do with our understanding of the families and what is normal or acceptable within that culture because no matter whose culture it is, is never an excuse for children to suffer the hurt and humiliation of abuse, neglect or exploitation. At the same time one cannot take the stance of accepting inhume treatment of children in the name of cultural adversity. By understanding these cultures children will receive appropriate services if cultural factors which shape the family play a role in the allege maltreatment. Given the many cultures and sub-cultures and societal influences affecting the way in which a country defines abuse globally is usually a formal task in terms of some of the salient cultural factors which are being played out in child abuse situations among ethnic groups and which should be culturally relevant as evidenced by many empirical studies.

While much research has been carried out to assist health professionals to detect and manage child abuse and neglect culturally and cross-culturally little attention is given to the context of cultural diversity and its influence which should be routinely incorporated to establish a professional standard of cultural competence. How

Beatrice E. Kirton

30

culture and community impact on and influence child maltreatment is a subject which warrants intense research because the intervention that works best for one culture group may not be the best approach for another and should be tailored to each community. Research that explores the relationship between cultural practices and child abuse and neglect must include how this is viewed in different cultures and sub-cultures, and how social workers respond to systemic stresses on low income Caribbean families must be acknowledged and addressed. Respecting family values while ensuring the child's safety in the home produces some common areas of misunderstanding between professional child care workers and cultural minority families because cultural diversity is fundamental to successful outcomes for the family as a whole and can open their eyes to areas of crucial understanding of the role of culture in Caribbean family life. In response, social service authorities need to thrive toward greater equality of conditions which will enable more families to cope thus reducing the circumstances which causes families to abuse or neglect their children.

Faced with the evidence of the harm done to children by family deprivation in Caribbean culture and sub-culture and its rapid growth forces us to recognise that how an individual child reacts to being abused will depend on the complex interactions between the child's own personality and predisposition, his or her unique family circumstances and relationships and the nature, severity and duration of the abuse.

This argument can be further developed taking into consideration that for many children from socially disadvantaged backgrounds, abuse or neglect from their parents was just another factor in a generally abusive environment. Out of this theoretical paradigm comes a very clear notion that not all children who are disadvantaged and deprived are necessarily abused but are vulnerable to being at risk.

It is here that Caribbean nations need to adjust and enhance themselves in fulfilling the needs of and capacities of its citizens by striking the right balance between protecting high risk children and preserving vulnerable families.

CHAPTER 2

THE HISTORY OF CHILD ABUSE AND NEGLECT

It is hard indeed to have a clearly formulated opinion that child abuse and neglect is a historical concept because it continues to rear its ugly head in the lives of children. Despite being widely condemned, it remains a persistent threat to society, which although recognized as a moral panic is by no means resolved, and the resulting injuries that children suffer are still far from being understood.

It has been argued, and rightly so, that our children are our future and what they therefore need is a future that is full of promise. Social scientists have argued that society, in its whole must make irreducible needs the highest priority for all children in order for them to grow, learn and flourish.

Psychological studies have concentrated on the interaction between children and families and have found that it is not easy to assess psycho-social development and deprivation as it is to assess physical development. According to this thinking the child who is at risk physically is probably also at risk psychologically and socially, and because the child is a growing person in a sequence of evolving life stages under changing circumstances, the role of the parent must unavoidably change and develop at the same time. Some of the work done by practitioners in child abuse and neglect has influenced psychology in the form of social learning theory. This approach is concerned with guiding parents away from improper methods of child rearing particularly when they act out their childhood traumas on their children, and because they are so much in need of their parents nurturance, and have so few resources to defend themselves they make the most highly charged powerful attraction or parental abuse.

In both developing and developed nations children are subject to poor parental and post natal care where malnutrition, disease and poverty are widespread. Despite this bleak picture a cherished belief is that human nature compels parents to rear their young with tender loving care thus mitigating harmful environmental and social conditions which are confronting our precious treasures.

Drawing on early times, there was never a definition of childhood neither was there a definition to differentiate it from adulthood. Treatment of children during this period was accordingly based on the perception of children as adults in need of training leading to generally rigid and brutal treatment. The harsh reality which is central to society at the time was its attitude toward children which traditionally consisted of the belief that children are their parent's responsibility to treat as they so desire. There is currently a trend in modern day China where parents have been restricted to having only one child as a means of controlling population and improving overcrowding. As a consequence of this, closing the gap between the desired number of children people want and what actually happens remain realistic. For example, the killing of baby girls is considered almost a form of birth control because male children are traditionally favoured.

The stories of Isaac and Moses show us that the killing of infants was part of Hebrew social custom. When the western world became influenced by Christian religion it used its influence to counteract infanticide. Laws were established adopting the principle that the State can intervene in the family on behalf of the child still the killing of babies especially illegitimate ones continued through the 19th Century.

To understand why child abuse is now seen as a social problem, we need to go further back to see how humankind has fallen short of the goals set by the United Nations, and to recognize that we live in an ever changing society where the way we react to one another and to children is part of that change.

The basic patterns of evolution of childhood began to be traced to the overall evolutionary direction of parent/ child relations.

This is evident in the historical record where evidence of child maltreatment and infanticide remained widespread among all historical records and is well documented. This way of seeing child abuse is critical because it gives some insight into how it has become part and parcel of the way some sectors of society define certain social conditions as risk factors. Gough D. 1987 suggest that definitions of child abuse have two things in common. Those are that the child is harmed, and that someone is responsible for that harm, and raises an important question about how child abuse is defined in terms of children's rights or lack of them, and the kinds of minimum conditions necessary in child rearing in respect of their needs. Wendy Stainton Rogers 1992 explains that we cannot begin to understand the current situation relating to child abuse and the way we respond to it until we have traced back through the events that have led up to what happens now. The protection of children from outright abuse was carried one step further with the founding of the American Society for the Prevention of Cruelty to Children in the United States of America in 1875. Up until the late eighteenth hundred, there were no laws to protect children. This meant that children were grossly maltreated in the privacy of their homes because they had little protection and no one to turn to for help. This raised an important concern about how children are treated in terms of their rights and led to major concerns about the case of little Mary Ellen.

Mary Ellen Wilson was an eleven year old girl child who was grossly mistreated by her step-mother. She was shackled to her bed and badly beaten. Too tiny and ill formed for her age; it was quite evident that she was also malnourished. Some of her scars were visibly healed giving a clear picture of long term sustained child abuse and neglect. Mrs. Wheeler, a casual visitor to the step-mother was so appalled by what she saw highlighted Mary Ellen's plight by reporting the severe and obvious abuse and neglect to the Authorities. Mary Ellen was presented to court in an abusive state befitting the treatment of an animal, and so they found that no law had been broken. This situation changed the face of parental authority in North America.

The main reason why animals had better treatment than children was that parents knew what was best for their children and had an absolute right to raise them as they perceive to be right. It meant that when children were grossly mistreated within the privacy of the family they had no protection.

Mary Ellen Wilson's case set into motion an organised effort to battle child abuse and neglect. Consequently, toward the end of the nineteenth century, a number of reforms began to question the sanctity of family privacy when it comes into conflict with the needs of children, and in 1912 the U.S. Government established the Children's Bureau to oversee the health and welfare of children.

Behlmer G.K.1982. noted that social historians undervalued the enormous amount of work carried out by the Society for the Prevention of Cruelty to children in New York in 1871, and the National Society for the Prevention of Cruelty to Children in the United Kingdom in 1883 who were working toward the prevention of maltreatment to children long before it was seen as a matter of wide public concern. It was not until the mid twentieth century that the medical profession entered the fight. Subsequently, one of the first physicians to speak out was Professor John Caffey 1946 when he commented on children who had unexplained fractures and a type of traumatic brain injury and speculated that they may have been inflicted by parents. In 1962, Kempe and his associates have identified and published their research findings which described the scope of child abuse and neglect, which drew significant attention to the problem and extensively documented research on maltreatment to children internationally since early findings. These pioneers through their research found evidence that those caring for young children were capable of neglecting, inflicting injury and abandoning them. Kempe's documentation presented clearly all the features which eventually came to be recognised as the "Battered Child Syndrome" and alerted societies to aspects of child health, which were detrimental to the healthy development of the young child. Since that time, particular pathology and epidemiology of child maltreatment have shown that in every society more and more children are becoming victims of social, emotional and physical deprivation, and sexual abuse which later entered the definition. Although the precise magnitude is not known, the problem is large enough to be seen as a public health problem, and has gained the attention of health care professionals and child care advocates because of its negative impact on the wellbeing of children world-wide.

Despite differences in emphasis and approaches in explaining child abuse and neglect in Caribbean nations, there is general agreement that child abuse and neglect arise from a complex interaction of parental characteristics, attributes of particular children and environmental and social stresses. It is generally recognised that intergenerational transmission of abusive parenting patterns, failure in attachment and bonding processes have also been importantly linked with child abuse and neglect. Helfer, Ray. E.

Societal abuse and neglect of children from a cross cultural perspective can enhance our understanding of this disturbing aspect of human behaviour. Meanwhile, the question of children's needs may be summed up in the context of child care objectives, not as a rescue operation but, in its wildest sense is relevant or important to all children whether they live with their own families or whether they have special needs in their social or emotional development. At first sight, the basic needs of all children do not seem too exacting or difficult to satisfy under ordinary circumstances, but when these are not met by society which is the main source of provision; these needs exert such pressure that parents cannot easily recognise the needs of their children. Conditions such as poverty, inadequate housing, poor health, inadequate nutrition and unemployment have been seen as either contributing powerfully to the incidence of child abuse and neglect in Caribbean society or so damaging to the children as to outweigh the proportion of child abuse and neglect which occurs because of parental psychopathology. Gelles, R. 1973. Cross culturally, mothers who are isolated in child care tasks without others to relieve them periodically are more likely to be harsh with their children because the once availability of the biological alternative caretaker to relieve the parent from an unremitting burden of child crew is no longer available. Minturn, Leigh and Williams, W. Lambert 1964. Far more deeply involved and vulnerable is the problem particularly in a heterogeneous nation where it is accepted that what may be unacceptable practices in one culture may be common place in another has produced a useful historical perspective from which to view the remarkable variation in the human species in the treatment of children. Radbill, Samuel. 1974.

In the Caribbean today, with its gradual progress toward universal education opportunities, political and economic integrity and changing patterns of socialisation, many efforts and constructive plans are put in place for the proper care of children. Great advancement has taken place in the area of maternal and child health including a network of health and social services which covers the entire Caribbean population. To this end, all Caribbean children now have access to basic health care therefore reducing the infant mortality rate.

These favourable developments do not augur well for the proponent of child abuse in the Caribbean region. Recent research indicates that a substantial and growing number of children throughout the Caribbean remain victims of serious acts of violence in their homes. It is estimated that a growing number of children are in need of protection against all forms of abuse and neglect.

Professionals who have a responsibility for intervening in cases of child maltreatment in the form of child abuse and neglect are of the view that child abuse occurs as a result of multiple forces that impact the family and that these negative interactions eventually result in child abuse and neglect. They have recognised that the multiple and interactional causes of the problem when individualised determines that what might be factors that may cause child abuse in one family may not result in child abuse in another family. For example, there is limited understanding of why some parents who were maltreated as children abuse or neglect their own children, and why other parents with a similar history of being abused as a child do not

It must also be borne in mind that while certain factors may be present among families where child abuse occurs, this does not necessarily mean that the presence of these factors will always result in child abuse and neglect. Therefore, it must be emphasized here that those Professionals who have a responsibility for intervening in cases of suspected child abuse must be cognisant of the multiple causes of the problem and use an individual approach in their treatment of children and families. Here again, while particular factors may often be identified in certain types of cases does not mean that these factors will always be present or that their presence will always lead to child abuse.

Characteristics of Abusive Parents

Why does a parent abuse his/her child? The answer to this question is neither simple nor straightforward. Research suggest that abuse is the result of a number of factors interacting together in the parent/child relationship, such as the characteristics of the parent and child in the way the parent behaves toward the child and circumstances of children's lives that might contribute to pro-social behaviour. These include: the quality of the family environment, various social and cultural factors and a precipitating crisis or event such as divorce or other socioeconomic stresses. Child abusing parents have been found to possess many traits including a tendency to be rigid in their discipline, domineering, impulsive, immature, self—centred, hypersensitive, and low in self esteem or problems with coping and self control. The existence of child abuse and neglect is ample testimony that these parents cannot always control their aggressive impulses. Some theorists are of the opinion that child abusive parents had unhappy childhoods or they may themselves been abused or neglected and deprived of basic mothering. As children, they would have learnt from their own parents to be aggressive and in turn criticize their young children while making unnatural demands on them. Parke R.D. and Collmer C.W. 1975. He further contended that not all persons who were abused as children became child abusers, nor were all child abusers abused by their own parents. Looking at the Caribbean experience, Research on child rearing practices, indicates that a significant number of individuals within the general population have experienced some form of child abuse. Such childhood experiences can have an influence on the child's physical, cognitive, emotional and social development. This influence can last through childhood and extend into adulthood. Research also recognised that maltreatment by parents is a symptom of extreme disturbance in child rearing, usually aggravated by other family problems such as poverty, alcoholism and drug abuse or forms of anti-social behaviour. It can be argued that a disproportionate number of abused and neglected children can be found in large, poor or single parent families which tends to be under stress and have trouble meeting children's needs. Sedlak A.J. and Broadhurst, D.D 1996.

Other characteristics associated with abusive parents include: low intelligence, hostility, isolation and loneliness, anxiety, depression, low frustration tolerance, immaturity, dependency, drug or alcohol abuse, a lack of parenting skills, marital difficulties, a lack of knowledge about child development, domestic violence, unemployment and financial stress. In some situations, single parents may be at high risk of abusing their children due to high levels of stress and low income. The parents earlier experiences, particularly their experiences with their own parents and significant others are also powerful influences in the way they adapt to, cope with and enjoy parenthood.

A considerable body of evidence has recognised that all parents need certain psychological and tangible support in today's permissive society; including those who have been well nurtured as children and whose current life situation are favourable. Even for parents who display competence, are reasonably in mind and body, are desirous of being a parent and able to work and earn a decent living will find that child rearing is not easy in this complex world. Parents whose nurturance has been grossly inadequate or traumatic and those whose current life situations are unfavourable for any reason, their capacity for healthy development as a parent is impaired to varying degrees and may need even more help. Well meaning but misguided efforts on behalf of the child that ask more of the parent than he is able to give are likely to provoke anger in the parent and may even cause him to retaliate against the very child he seeks to help. Naylor, A.K. 1970.

The need for helping parent figures in difficulties to be on better terms with their children must be emphasized because it seems the importance of such work is not always sufficiently recognised which is relevant to many children in a wide range of situations. In response to the above, parents need to develop true empathy for children and must involve taking time to listen and to see the world from a child's point of view. Empathy for children can be developed by learning all that can be learnt about child development from birth through adolescence, and the parenting skills appropriate for children at different ages. With this knowledge, parents can increase their understanding of their children's behaviour and are less likely to hold unrealistic expectations of them. According to Bronson, W.C. 1974, there may be some characteristics of the mother/child interaction which do not change overtime. Although such wide variations exist in mothers behavioural responses to their children's requests for attention there is no way to predict the specific content of the maternal response.

There is the general feeling that the majority of parents love their children, and would do anything within their power to protect them from harm. However, due to an adherence to family traditions and ignorance here in the Caribbean physical abuse is considered an accepted form of punishment for children whose parents feel that they have gone against their parents express wishes. And when physical injuries in the form of broken bones, bruises or lacerations do occur these parents become very obstinate and deny or refuse to accept that child abuse has occurred. They would argue that it is a necessary form of correction and would use the adage that to spare the rod is to spoil the child as a means of justifying their actions.

Unlike neglectful parents, who tend to be apathetic, incompetent or irresponsible, abusive parents tend to be overly involved with their child. Wolfe, D.A. 1985. Often deprived of good parenting themselves they tend to be greatly upset by behaviours that most parents accept as normal. Reid, J.R, Patterson G.R., and Loeber R.1982. This abuse may begin when a parent who is already anxious, depressed or hostile tries to control a child's behaviour but loses self control and ends up beating the child in the presence of others without the modicum of guilt or remorse. They would become aggressive and rebuke anyone who tries to intervene with remarks that the child is theirs and they can discipline the child as they want to without interference from anyone. This type of behaviour does not auger well for the healthy social or psychological development of the child. Evidence has shown that parental hostility has a particular harmful effect on a child's development, and the distortion perpetuates itself from generation to generation.

Behaviour scientists generally agree that there are things parents should do to stimulate, support, guide and provide structure and discipline in a non-violent and safe environment, and there are certainly things they should not do such as bringing up children in an unwelcoming and non—nurturing environment where violence is the only solution to concomitant problems in childrearing and discipline methods.

Many parents, as child abusers in Caribbean family life have learnt as children that violence works because of their own experience as observers of domestic violence having grown up in a family where parents hit each other, where, as children they were beaten by their own parents or actively participated in sibling rivalry have emulated this behaviour in the rearing of their own children. M.A. Straus, R.J. Gelles, S.K.Steinmetz 1980.

One study found that abusive parents tend to lack certain guidelines for managing children's behaviour and tend to be consistent in their methods of discipline. Young, L.1964.

Because of this erratic behaviour by these parents, children never know when or what to expect in terms of punishment and for what reason, and if erratic punishment is not effective, the child is then blamed for provoking the parent and is labelled as defiant causing the parent to react with intensified aggression. Consequently, these children are subjected to a life of anxiety and uncertainty,

Children at Risk

It is precisely because children are valued that their social, physical and emotional capacities be developed and that their need for love, security, recognition, stimulation and responsibility are met, usually within the care of their natural parents and through the influence of society. The social deprivations which afflict a part of Caribbean population, makes it difficult for such objectives to be accomplished and has a negative effect on the quality of child care. It is frequently said that we live in a permissive society, and the dangers inherent in such a society can have a continuous and negative effect toward the care of future generations. Studies have shown that the parent, who is both warm and permissive, tend to be most suitable and desirable and that the children of such parents are likely to be socially assertive and independent. These parents tend to be emotionally healthy, their aggression is positive and not destructive and they apply normal and reasonable restraint in their method of child rearing. But where emotional bonds are not formed in terms of complex parent-child interactions due to ambivalence and hostility towards their children, parents may be helped in some way to accept their children through consistency, good enough discipline, a nurturing and loving relationship and knowledge of appropriate parenting skills. According to Staub. E. 1979, even if parents know what kind of person they want their children to be, few are well informed about how to accomplish such goals. For example, some of them do not know how to relate positively to their children, what method they must use to discipline them or what appropriate steps should be taken to help them develop into certain kinds of persons. Given the uncertainty of how to set clear goals and the knowledge to accomplish them, it is not surprising that children with adverse characteristics or abnormalities can make a parent hostile toward a child they wished they did not have. In this respect, child abuse can be visualized as part of a continuum which includes equally harmful interactions between parent and child. In view of these trends and tendencies, it is generally accepted that certain children are more physically and emotionally vulnerable than others to suffer abuse. Psychological theory has determined that the child's age, his physical, emotional and social development can greatly increase or decrease the potential for abuse depending upon the interactions of these characteristics with parental factors previously discussed. Studies in parent-child relationships have indicated that the likelihood of maltreatment to children increases when parents who had troubled childhoods, or think poorly of themselves find negative emotions hard to handle. They tend to have relationship problems with children who are particularly needy or demanding, who cry a lot, who are unresponsive, who have failing grades at school, the individuality of the child, the child who is unable to fulfil parental expectations, the child who is the result of a rape situation, the child who resembles a father who has deserted the family and the unplanned or unwanted child. These children are perceived by their parents to be difficult to manage and may also, have certain disabilities which may increase their vulnerability to abuse. Their greater needs may stem from being developmentally delayed or physically or educationally challenged, have poor health, difficult personalities, physical disabilities, be hyperactive or mentally retarded. Reid et al 1982. Although most parents are caring and nurturing, there are those who cannot or will not take proper care of their children, and these children end up being hurt or worse off being killed. According to Belsky (1993) maltreatment, whether perpetrated by parents or other care givers is either deliberate or avoidable endangerment and can take many forms which are likely to be accompanied by one or more of the others. For example, a child who suffers serious neglect can also be a victim of emotional or psychological abuse, and its effects may be difficult to distinguish from signs of other developmental problems such as developmental delays or emotional disturbances.

CHAPTER 3

UNDERSTANDING CHILD ABUSE AND NEGLECT: A CARIBBEAN PERSPECTIVE

Understanding the nature and causes of child abuse and neglect has challenged Caribbean society since the early 20th Century. If there is one fact that has been learnt during that time is that there is no single cause of this phenomenon. Researchers continue to produce evidence and some awareness that there is no single cause for child abuse and neglect as it occurs across all social, economic, religious and cultural groups. It continues to spread at an alarming rate and continues to have devastating effects upon families in every part of the globe socially and economically. At the same time a broad spectrum of the world community including professionals at all levels of maternal and child health have demonstrated intense concern over the problem and the harmful and long term effects on the victims and their family. In addition child abuse and neglect occurs across all socio-economic boundaries. It continues to be a part of human behaviour all over the world and throughout the Caribbean territories. It is described as a serious and pervasive phenomenon that affects not only children but also the family and society in general.

According to the general definition, child abuse is a term that refers to maltreatment of a child by a parent or person who is responsible for his welfare under circumstances which indicate that his health and wellbeing are jeopardized to the point where it can be considered a criminal activity. Although many people believe that child abuse occurs only when a child receives a non-accidental injury, the act actually includes several distinct types of ill-treatment which can include any behaviour that is abusive resulting in demonstrable harm or injury, or a combination of physical abuse, sexual abuse, emotional or psychological abuse, neglect, abandonment and other unconventional forms of ill-treatment to a person under the age of eighteen. They can be inflicted by a parent, a caretaker or other adult known to the child, These forms of maltreatment are likely to prevent such a child from reaching its full potential and by its more controversial definition is considered a felony. Child Abuse Breaking the cycle, 1989. These forms of cruelty to children differ considerably from accidental acts to wilful acts and are often of a repetitive nature characteristic of the "Battered Child Syndrome".

Another form of child abuse observed in Caribbean culture is ritualistic abuse performed as idiosyncratic beliefs and folk medicine performed for the treatment of childhood illnesses or for the protection of children from evil spirits. This form of treatment can be very detrimental to a child's healthy development and extends beyond the usual definition of child abuse. For example, a parent putting a sedative in the baby's formula to stop him from crying or to induce sleep and parents refusing to seek attention for a child who has a serious medical condition on religion grounds. These culturally diverse child rearing practices place the professional counsellor in a precarious position in determining the extent of child abuse, or, whether child abuse has occurred. Despite any uncertainty, these professionals' sense of personal and professional responsibility in protecting children from abuse and neglect must remain intact. In studying Caribbean traditional child rearing practices there are those that are associated with healthy functioning children just as there are those practices which lead to unnecessary physical and psychological trauma to children. For example, behaviours to children that would be considered unacceptable are belittling, insulting, yelling and name calling. Although these actions may not result in observable injuries they are nevertheless considered abusive by standards of negative child care and development and one cannot pretend that the facts are otherwise for while this behaviour might not seem initially to be serious it is worth remembering that prompt intervention with such vulnerable families may prevent minor abuse from escalating into something more serious.

Understanding the nature and causes of child abuse and neglect as they relate to children and families in Caribbean territories, clearly it would be naïve not to have some awareness that the personality and behaviour of a child are the result of many different factors both genetic and environmental. These can have an influence on their behaviour, and the way parents react to them can be either positive or negative depending on the circumstances that influence the behaviour and the vulnerability in relation to the children. Just as importantly, due to the intricate nature of the definition it is difficult to understand what really constitutes child abuse and neglect, whether it is a problem related to disadvantaged families or the stresses of society to which many children in the Caribbean are exposed.

Over the past decade or so, the phenomenon of child abuse and neglect continues to spread at an alarming rate and continue to have devastating effects upon families. Many experts have argued that one factor that has contributed to the abuse and neglect of children is the marginal status that children hold within society as evidenced by the fact that millions of children are allowed to live in economically and socially impoverished environments. These children need protection from these adverse situations through a conscious effort on the part of their community to promote their total development. In a similar vein, parents who cannot meet the needs of their children are being blamed for their failures whatever their social conditions. Central to current thinking the frequently occurring spate of reports regarding cases of child abuse and neglect tend to highlight the inadequacies of individual parents without considering whether or how the inadequacies of an unequal society may influence their behaviour. In the Caribbean, like other underdeveloped, developing and developed countries abused and neglected children began with concern about family life with its changing functions and dysfunctional characteristics. Of critical importance is the magnitude of the problem to be addressed and the stresses on the family it evokes.

While there is a combination of factors which have been shown to be associated with various types of abuse, there is need for further investigation into the factors that exacerbate the risks associated with child abuse and neglect. Research indicates that a high percentage of parents who maltreat their children can relate and describe a history of abuse or neglect in their own lives which can create a predisposition to abuse or neglect their own children. This is associated with such factors as low self-esteem, feeling unworthy or depressed, and experiences rejection or anguish in relationships. Some are often pre-occupied with trying to find ways to get their own needs met and performing child care is often performed mechanically and at their own convenience without sensitivity or emphatic action in response to the child's perceived needs.

Parents who are under extreme stress of economic hardship are more likely to mistreat or neglect their children because they cannot cope with the social and material pressures of their lives Elder G.H. Jr. 1974. Other contributing factors which can lead to child abuse by parents are symptoms of extreme disturbance in patterns of child rearing which is usually aggravated by other family problems such as poverty, drugs and alcohol or other anti-social behaviours. In fact, child abuse and neglect reflect the interplay of many contributing factors involving the family, the community and the larger society. It must be emphasized that while certain factors may often be present among families where abuse and neglect occurs this does not mean that the presence of these factors will always result in child abuse and neglect. Although most neglect cases tend to occur in disadvantaged families, it is not the general rule that most low income parents abuse or neglect their children. Sedlac A.J and Broadhurst D.D. 1996. For example, wealth does not guarantee a safe home for children. In fact, wealth may simply make it less likely that abuse and neglect will be reported to the authorities which can have the potential for negatively impacting the healthy growth and development of those children since they cannot be expected to thrive in a home in which fear of violence is a relentless fear.

The most significant approach for determining the spectrum of child abuse and neglect within Caribbean society lies in recognising the social and economic factors that contribute to the problem. For example, is the standard of living of these vulnerable families a predisposing factor being a single parent or does psychological factors encourage or cause this major public health problem that affects the physical and mental health of family members; and which is detrimental to the child's growth potential? The contribution of sociology and anthropology help us to understand that there is some fairly objective means for determining the standard of living enjoyed by other households in the society. On the other hand is the need to measure the level of income a household has as it relates to prevailing community standards. There are several other important factors of deprivation in addition to levels of income which are described as fundamental human needs and are provided through meaningful relations. These are employment, housing and material goods and services. Lystad.M. 1986. In addressing the problems of deprivation and its impact on child abuse and neglect in the wider Caribbean, it is important to give special attention to how wealth and income are measured and how major inequalities among individuals and households influence parental behaviour toward their children especially in rural and urban areas with high levels of stress due to financial difficulties, unemployment, overcrowding, poor housing, substance abuse including alcohol and low social support. This distribution reveals that poverty and low income which is insufficient to secure a minimally adequate standard of living is built into the fabric of Caribbean society since a large portion of this population own little or no income generating wealth, nor are they assured access to gainful employment. The overwhelming majority fail to have any broad social expectations almost as though they have learned that such expectations are beyond their reach or control. To begin with, in these deprived areas there is a substantial proportion of the population actually living below the poverty line. This heterogeneous and varied group of people tend to endure circumstances that differ almost as markedly as their ability to cope with problems affecting their children, and where there is little or no opportunity to escape the poverty in which they found themselves. In this connection, a number of observations are made. Firstly, there is never complete uniformity among people sharing similar conditions of living standards, and secondly, there are seldom any real consistency underlying the attitudes of individuals. Never the less, researchers have observed the emergence of a fairly clear pattern which gave a vivid profile of how these deprived communities respond to levels of income and how this is dispersed in meeting the economic needs of their family. The general consensus being that some families find themselves in financial difficulties because their total income is insufficient to allow them to obtain what is considered the minimum subsistence level which is necessary for physical efficiency. Others had an income which would have been sufficient were it not that some portion of it was used either usefully or wastefully either by way of need or greed; but most seriously, there are those families where the bread winners wages is so small that it cannot support even the smallest family because the number of dependents stretches the income further than it can go.

It is certainly possible that the problems experienced by deprived families can stem from and are associated with low income and a poor knowledge base that cannot be seen as the major contributing factor in abusing families. What's important is to recognise that homes under intense stress can do more harm to a child than homes where the family suffer from low income. Sedlac & Broadhurst 1996. It can also be argued that when deprivation occurs against a background of multiple stress then child abuse and neglect can occur because having a basic income above the poverty line is not an adequate guarantee for survival if there is little security to that income so that levels of poverty and deprivation will continue to exist especially in families with multiple social and economic problems. Similarly, families who fail in meeting the needs of their children are seen to be more complex. The reality is that deprivation is a great deal more than a shortage of financial resources but also a profound and permanent sense of insecurity which afflicts families with multiple forms of deprivation Marsden. D.1973. Unfortunately, the analysis of poverty and deprivation have not revealed the necessary or significant information through which poverty, family instability and high concentrations of disadvantaged families combine to produce high rates of child abuse and neglect. Never the less, while research shows an association between child abuse and neglect and poverty it is not to suggest that poverty causes child abuse and neglect since the majority of families parent their children effectively despite their poor conditions. At the same time, it must be emphasized that while certain factors may often be present among disadvantaged families, this does not mean that the presence of these factors will always result in child abuse and neglect.

Given the reality that most parents probably behave inappropriately from time to time it is wise to consider the many cultural and structural conditions that contribute to physical violence and aggressive family interactions. Studies have found that children within families and environments in which these factors exist tend to be particularly vulnerable to social problems of all kinds and are deeply rooted in cultural, economic and social practices. These interactions are likely to guide children from these communities through a series of conflicting developmental tasks while inculcating the dominant views of society, and at the same time preventing them from reaching their potential. Mc Adoo, H.1974.

Since we understand too little about the family level differences that produce this diversity of consequences, we must realise that family life is not easy in a complex society especially for those parents particularly in the low income urban areas of cultures and subcultures where there are problems of poverty, deprivation and drug and alcohol abuse, whose nurturance has been grossly inadequate or traumatic; and in those whose current life situation is unfavourable for whatever reason. To understand more clearly this group and be able to provide support for its culture, one must be aware of its unique qualities and the variations of lifestyles and structures, to give special attention to its social and economic wellbeing and to provide support for its lifestyle and orientation. Because of the many negative stereotypes that have been perpetuated for centuries on this indigenous group in Caribbean communities with their cultural biases, it is difficult to obtain an objective picture of their negative commonalities coupled with unique physical characteristics which have led to the reinforcement of cultural similarities that has been strongly resistant to total assimilation into the majority society.

In order for child care professionals to work effectively with these vulnerable parents and their children it is necessary to be sensitive to their needs and desires and to understand the cultural differences in Caribbean child rearing practices which are occasionally viewed as unnatural to those outside of the culture but usually make sense within the context of the environment in which they evolve.

The general tendency is to view the family as the causal factor of each success or failure which is essential to strengthening their individual identity and adapt to life stresses. It is imperative that the family's point of view be considered which in turn requires an acknowledgement of the culture from which they come, and which is fundamental in getting a better understanding of them and their concerns. Regis, H.A. 1991

There must also be an awareness of the family's structure, valued lifestyles, beliefs about child rearing, socializing processes and the way they adapt to stresses with particular reference to success or failure in coping with the demands of their environment in a rapidly changing society. Towney, R.H 1931. This insight is of great practical importance for the understanding of child abuse and neglect and at the same time directs us to examine the association with such factors as low self-esteem, feeling of unworthiness or depression, the experience of rejection or anguish in personal relationships in particular. In addition to misery and despair some of these families are often pre-occupied with trying to find ways to get their own needs met where child rearing practices are performed by merely going through the motions.

CHAPTER 4

RECOGNISING AND RESPONDING TO CHILD ABUSE AND NEGLECT

Most children grow up in families where they are safe and secure with loving parents who want the best for them physically and emotionally. Others are not so fortunate and can experience episodes of abuse and or neglect according to the general definition which is defined in various ways. Some limit the term to physical abuse resulting in visible injuries while others extend the definition to include sexual abuse and neglect. An even broader definition includes psychological abuse which can hardly be considered as non-accidental in Caribbean territories.

Research continues to produce evidence and some awareness that there is no single cause for child abuse and neglect. The phenomenon continues to spread at an alarming rate and has devastating effects upon families in every part of the globe as it occurs across all social, economic, religious and cultural groups and involves every class, creed and race. At the same time, a broad spectrum of the world community including the Caribbean have demonstrated intense concern over the problem and the harmful and long term effects on the child victim and his family, yet the complex origin and profound consequences are only just beginning to be fully recognised. It is also considered a problem for every nation and every community rather than an individual problem. Researchers have attempted to measure the scope of child abuse and neglect from samples of known cases and have concluded that it continues to be through the ages a part of human behaviour which no society can afford to tolerate if we are to believe that children are generations of the future who need to be valued and protected from any form of maltreatment, and that the family as an institution is to be preserved. Abuse and neglect of children is an act of deliberate violence to, or, the sexual assault of a child or the intentional withholding of care by a parent, adult caregiver or other parents with whom the child is familiar. Even without physical damage from the trauma of abuse or associated affects of neglect children cannot expect to thrive in a home in which fear of violence is a relentless fear. With growing concern for healthy child growth and development however, the problem of child abuse should be considered in a much wider context which involves the magnitude of the problem to be addressed and the stresses on the family it evokes. While a combination of factors have been shown to be associated with various types of maltreatment, there is a need for further investigation into the factors that exacerbate the risks associated with child maltreatment. There should also be life skills programmes to increase parents awareness of the societal and personal factors that underlie the perpetration of child maltreatment as parents who are under stress of economic hardship would mistreat or neglect their children because they cannot cope with the social and material pressures of their lives. Elder, G.H. Jr. 1974.

The kind of physical care the child receives affects much more than his bodily health. First of all, his social and emotional development is also affected by the nature of his care. At the same time, we need to recognise that throughout history and across the world parents have control over their children and with this comes the possibility of maltreatment at any given time. These forms of cruelty differ considerably from accidental acts to wilful acts and are of a repetitive nature characteristic of the classical "Battered Child Syndrome" Research into childhood injuries indicate that there is little expert consensus about the causes of child abuse and neglect, or how best to predict which children are at risk of future abuse. However, there are signs which may be termed "accidental injury" and which are not inflicted but can be inferred from the nature of the injury. These childhood injuries have determined that healthy children collect bruises from time to time. It may be that some children are especially prone to accidents which are common in childhood and are usually not serious and are referred to as unintentional or accidental. Children are also vulnerable to particular types of accidents depending on their age and stage of development and are exposed to hazards as part of their everyday lives as they play whether at home, in the park and in the school play ground. As part of their healthy development they are susceptible to bruises, bumps and cuts. For example, in a preschool environment, play is the hub of all activities where children can sustain injurious accidents such as scrapes, scratches and bruises usually to their arms and legs in particular, while older children receive injuries from falls while riding their bicycles, climbing, skateboarding or in scuffles among their peers. These children are likely to receive broken bones, cuts and bruises which are clearly related to each particular accident. With such a shadow of uncertainty regarding the safety and wellbeing of children, professionals involved with families and the public in general need specific information and awareness regarding the incidence and indicators in order to determine whether reports of child abuse are substantiated or unsubstantiated, and how to respond to any concerns. Furthermore, it is important to understand that child abuse thrives in secrecy and privacy and can only be treated and prevented through recognition and responding. Bakar, D. 1971. Given that there is no precise agreed working definition for determining the indicators of child abuse with the intention of protecting children, it is of great practical importance in learning to recognise the signs and symptoms. The first step in helping abused children and children at risk of abuse is for practitioners in the field of child protection to be familiar with the working definition, the factors that have been used for arriving at these definitions and a better understanding of what constitutes child abuse and neglect as it relates to multi-cultural norms and communities within Caribbean society, and which would lead to a greater likelihood that all forms of abuse would be identified, reported and investigated. This familiarity can help both in treating its milder manifestations and in avoiding groundless suspicion of its occurrence, therefore alleviating the moral panic and tension on the family generated at times by overzealous interference by some child care agencies; since the presence of a single sign or suspicion does not prove that abuse has taken place or is likely to happen.

Continuous research indicates that reported cases of child abuse and neglect within the Caribbean continue to increase over the years which reflect an increase in the amount of children abused and neglected. Most experts believe that the vast increase in additional reports is a result of better identification on the part of some professionals and lay persons. As a result, more children now stand a better chance of survival yet many continue to fall through the cracks due in part to inadequacies in recognising and reporting suspicions and concerns related to child maltreatment. According to some experts in the field of child health and development, one reason for this lack of intervention is that certain clinicians and professionals still fail to report large numbers of maltreated children they come in contact with. While there might be certain unchangeable attitudes and beliefs, in order for screening decisions to be made professionals working with children on a regular basis can play a vital role by reporting to the statutory authority any instance where there is suspicion that a child has been harmed or is at risk of being harmed.

The early intervention role played by these professionals in responding to child abuse and neglect intends to assess any reports to determine whether referrals are substantiated. This calls for strict guidelines in assessing allegations of child abuse and neglect in terms of the appropriateness of the report given the wide range of its functions. There are a number of different perspectives which could be examined in an attempt to understand the extent to which power and responsibility are the realm of containment, control and alleviation of some of the major problems associated with the intervention process. For example, whether the agency has a limit to what they will investigate or reject due to a lack of casework resource to investigate each and every referral that it receives. Do they reject some referrals before carrying out an investigation while using their own discretion or whether there is ambivalence among some professionals and the public at large to slow response or lack of intervention by the investigating agency when reports are made? While there is no evidence to suggest that the proportion of reports that an agency receives warrants investigation, it does appear that this optimistic thinking can leave children unprotected allowing the abuse and neglect to continue. To bring this point home, the diversities of childrearing and child protection assumes knowledge of and belief that a child has a right to have his needs met which should commence with an investigation, an assessment and any necessary action to protect the child. It is at this point that any attempt to standardize a definition and criteria for intervention should be encouraged.

Other contributing factors which can lead to child abuse and neglect by parents are symptoms of extreme disturbance in child rearing which is usually aggravated by other family problems such as poverty, drugs and alcohol or other anti-social behaviours. Studies have found that even though most cases of child neglect tend to occur in disadvantaged families, it is not the general rule that most low income parents neglect their children. Sedlac, A.J. and Broadhurst, D.D. 1996. According to research findings, the more understanding gained about the extent of child abuse and neglect, the more we come to recognise that it reflect the interplay of many contributing factors involving the family, the community and the larger society.

The most significant approach for determining the spectrum of child abuse and neglect in any society lies in recognising the social and economic factors that contribute to the problem. Research evidence shows that there is an association between socio-economic status of a family and an increase risk of child abuse particular neglect, physical abuse and emotional abuse. One common theory is that these forms of abuse occur not as a result of personal short comings but as the result of poverty, isolation and other factors outside of the control of the individual, but rather from living economic situations that render working class and unemployed people disadvantaged so that they are unable to meet the basic needs of their children.

While children of families in all income levels suffer some form of maltreatment, research suggests that family income is strongly related to incidence rate. However, little is known about the nature of this relationship and what processes underlie and interact with poverty to increase risk although there is a growing body of research into the characteristics of vulnerable families and the types of risk factors associated with abuse. For example, whether the standard of living of these vulnerable families is a predisposing factor or being a single parent, or what social and psychological factors encourage or cause this major public health problem that affects the physical and mental health of family members; and which is detrimental to the children's growth potential. In a recent qualitative study examining the relationship between poverty, parenting and children's wellbeing in diverse social circumstances, the sociological approach presumes that there is some fairly objective means for determining the standard of living of these families compared with the standard of living enjoyed by other households in the society. On the other hand, the economic approach needs to measure the level of income a household has as it relates to prevailing community standards. In addition to levels of income there are several other important factors of deprivation which are needed to provide a reasonable sense of security such as employment, housing, medical services, material goods and services and other basic needs which are fundamental human needs and which are provided through meaningful relations. Lystad, Mary.1986.

In addressing the problems of deprivation and its impact on children and families within Caribbean society it is important to give special attention to how deprivation and low income is measured. It can be concluded that the way wealth and income is distributed among the classes in Caribbean society involves major inequalities among individuals, households, ethnic groups and social class. This distribution reveals that poverty or income which is insufficient to secure a minimally adequate standard of living is built into the fabric of Caribbean society since a large portion of this population own little or no income generating wealth, nor are they assured access to gainful employment and are doomed to remain in the state of poverty. Also, how to some extent these can be associated with their struggle for survival and the concomitant problems affecting their children where there is little or no opportunity to get out of the mire of poverty in which they found themselves.

To determine the link between economic stress and child abuse and neglect, a great deal of focus is needed to determine the extent to which low income families mismanage their resources. Research explored the experience of families trying to make ends meet on limited budgets by describing their spending patterns and their financial challenges to assess the impact of financial deprivation on poor outcomes for children. For example, some families experience economic difficulties because their total income is insufficient to allow them to obtain what is considered the minimum necessity for physical efficiency, some had an income which would have been sufficient were it not that some portion of it was pre-empted by other expenditure either useful or wasteful, some where the breadwinner's wages are so small that it cannot support even the smallest family and some, where the number of dependants in the family stretches the income further than it can go. Despite evidence to support the fact that the problems experienced by deprived families can stem from and are associated with low income and a poor knowledge base, these cannot always be seen as the major contributing factor in abusing families. It can be argued that homes under intense stress can do more harm to a child than homes where the family suffer from low income. Unfortunately, when deprivation occurs against a background of multiple stress then child abuse and neglect can occur because having a basic income above the subsistence level is not an adequate guarantee for survival if there is little security to that income. Therefore, levels of poverty and deprivation will continue to exist especially in families with multiple social and economic problems. Marsden D.1973. Research studies have indicated that factors which have contributed to the abuse and neglect of children is the marginal status disadvantaged families hold within Caribbean society. This is evidenced by the fact that they and their children's needs and concerns must be better understood to alleviate the economically and socially impoverished environments which they are allowed to endure. It is important also to give special attention to the lack of those basic resources necessary for helping families who fail to meet the needs of their children if we are to break the cycle of child abuse and neglect, and until we begin to value families with fulfilled needs and privileges the problems of protecting children from the different forms of abuse will be an unfulfilled promise since there is no more a way to determine how much abuse is unreported than there is a way to determine how much is occurring.

Despite vigorous debate overtime regarding a concise definition of child abuse and neglect little progress has been made to improve the definition which requires careful analysis of the objectives and a clear perspective on developing a precise and scientifically valid system of defining, classifying and measuring child abuse and neglect. To this end, and in the face of increasing pressures and limited resources, Caribbean child care professionals and policy makers have pooled their expertise and presented a framework for defining and measuring child abuse and neglect. This is meant to be comprehensive and precise to the legislation as adopted across the Caribbean and should lay the ground work for better identification and reporting efforts, with the intention to improve the plight of Caribbean children from all forms of ill-treatment and in support of their families.

This framework included an International conference on child abuse and neglect "breaking the cycle" which was held in Trinidad and Tobago. The main focus of the conference was to obtain and exchange data and experiences on both the local and international level with regards to improving the Social Service Delivery Systems in the Caribbean region. A steering committee arranged by the University of the West Indies, Mona Campus, Jamaica. At this forum it was recognized that there is a need for accurate and reliable data on the occurrence of child abuse and neglect in the Caribbean, and which would be integral to developing a knowledge base for intervention and prevention strategies in the fight against this phenomenon. Subsequently, a territorial working group representing the Department of Child Health in association with P.A.H.O. and U.N.I.C.E.F. collaborated and organized a regional workshop on child abuse and neglect held in St. Lucia in 1990. The objective of this workshop was to develop a standardize framework for the collection of data and to develop a working definition of child abuse and neglect as a concept and a practice which would lead to the development of a documented accessible resource of available data, resources and shared experiences. Other efforts have been made to address the lack of relevant information that can be misdirected or fragmented. This was done by way of regional seminars, workshops, Symposia and conferences and to give experts in the field a better understanding of the characteristics of child abuse and neglect with an internationally agreed policy for prosecution of offences in order to effectively prevent and treat child abuse and neglect.

Clearly, there seems to be a failure to date by specific Governments across the Caribbean to give sufficient attention to this issue probably through lack of insight to the magnitude of the problem, or, to make a concerted effort in the fight to protect children from acts of violence within their homes and communities; or to monitor the extent to which existing laws, policies and services are matching the needs of children and families especially within the context of child protection.

Recognising Child Abuse and Neglect in the School Setting

Each form of child abuse and neglect, that is, physical abuse, sexual abuse, neglect and emotional abuse can be found among children from Preschool to Tertiary education.

Every day, the safety and wellbeing of some children across the Caribbean are threatened by one or another form of abuse. Intervening effectively in their lives is not the sole responsibility of any single agent or professional group, but rather, a shared community concern.

Children spend a large portion of their time which gives school personnel such as teachers, guidance counsellors, school social workers, the school nurse and psychologist and other employees more access to students, and who would be in a better position to have a reasonable cause to believe that a child or adolescent under eighteen years of age in a school environment has been physically abused, neglected, exploited or sexually assaulted. These personnel must be aware that it is their moral obligation and responsibility to report their suspicion and or concern to the principal in charge of the facility who has a legal mandate or personal responsibility to make a verbal report in the first instance to the Child care Authority or Law Enforcement.

When a child turns up at school with consistent signs for concern, this should cause the teacher to take a closer look at the situation and consider the possibility of child abuse or neglect. To decide if a particular child is a victim of abuse the teacher may also have to think about and deal with changes in the child's behaviour in the classroom. Sometimes teachers are overwhelmed at the thought of taking on yet another responsibility but they cannot afford to ignore the reasons why children cannot learn. Presumably, in every school there are teachers who will make the point that their responsibility toward children in their classroom begins and ends with the teaching of English, Arithmetic and verbal reasoning rather than dealing with home difficulties. Unfortunately, however, it is an indisputable fact that while there are some teachers being effective in observing and monitoring children's behaviour in the classroom, one will be least effective, and when there are many doing so one will inevitably be the worse. A wise and sensitive teacher uses time and opportunity to observe the needs of individual children and can often identify those who stand most in need of affection and support through the child's appearance or behaviour, or during routine interviews with parents. From assessing the child's performance, academic and psychological clues can also provide some evidence of possible abuse.

While some forms of abuse may be quite obvious, many times, observing it in the classroom is much more difficult. This is especially so because most teachers are not trained to recognise such students. Despite the lack of skill in being able to recognise other forms of abuse in the classroom, physical signs can readily be observed quite often by the appearance of skin or bone injuries, bruises or fractures some of which may be mild and others quite severe. Other physical signs of abuse which might be readily observed by teachers are a lack of care and attention which are manifested in conditions such as malnutrition and sluggishness. Disruptive and antisocial behaviour in the classroom can often be a clue to the presence of child abuse and neglect and may exist alone or may accompany physical signs. These can range from observation by the teacher or other school personnel to graphic statements by children that they have been physically or sexually abused. Conversation with parents can also provide the teacher with clues to how the parent feels about the child and can be indicated by the parent seeing the child as "wicked" or "hard ears", seems unconcerned about the child, behaves in a strange way, fails to keep appointments or refuses to discuss problems the child may be having in school. Research indicates that there are some clues which, rather than signal the presence of one particular type of abuse or neglect may be general signs that the child is experiencing abuse and or neglect at home.

Academic performance can be a tip off to the presence of child abuse and neglect. This is particularly true when there are sudden changes in the child's performance. For example, previously good students who suddenly seem disinterested in school or observed by the teacher to be no longer prepared for class may be emotionally abused. Children who suddenly refuse to change for Physical Education may be concealing evidence of beating or sexual molestation.

Academic difficulties may have a variety of causes and the presence of an academic problem does not prove that child abuse or neglect exists but the possibility of child abuse and neglect must be considered along with other possible causes when the problem is assessed. Of course, caution must be exercised in assuming that a child has experienced abuse because the presence of a single indicator does not prove that abuse exists; however, the repeated presence of an indicator, or the appearance of serious injury should alert the teacher to the possibility that child abuse or neglect exists. Research indicates that abused and neglected children often demonstrate significant learning problems in academic areas.

As a focal point of the community, schools must be prepared to do their part. The abused or neglected child as any other child who has difficulty is entitled to special help in an effort to enhance his learning. When children fall behind educationally due to forms of abuse and or neglect, emotional disturbance and behaviour problems are likely to arise. These are crippling handicaps a child has to face due to lack of aspiration on his behalf either in his parents or his teachers.

CHAPTER 5

MANDATORY REPORTING: ETHICAL & PROFESSIONAL ISSUES

The protection of children from forms of abuse involves identification, investigation and intervention which can be successfully guaranteed by the reporting of suspicion to the appropriate agency that is responsible for the protection of children. When a person believes or suspects that a child is a victim of abuse or neglect, it then becomes the responsibility of the social service agency to conduct a thorough investigation to determine whether abuse has taken place to the detriment of the child's physical and mental health.

To intervene in cases of child abuse and neglect, there is basically one area of law which can be critical to the protection of children such as the legal requirement of certain professionals to report suspected cases of child abuse. This provision of law establishes various protective services for abused children and designates the public and private agencies to deal with the problem through mandated reporting of suspected cases of child abuse and neglect.

The legal requirements to report suspected cases of child abuse and neglect is legislated with laws to monitor compliance and sanction non-compliance. It therefore behoves all jurisdictions nationally and internationally to possess mandatory reporting requirements of some description. Because of the alarming statistics on the phenomenon of child abuse and neglect, Federal and State Laws across the Americas have established Mandatory Reporting Laws for the protection of children. These Laws initially focussed on requiring physicians and other medical personnel to report cases to a State Agency that would investigate the complaint and initiate appropriate action. However, while reporting has increased generally through mandate policy, research indicates that many reports are not ultimately made by clinicians because they either do not have enough evidence to support a reasonable suspicion or they do not know what constitutes reasonable suspicion. Wilson C. and Gettinger, M.1989. In the case of sexual abuse, many clinicians believe that it is more serious than physical abuse or neglect and as a result are more incline to report these types of cases. Nightingale N. and Walker E.1986. As the scope of the statutes widened, it included a broad variety of people who might, in the course of their work with children become aware of any case of suspected or actual incidence of child abuse and neglect. As a consequence, in 1967 all jurisdictions in the United States adopted some form of legislation regarding professionals who are mandated to report their concerns, suspicions or observations. Conversely, According to Bell and Tooman 1994. In the United Kingdom Mandatory Reporting of child abuse and neglect was not included in the 1989 Children's Act on the grounds that organisations of Welfare, medical and other professional services rendered such a directive unnecessary. The argument being that the political and economic changes in the United Kingdom over the past decade have significantly altered the provision of Health and welfare services including the Child Protection System, and that these changes warrant a re-examination of the necessity to introduce Mandatory Reporting.

In the English speaking Caribbean, there are relatively no laws in place that mandates the reporting of child abuse and neglect. While there are laws that offer children some protection, they may not be sufficiently well known. Despite these and other difficulties, data is evident that Jamaica and Belize have mandated the reporting of child abuse and neglect. However, without the necessary research, it is difficult to gauge its success because under-reporting and at times inappropriate reporting can create a big problem in the fight against child abuse and neglect since many abused and neglected children are not identified. In the case of Barbados, where there are no mandatory reporting laws anonymity is guaranteed to all reporting individuals which is a step in the right direction.

As a small nation state, with close knit communities, any attempt to mandate reporting of child abuse and neglect in the Caribbean will be viewed with careless optimism and fraught with scepticism laying a platform for inefficiency, irresponsibility and complacency among some professionals who would rather accept anonymity in reporting rather than a mandate.

While referring to mandatory reporting and the rules of confidentiality, some Social Service Departments in the region have a policy of not agreeing to anonymous reports on the basis that having basic and relevant identification of the reporter allows them the opportunity to call back for any pertinent information which was lacking in the report, and also to wean out any malicious calls or false reports. Never the less, they have the option of using their own judgement on anonymous calls bearing in mind that confidentiality is the cornerstone of the therapeutic relationship.

In exploring clinicians decision-making objectives about mandatory reporting, cross cultural studies have reportedly found that the reasons attributed to under-reporting are multi-faceted and multi-cultural, and have determined that a variety of factors appear to influence the process through reasonable and rational fears. These include concerns about not being free from certain liabilities through lack of privileged communication which would free them from certain liabilities despite their professional integrity and moral responsibility. This leads to the question of ethics versus priority in mandatory reporting which strikes a balance between who is to report and to whom reports are to be made. This becomes a thorny issue between professionals in particular and the public in general where concerns arise in terms of, if I report my concerns who would I be offending and who would I be protecting, or, am I acting out of spite and be accused of not minding my own business, or, am I acting in good faith to protect the child and support the belief that the child has been abused. Furthermore, am I in breach of privileged information which is a privilege of confidentiality between the person who is aware of the abusing family and the child? The question which needs to be asked therefore, is, in child protection can there be a lesser intrusive means of acquiring the necessary and meaningful information to establish that a child is being abused and is in need of urgent protection.

This raises another question regarding the importance of principles versus practice underlying treatment and prevention and a range of phenomena in child protection, and between the causes and effects of proper reporting and investigation. For example, do the principles underlying reporting approaches and attitudes, and the circumstances in which they need to be used are in the best interest of the child. Other stumbling blocks to reporting by some professionals include: the misunderstanding of reporting laws, fear of making an inaccurate report, a poor impression of the child protective services, fear of retaliation and reprisal, denial by victims, fear of negative personal consequence, fear of being sued or loss time from work, personal and emotional reasons and a lack of understanding of what constitutes maltreatment.

Other professionals who are more likely to be in contact with children and are reluctant to invoke the procedure are medical practitioners, teachers and police officers.

For example, according to the research, it was found that doctors are unsure that the injury or condition is undeniably attributed to abuse, that any reporting will negatively affect the doctor/patient relationship, court proceeding report is too time consuming and will take them away from other patients and lack of understanding of the system. Infants and children are often brought to the Doctor for treatment of childhood illnesses. However, when the diagnosis goes beyond the normal diagnosis of an illness, the Doctor should be alerted to the possibility of child abuse and discusses this with the parent objectively while avoiding accusatory or judgemental statements before reporting his concern or suspicion to the appropriate agency.

There is a need for police officers and social service departments to work more closely in co-ordinating their role in child abuse and neglect cases. It is only recently that the connection between children who ran away from home and deviant behaviour were correlated. In Barbados, it was once thought that these "Runaways" were in need of proper parental care and control, and so, they were taken into custody and placed in detention until it was realised that these children were trying to escape sexual abuse within the home. To this end, in order for these officers to deal effectively and efficiently in child abuse and neglect situations it is important that they should be trained to recognise and determine if child abuse is indicated. In my experience, I found that mothers in particular prefer to report instances of alleged sexual abuse directly to a police officer because response time is important and minimum, and that child protection workers may not be able to respond as quickly.

Teachers are a particular valuable source when it comes to reporting suspected child abuse and neglect. This is because a teacher sees a child for a long period of time and is in a good position to observe any physical or emotional changes. However, some teachers are not sufficiently educated to recognise the signs of abuse or neglect or to recognise their responsibility to report any suspicions they may observe. Some do not see it as their responsibility to be involved in child abuse and neglect matters as it is not part of the school curriculum. They also feel that reporting will destroy their relationship with the child's parents. Some again express reluctance to report because they do not get feedback from the child care agency when they do report.

The full use of reporting will depend on acceptance and understanding by teachers and their ability to execute their mandate. Regardless of how resentful or inferior they may feel, they should take responsibility for seeing that the child is protected from further abuse and not because of the procedures on protocol followed by their particular school when it comes to reporting child abuse and neglect.

Since measurable data is inadequate to test the working hypothesis of the problem, why mandate reporting in the Caribbean region? The effectiveness of mandatory reporting as a new concept in Caribbean societies rest on definitive knowledge of child abuse and neglect, and its reporting protocol needs to be understood and supported by both professionals and policy makers; and should be based on a strong sense of commitment and on the belief that it will work. Obstacles to be overcome therefore, include perhaps an over attachment to the value of self-determination. It is the balance of these which lie behind many of the issues surrounding the decision whether to mandate.

The protection of children from abuse and neglect, calls for the best efforts of all those involved in the child care system, because society has a social responsibility toward the wellbeing of children. Reporting laws have been designed to identify children in need of urgent protection to enable the child care system to respond with protection for the child and help for the family. Legislating the reporting of suspected and known child abuse and neglect as mandatory will cause specific and ethical difficulties for practitioners.

Although there is widespread agreement about the need for a multidisciplinary approach to child protection, the extent to which various professionals wish or can be compelled to comply with mandatory reporting can vary. For example, social workers, teachers and the police work within hierarchical structures where superior officers can take action to promote compliance. On the other hand, General Practitioners, consultant paediatricians or head teachers may work more independently and with less opportunity for the exercise of bureaucratic controls and for various reasons.

Power struggle, status issues and conflicting responsibilities by these professionals can interfere with the primary task of protecting children, and no matter how well procedures are prescribed and how sophisticated in allowing professionals the exercise of discretion in complex situations, several questions and broader ethical issues pertaining to mandatory reporting need to be addressed. One cannot assume without empirical calculations how successful this type of reporting will be enhanced, or the extent of its success without the relevant research to thoroughly assess the impact on individual professionals and lay persons who are expected to report without the requisite knowledge and procedures to facilitate the identification and reporting of child abuse and neglect.

Education and Training

Perhaps, the most effective method of encouraging reporting by professionals and individuals within the appropriation who are mandated to report is a well articulated and continual outreach information programme for local department staff, persons and officials who are required to report and any other appropriate persons to encourage the fullest degree of reporting of suspected child abuse and other forms of maltreatment. The programme should include but not limited to responsibilities, obligations, powers under the title and include such matters as the recognition of child abuse and neglect, the what, how, where and when to make their report including issues pertaining to anonymity, immunity and procedures of the child care agency for reporting as well as the family court and other duly authorized agencies. Accordingly, the reasons attributed to underreporting are multifaceted, and include reasonable and rational fears of retaliation and reprisal, personal and emotional reasons for not reporting, denial by victims, family and policy makers from lack of prosecution and lack of mandatory reporting Laws by professionals. The system of potential responses to child abuse and neglect is dependent upon the investigation of the child abuse victim and the subsequent reports, and once a report has been received the process of investigation begins in order to determine whether the allegation of abuse is valid. Experts generally agree, however, that increases in rates of child abuse over the years reflect an increase in the number of reports of abuse and neglect rather than an increase in the actual number of children being abused This is important since there is no way to determine how much abuse is underreported than there is to determine much is occurring. Added to this potential uncertainty are the vastly different manifestations of child maltreatment. A look at several studies from within the region Child abuse, Breaking the Cycle 1989 give some idea of the extent of the problem as it existed throughout the Caribbean. Despite the inadequacies in data gathering, one can draw the general conclusion that child abuse in all its forms is a phenomenon of great proportion to be urgently addressed. Otherwise, one cannot fully understand the extent of the problem from a total Caribbean perspective, or recognise a correct method of intervention.

CHAPTER 6

PREVALENCE OF CHILD ABUSE AND NEGLECT IN THE CARIBBEAN: A COMPARATIVE ANALYSIS

Children are most likely to be abused or neglected when incomes and educational levels are low, when mothers head the household, when the environment is unstable and when day care is not affordable. In the environment where the risk of abuse is high, many children were left unsupervised, families were socially isolated and both houses and families were rundown. In these at risk environments, sometimes the childrearing habits go dreadfully wrong and instead of successfully raising their children parents may beat maim and sometimes kill them. According to the definition, a physically abused child is one who has been physically injured because of intentional acts or failure to act on the part of his or her care parent or care giver, and the acts or omissions violate the community's standards concerning the treatment of children.

Research literature of the 60's indicated that abuse of children has been present throughout history and the attitudes of Caribbean people towards child rearing is heavily influenced by its culture and colonial experience where children were expected to be seen and not heard and where parents had the authority to chastise their children by beating them regardless of society's condemnation.

Like any other outcome of childrearing child abuse has no single cause. It appears to result from the interactions of many factors which include the personality characteristics of the parents, the social and economic strains on the family, the personality characteristics of the children, the isolation of the family and the cultural acceptance of violence. Starr R.H. Jr.1979.

Each year, thousands of children are traumatized by physical, sexual and emotional abuse, or by them being seriously neglected by parents and other caregivers making child abuse and neglect as common a tragedy as it is shocking. The incidence of these caregivers consciously and willingly commit acts that harm the very children they are suppose to nurture is a sad fact of human nature that is found in all ethnicity and class.

The sad and deplorable fact is that for every incidence of child abuse and neglect that gets reported, it is estimated that much more go unrecognised and unreported

On the 11th October, the United Nations released the first United Nations Secretary General study on violence against children which addressed violence against children within the family, schools, alternative care institutions and detention facilities, places where children work and communities.

The report included the following overview statistics:

In the year 2002 almost 53.000 children died worldwide as a result of homicide, up to 80 to 98% suffered physical punishment in their homes with one third or more experiencing severe physical punishment resulting from the use of implements, 150 million girls and 72 million boys under 18 years of age experienced forced sexual intercourse or other forms of sexual violence.

In 2004, 218 million children were involved in child labour of which 126 million were in hazardous work.

Estimates from the year 2000 suggest that 1.8 million children were forced into prostitution and 1.2 million were victims of trafficking.

Since Kempe 1962 "The Battered child syndrome", societies worldwide have begun to realise the true prevalence and significance of child abuse and neglect and its intense causes and suffering and personal problems in families.

However, international statistics are controversial and suffer from a number of limitations which should be treated with caution. First it should be noted that any data collected constitutes a conservative estimate of the extent of child abuse and neglect not reported to the child protection agency, or cases which were not substantiated. In addition, there are significant gaps in the data because of differences in collecting and managing cases. However, much of the research that has been done on child abuse and neglect statistics indicates that the number of children reported as abused or neglected has increased substantially in most parts of the world. For example, In the United States, according to child maltreatment statistics in the federal fiscal year 2006, there were 905,000 victims of child abuse and neglect. Of these, 64.1% suffered neglect, 16.4% were physically abused, 8.8% were sexually abused, 6.6% suffered emotional or psychological abuse and 2.2% were medically neglected. In addition, 15.1% of victims experienced other types of maltreatment such as abandonment, threats of harm to children and congenital drug addictions. In the United States, there is a system of mandatory reporting of cases of suspected child abuse and neglect.

By contrast, management of child abuse and neglect in the United Kingdom is based on voluntary cooperation at a local level and recognition of child abuse and neglect through reports to the child abuse register. Child abuse registers are established throughout England and Wales. Between 1977 and 1982, there were 6,532 children placed on the child abuse register.

One study of the extent of child abuse and neglect showed that the various agencies were concerned with this problem. These are: The Social Service Department was the primary agency in the management of all types of abuse but the police department were particularly concerned with the sexual abuse cases, the Hospitals played a significant role in seriously injured children; and health visitors and the National Society for the Prevention of Cruelty to Children were involved with cases of neglect in particular.(Source: Susan J. Creighton. The International Journal on Child abuse and neglect vol. 9 no. 4, 1985. An epidemiological study of abused children and their families in the U.K. between 1977 and 1982)

How much child abuse and neglect is there in the Caribbean? On the threshold of the 21st Century, child protection efforts have been evolving from strategies of limited intervention to broader pro-active intervention and prevention. This has led to the finding that too many children in the Islands of the Caribbean are still victims of inhumane treatment that violates their rights because there is no systematic data collection of all types of child abuse and neglect in most of the Islands and investigations are seriously lacking. While data on the prevalence of child abuse and neglect in the Caribbean may be a misrepresentation of the actual number of children who are victims of abuse and neglect, it should be noted that the information that is available constitutes a conservative estimate of the extent of child abuse and neglect across the Islands bearing in mind that estimates may be higher in some territories than in others. Because estimates of the problem is provided only through compiled statistics from the police department and child welfare agencies who rely on reported incidence, and so, these statistics only reflect a part of the problem. As awareness increase information that is available points to a major public health challenge for social workers and other professionals who are engaged in child protective services.

In the Caribbean in recent years there is increasing evidence that rates of child abuse and neglect have increased due to the attention focused on the problem. For example, according to statistics from the Child Care Board Barbados, there have been a number of reports of child abuse and neglect conveyed to that Agency. The following data outline the quantities trends of abuse and neglect over the period April 1998 to March 1999. There were 304 cases of physical abuse, 282 cases of sexual abuse, 477 cases of neglect, 45 cases of emotional or psychological abuse and 05 cases of abandonment.

In St. Lucia for the first half of 2007 The Division of human services recorded 141 cases of child abuse consisting of 56 cases of sexual abuse, 45 cases of physical abuse, 24 cases of neglect and abandonment and 16 cases of emotional or psychological abuse.(Country report on human rights practices 2007. Bureau of Democracy Human Rights and Labour; March 11th 2008)

In the Island of Dominica the incidence of reported cases of child abuse and neglect doubled between the years1990 and 1993 from 127 to 252 (Taylor, 1997. This figure reached a high of 416 in 1994 and dropped to 260 in 1995. The reported incidence continued to rise in subsequent years reaching 267 in 1997 and 303 in 1998, a trend that is probably due to issues of sensitization and service access.

Neglect represented the second highest number of cases reported in Dominica for the period 1995 to 1998(Sharpe, 1992)

According to Eldemire, 1992, sexual abuse was the most prevalent form of child abuse in Dominica in 1998, comprising 41.6% of cases registered in the child abuse Register.

According to statistics obtained from ST. Vincent and the Grenadines Social Welfare Department, during the period 1995 to 1999 there were 197 cases of sexual abuse, 407 cases of neglect and 261 cases of physical abuse. There were no statistics available for emotional or psychological abuse or abandonment.

In Jamaica, the Child Abuse Mitigation Project (CAMP), a response to violence against children project based at the lone paediatric hospital in Jamaica and funded by UNICEF in 2004, stated that during that year many children were hospitalized due to abuse and neglect. Accordingly, children were victims of 70% sexual crimes reported to the police in that year. The hospital documented 560 cases of child abuse and neglect, and unintentional injuries. 704 children were rescued from threats of further abuse and neglect. Violence inflicted injuries included physical assault 45%, injuries to the head 36.8%, sexual assault 16.4% and gunshot wounds 1.3%.

The Research Directorate of the National Domestic Violence Hotline of Trinidad and Tobago provided the following statistics on child abuse and neglect: Between January 2005 and August 2005, there were 135 individual child clients less than eighteen years of age. Of these, 39% were male and 61% were female. The abuse reported by them or on their behalf was distributed as follows: There were 71cases of physical abuse, 126 cases of emotional abuse, 34 cases of sexual abuse, 13 cases of incest, 61 cases of verbal abuse, 9 cases of financial abuse, 23 cases of threats and 64 cases of isolated neglect. According to the report, these statistics represent only the cases that have been reported and do not represent the entire picture. The extent of child abuse and neglect according to the previously documented statistics is an indication that the problem is very serious and occurs across all socio-economic groups and family systems. Within the Caribbean region, large numbers of children are believed to be affected and the incidence is higher than official figures indicate suggesting that there is significant under-reporting. In short, Government statistics are only the tip of the iceberg and do not indicate the actual rates of child abuse and neglect.

Another difficulty experienced by child protection agencies and the police Department in the collection of accurate statistics on the rate of child abuse and neglect within the Caribbean lies in the context of a common finding that White, mulatto and upper class black families are underrepresented in detection and reporting which therefore merits particular attention.

Although it can be assumed that children are at risk of maltreatment in these family structures, there are no studies available that have actually tested the premise or investigate the relationship between these families and child abuse or neglect.

Much of the research which has been done on parental factors and child rearing practices, however, did not target this group which it is assumed to be due in part to their status in the community and the attitude that what happens in their family must remain in their family with little or no regard to the negative impact this attitude may have on their children and the family as a whole. In this regard, therefore any attempt to assess relationships between these family structures and maltreatment has been somewhat non-existent.

Clearly, there has been a failure to date to investigate the role of parental characteristics for abuse within this group. It is apparent that little is known about the degree of risk, what factors influence the risk or under what conditions these families care for their children. Because of a lack of criteria for intervention in the lives of these families, it may be assumed that the weakness or lack of intervention lies in a misled emphasis that no consistent profile of child abuse perpetrators has emerged because research studies have failed to typify offenders due to their class structure, profession or wealth.

The failure of social workers and researchers in any attempts to engage these families in research has been attributed it would seem is due to the lack of informants and an attempt to elaborate on why the under-representation occurs, or the process of how abuse occurs in such families.

CHAPTER 7

CARIBBEAN FAMILY LIFESTYLES & STRUCTURE

Despite the changing lifestyles and ever increasing personal mobility that characterise modern Caribbean society, the family remains the central element of contemporary life. This institution characterises three basic types of family structures that affect child rearing values and lifestyles. These sub-groups belong to the nuclear family, the extended family and the single parent family whose primary function is that of nurturing children and preparing them for adulthood. The nuclear family is identified as the marital union and the common law union where parents live together but are not legally married. Industrialization and the proliferation of ideas have led to the increase of nuclear families which is a practice common among the minority of affluent and middle class and is the unit of choice who provide for many a safety net for the family tied into an established framework of kin and neighbour relations.

Family forms long established in the Caribbean is the extended family. This group includes two or more generations as a close knit band of extended lineage such as aunts, uncles, cousins and grandparents who are closely connected and are living in close proximity and if they do not live together they keep in contact with one another and provide the safety net or place of refuge where children can resort to in good or bad times. It is considered the most important group a person belongs to and continues to play an important role in contemporary

Caribbean society. These families tend to provide both emotional and economic support to its members while developing and maintaining cordial relations. Within this family form the grandmother is highly valued as their knowledge is seen as relevant to current situations since culturally their way of life has changed very little through the generations.

It is recognised that in present day society industrialization through its many processes and geographical relocation took away some of the functions that were previously provided by the network of the extended family thus eroding the important role it performed in offsetting some of the detrimental strains experienced through economic insecurities and practical and moral support systems of the nuclear family and the single parent family giving them back the responsibility of providing the care and control of their own children.

Then there is the single parent family who arrive at single parenthood through a number of circumstances and motivations. There are those who see single motherhood as a desirable role, those who experience the critical event of divorce and those whose pregnancies were not planned. These alternative lifestyle parents more often perceive themselves as less fortunate than the traditional lifestyle parent.

Nevertheless, despite these and other difficulties family life is very important to Caribbean people and many of today's living group arrangements are based on shared social and economic advantages which can almost be identified with the former western nuclear families with traditionally shared ideology or joint ownership of resources. These units comprise two parents living together with their children either in a common law relationship or social contract rather than a legal marriage which involves an ideological commitment that the relationship should be viable only as long as it is emotional and financially meaningful. Kornfein, M. Weiser, T.S. and Martin, J.C. 1977 have distinguished two groups of families within this category. Those strongly committed by personal and social philosophy and those who ideally would like to marry but are confined to this status because of legal, economic or other pragmatic considerations. They found that the latter group behave in many ways that resembles the more traditional married relationship in that they tend to give the children the father's surname.

In this family form, the mother remains a housewife and devotes her time to looking after the home and keeping the family functioning while taking care of the needs of her spouse and children. She sees her role as raising her children to be a source of love and satisfaction and get them to follow family roles by instilling in them respect, moral values and with the ability and strength of character to distinguish between right and wrong. The father is designated as the material provider and is almost always employed.

Gender Roles

When talking about stability and functionality in Caribbean family life, the logical starting point must be in evaluating the role of each parent and their relationship with their children, and how they influence their children's development.

There has been much debate concerning a father's participation in the rearing of his children. It is important therefore to focus on the rearing of male members of the family since it is often stated that women are responsible for raising the dysfunctional males in the Caribbean society. It is further stated that if women instilled the right values in their male children from birth, we would not be faced with a society where there is overt inequality between the sexes in all spheres of life. However, in the context of family life, this argument becomes problematic and intensely subjective since the family unit does not function in isolation from the larger society which has its own established code of behaviour. It was once felt that children belong exclusively in the woman's world and so the males abandoned their responsibility to the family while they took comfort in male exploits by playing cricket, slamming dominoes or socializing in rum shops. If we are to change the stereotypical notion of what is or is not appropriate behaviour for each parent, it is necessary to inculcate the value of total family roles and responsibilities for all members regardless of their gender. It stands to reason then, that family members should influence one another in several ways such as the things they do, how they think, their health priorities and most of all their emotions all of which are affected by the relationships they share with the rest of the family. However, as long as gender role stereotypes continue, they will affect differences in the roles of fathers and mothers

The Mother's Role as Home Maker and Child Rearing

As alternative lifestyles have emerged where the question of a mother's place in the home is a sensitive one, there are hopeless ambivalent attitudes towards her parenting responsibilities. Traditionally, the Caribbean husband preferred his spouse to remain at home to raise the children and take care of the home while he worked. This female role of mother and housewife made women dependent on them for economic support thus putting them in a position of total economic dependence and full participation in a patriarchal and paternalistic gender ideology, and devoted themselves fulltime to caring for their family. Any previous investment they had made in education training or employment lost its value as they concentrated on their family and lacked the benefits gained by long time experience in the labour market.

However, despite arguments to the contrary, Caribbean women, as a result of their emancipation went on to achieve greater independence and in the process broke down the traditional role of home maker. More and more women are departing from their traditional role as housewife and entering the paid work force out of economic necessity. Many women also began to see openings for them in the labour market that were previously available only to men and they took advantage of these opportunities which dramatically changed the way the family worked as a unit, and therefore brought about a most significant impact upon gender roles where fathers as well as children had to make adjustments in their own roles in the home. This improved status of women in the work force became an essential part of the economy, and a significant number went on to combine a career with the task of raising a family with the provision of day care either within or out of home while fostering a stable environment of love and security for the family.

Despite the guilt some working mothers may feel over being away from their children, whether the job is on a full time basis or part time, these women often feel more competent, more economically secure and more independent. Their self esteem tends to be higher than that of home makers whose work is usually undervalued. As for the Caribbean mother from the lower echelons of society many have to give up their position as home maker to find employment to supplement child maintenance or when this is not forthcoming, to get away from the humiliating dependence on the husband, to achieve personal independence and to get away from boredom, isolation and the mental and physical ordeal of domesticity and to take some of the pressure off having to bear sole responsibility for raising the children. Because many of these mothers might have been out of the job market for many years raising a family, or are new to the job market and have minimal or basic qualifications, their choice of employment is limited to working in factories, baby sitting, domestic service, home helpers and in agriculture or in retraining programmes. By making satisfactory arrangements on if the mother is in full time employment, these mothers can make the job situation work if they are happy with their choice of employment and the children are not deprived.

By and large, the more satisfied a woman is with her life and work status, the more effective she is likely to be as a parent. Parker, R.D. and Buriel D.1998.

Research indicates that school aged children especially girls of working mothers seem to have two advantages over children of stay at home mothers. That their lives are more structured with clear cut rules, giving them more household responsibilities; and they are encouraged to be more independent and competent Boys of working mothers on the other hand, seem to be negatively affected due to mother's new role because of her concept that among Caribbean mothers, their sons must be socialized to accept the traditional gender role as natural and just, and which is likely to help them maintain their male dominance. These mothers felt that for their sons to be involved in household chores will rob them of their masculinity and label them as passive while exhibiting feminine traits and are therefore not encouraged to do household chores. The manner in which chores were allocated to boys was indicative of traditional role expectations. They felt that boys must be masculine, active, aggressive, tough and dominant in order to maintain a positive masculine orientation, whereas girls must be feminine and submissive in preparation for their positions as wives, mothers and home makers. This traditional socialisation pattern of males in Caribbean family lifestyle is seen as the biggest road block to active participation by fathers in child care and underscores the necessity of fathers' involvement with children from birth. Since they were not conditioned to be part of the domestic scene, they were considered incompetent or unwilling to take on traditional women's tasks such as cooking cleaning and child care because they saw these as woman's work.

The colonial experience from which most stereotypes of Caribbean people evolved contains certain kinds of autonomy that they are eager to preserve. However, despite the cherished illusion of motherhood, many of these working mothers are able to overcome the job and child care problems, and with a realistic appraisal of their situation, they saw the dual role as successful and rewarding. Under these circumstances, mothers in particular must play a critical role in guiding their children into those gender roles which are deemed appropriate to modern society. This new status of the Caribbean woman carries with it some challenges and anxieties for the Caribbean man who saw himself no longer the sole authority or bread winner in the home but has to share the responsibility of home maker and child care with his partner who is now demanding equality.

Role of the Father in Caribbean Family Life

Historically, Society has played a part in defining the role of fathers in the structure of the family, and expected more of fathers than modern society. Research evidence indicated values and attitudes concerning the role of fathers are changing. They are now expected to engage in all aspects of child care and child rearing activities by assuming a greater multiplicity of roles than ever before. They are also expected to be more than just financial providers but embrace the more multi-dimensional notion of fatherhood that has now become the norm In the Caribbean within recent times there has been increased involvement in the relationship between fathers and their children, and this relationship has taken on a more conventional role. Some of these fathers have begun to refine the roles expected of them as responsible parents and lamenting what they did not get from their own fathers in terms of nurturing or child care responsibilities

There is considerable discussion in academic, political and social circles and in society in general about the marginalization of the Caribbean man. Research into the traditional family life in Jamaica described the Jamaican father as promiscuous, physically neglectful and worthless, that they are absent from their children's residence and when they are socially present they are poor role models, neglectful in terms of financial support, harsh disciplinarians and possibly abusive to the children and mate, not setting good examples for their children, devoting quality time to their families or even being present. This behaviour vacillates from one extreme to another and can range from a consistent provider to complete abdication. Since fathers make different contributions to their children's lives there is evidence against such a generalization or concept which is frequently used to describe the Caribbean male. According to Ramkissoon, M. 2003, these characteristics are not all pervasive since many fathers are able to fulfil their role as provider economically, socially and psychologically.

The timing of fatherhood in relation to the development of economic self-sufficiency, maturity and personal responsibility are important predictors of the personal resources that men bring to fatherhood. Traditional notions of what it means to be a father requires a man to provide resources including earnings from a steady job to support his children. Furstenberg Frank, F.1995 suggests that even in the presence of strong emotional commitment to support his children, the inability to provide economic support seriously undermine his sense of competence as a father and ultimately his involvement with his children. Despite this lapse in emotional and financial contribution, middle class fathers still played a significant role more than ever before the emerging modern fatherhood. Conversely, the Caribbean man from a lower class family perspective where they are likely to be involved in much more employment situations such as under-employment, poorly paid employment and unskilled employment, are unable to fulfill their provider role as head of this economic unit. These occupational handicaps seemingly reflects the stereotype which has permeated all aspects of our society and has forced these fathers to be exceptions when it comes to being head of the household, maintaining the household financially and keeping the family unit together and contented which can have complex consequences for the entire family. For some of these fathers, the lack of a commanding paternal role made them withdraw psychologically and or physically from their children thus the quantity and quality of their investment in their children varies with social and ecological conditions. Westneat and Sherman.1993.

One of the most significant and welcomed change to family life in the Caribbean has been the attitude of men toward childrearing. The role of the father continues its transformation from a traditional one dimensional role to one that is more multi—dimensional to meet the current demands of parenting and the expectations that a father should be involved in all aspects of child care and child rearing activities.

There is evidence demonstrating that they are fulfilling care giving roles for their children. Leo—Rhynie. E.1993. Today there is little doubt that defining the role of fatherhood and the relevance of this role to children is significant resulting in a changed relationship between the parents. It is hoped that the gender and economic changes have had a major influence on the role of fathers in terms of how they view this change, whether it is to be involved in health, nutrition and education of their children, or whether they see their investment in their children tied up with the relationship of the mothers, the economic realities of providing maintenance for their children or the cultural norms of manhood.

Today, men are redefining the role of fatherhood as a result of women entering the workforce. Their work demands no longer prevent their becoming more involved parents. They are also responsible for teaching their children to be responsible through instilling discipline while they engage in full time employment. Supporting his family has become a shared responsibility and can no longer use their job as a basis for gender identity. However, child maintenance continues to be a major problem in some cases. It is hoped that the current or reformed legislation under the child maintenance law will seriously address this problem. The traditional negative assumptions about men and the roles they play as husbands and fathers are still being challenged.

The most obvious and direct way in which fathers can contribute to children's development is by helping to fill children' physical, emotional and intellectual needs. As we are all aware, the parenting role is a big one. Children have many needs, all of which cannot always be met by one parent. There is no longer any reason to doubt that fathers are significant contributors to child development. In the Caribbean within recent tines, there has been increase involvement in the relationship between fathers and their children and this relationship has taken on a more conventional role. Some Caribbean men are starting to realise what they did not get from their own fathers in terms of nurturing or parenting responsibility and are clearly beginning to define the roles expected of them as responsible parents. Years ago, in the Caribbean it was rare to see fathers diapering babies or dropping children off to school. Today it is far more common because most mothers now work outside the home so avoiding child care is no longer an option for these fathers. They are now more involved in the daily care of infants and children through taking them for medical appointments, taking care of the children even in the presence of their mother, playing and reading with them, assisting them with home work, school visiting and other outdoor activities.

Recent research indicates that men are doing more on the domestic scene and their role as father has taken more prominence in the development of the personality of the child. By working and meeting the needs of his family, many Caribbean men are fulfilling their traditional role as the major figure of authority. Their presence has a marked effect on the children's cognitive and emotional development, and appears to be particularly important in helping them avoid anti-social, delinquent and promiscuous behaviour. How he fulfils his role as a parent depends on how much time he spends with his family, his attitude toward child rearing and his own personality. For example, if he leaves home early in the morning and returns home too worn out from a hard day's work or after the children are asleep his influence on them will not be the same as if his work permitted him more time to spend with his family.

Despite their outstanding contribution to the stability of the family, there is still, however, the need for more Caribbean fathers to be more responsible to their families. It is well known that too many

Caribbean fathers neglect their responsibilities in terms of financial support, setting good examples for their children, devoting quality time to their families or even being present. This behaviour vacillates from one extreme to another, and can range from a consistent provider to complete abdication.

A widely held view is that most children in Caribbean society grow up without a father figure in the home, and that women are considered to be the most suited person to care for children. Because of these experiences, most Caribbean children are remarkably tolerant and resilient. They can understand that their parents do not share the same household, or that they have basic needs which are not being met adequately. Situations like these often put children in the position of not knowing the identity of their father which is contributed by the belief that the father's role in the home is not as important as that of the mother. This is characterised by the absence or irresponsibility of these fathers where mothers are forced into situations where they have to play the role of both mother and father. Clarke, E. 1957.

The biggest hindrance to active participation by most Caribbean fathers in child care is socio-cultural in terms of how active or passive they see themselves in their paternal behaviour and attitude. However, they are now doing more in the area of family life than they are credited with, and are going through a transition in which they are seeking to refine their role in the family, but while some are making the adjustment like sharing the housework and looking after the children others are finding the transition difficult.

Our Caribbean men and the wider society need to accept the view that the father's role in the home is as important as that of the mother, and. until then, men will never begin to fully take their responsibility as seriously as they should or aim to improve their behaviour in order to regain some respect in the family.

The Single Parent Family—Practical and Emotional Problems

Raising children in today's society is a complicated task rife with responsibilities of rearing a competent well adjusted socially capable child. However, the task becomes more difficult when it is attempted by a single parent. Mason, M.M.1995.

Many people believe that the dominant family form today consists of an adult man and woman and a child or children. The situation to which single parents are confronted can be caused by Divorce, the death of a spouse, desertion or separation of the adult, death or the desire to have a child outside of marriage or being a teenage single parent all of which can result in them being totally responsible for the upbringing of their children alone and has increasingly become a minority. Today, especially in the Caribbean family the image of a typical two parent family is no longer prominent. Research has indicated that the number of families in these single female—headed households continue to grow, including unmarried teenage mothers and their children some of whom are locked into cyclical patterns of family dysfunction. Research statistics have also indicated that some of these families account for between 30—50 per cent of all households and the most common means is through illegitimacy where the lone parent primarily the mothers find themselves at times to be both bread winner and caretaker. Children in these situations tend to experience many disadvantages as more and more financial pressures are placed upon their parent. In many Caribbean households, there is a large percentage of children some as young as five years who are responsible for parenting their younger siblings. This responsibility can at times include cooking, washing and doing major household chores. Some older children in fact take on the role of disciplinarian when the mother's health or confidence breakdown as a result of drug or alcohol abuse. There are also situations where the mother works at night and while sleeping during the day children are left to take care of the home and often cause children to miss out on school attendance. Children in these circumstances are also expected to provide emotional support to these vulnerable parents who freely express bitterness towards the absent father or boyfriend resulting in personal difficulties and frustration which are a result of the stresses experienced in the areas of caring for children, lack of finance and loneliness. These families, especially those from the lower socio-economic group because of their inherent inability to satisfy all its material and economic needs, their severe restricted social lives, frustration and anxiety in securing an adequate income, lack of preparation for the job market, proper accommodation and affordable day care leave them with a heightened feeling of inadequacy putting them among the poorest households in Caribbean society. Other hazards which affect these single parent families both practically and emotionally, and the way they behave toward their children are, unemployment, stressed filled employment, limited extended family support systems, low self esteem, poor health, relationship problems, separated or divorced, inability to cope with parenting and drug and alcohol abuse. These deficiencies make it difficult or practically impossible for these parents to fulfil all the responsibilities for which society holds them responsible, and which tend to have a marked influence on their living standards and methods of child care which are more likely to be guided by those external forces rather than by their own internal feelings or intentions. In other words, the difficulties experienced by these families and their inadequacies are influenced more by a lack of support and resources rather than by how they feel or what they do because when the stresses are removed they are better able to cope with their situation.

Apart from the difficulties of obtaining and maintaining a satisfactory income, the one parent family is more vulnerable. It is likely that a family in which a mother or a father has to bring up children single handed will think of itself and be treated by society as deviants from the marital norms and have to cope with the intractable, emotional and occupational difficulties to which they are confronted.

Even though some of these families consider themselves independent and self-sufficient the stress of childrearing aggravated by reduced social and economic circumstances, the lack of child maintenance, a supportive adult to share parental burdens and the attitude of society to their plight leave them overburdened and financially strained. Anyone who seeks seriously to understand how a deprived community lives will quickly come to appreciate that this is all a part of a general crisis. In this connection, a number of obvious points should be made. One crucial aspect is that poverty promotes further deprivation which can impair family behaviour and in turn can seriously impair parenting capacity. Unfortunately when we examine statistics in relation to the number of single parents, we examine figures but do we always relate those statistics to human beings with human problems which are often always impossible to solve. Sometimes when statistics are presented the picture call to mind are those of rows of files and card indexes and not of flesh and blood victims of cruel circumstances, or of an uncaring and indifferent society. In defence of the one parent family it isn't easy to relate cold hard facts to the desperate human problem and the actual hardship, misery and loneliness of people struggling to maintain some kind of family life within a unit that is not comparable with the family unit that most of us are familiar with.

In comparing the single parent with the parent who has the support of a partner it takes little imagination to see why life is so hard and unrewarding for them especially when coupled with the problem of being the sole source of authority and affection. Many are disturbed and distresses by growing indiscipline in their children and have great difficulty in establishing control which hardly help their situation. The single parent must learn skills which women rarely have to do like changing plugs or mowing the lawn. The kind of jobs husbands do as a matter of course though at times reluctantly so. Still a man about the house whom the majority of women take for granted is something the single mother has to do without. She must now learn to be the man and the woman fulfilling both roles as best she can for the sake of the children. Some of these mothers are desperate to get out for a few hours of socializing relieving some of the loneliness and frustration which their situation has forced upon them but are afraid of being condemned or reported to the authorities; hence they are often housebound because they have difficulties finding someone to look after the children.

The experience of being a single parent is different for women and men although they both experience greater role strain than in a two parent situation. Single parent mothers, however encounter more stress than single parent fathers because single parent mothers are usually given custody of the children in divorce cases and are considered the better custodian. On the one point of comparability the risk ratio between children living with the biological father alone as opposed to children living with the biological mother alone the results are similar. Yegedis,. B.L., 1992.

However, regardless of the sex difference single parents share similar problems and challenges. For both sexes, synchronizing the different responsibilities with time schedules is probably the most challenging aspect of single parenthood. A sizable body of research on single parent families have indicated that both individuals also differ in how they handle relations with children when they become single parents. Stuart, A. 1998. In stressing this fact, one recognises that one parent fathers have special needs and rights which need insight and sensitivity as well.

Caribbean fathers have long been stereotyped as irresponsible in their role as care giver as they have often considered the care of children as a woman's role and are neither geared to it in practical terms nor did they see themselves in a mothering role. However, in their quest to acquire the skills to enact the steps that are necessary to realise these goals of attempting to play an active role in their children's lives many hold on to such dreams in the future.

However, when the occasion arose for them to become custodians of their children they take their role very seriously and express competence as primary parents and tend to mellow in their approach to children upon assuming this status after a degree of anxiety about this new role because they do not have anything like the support network that single parent mothers have. Balky, J.1990. Admittedly, single parent fathers do really have a tough time in a world geared for women although they generally have a more healthy economic status than their female counterparts they also find themselves filling social roles for which they are not prepared.

One father felt that he has lost his identity since taking on the role of a traditional mum which left him feeling very isolated. Others have lost their self-esteem by not being able to work or join their friends at the games or go out with the lads. Here, a new style of parent child interaction emerged where men became less traditional, more discipline oriented, more concerned with the quality of child care they can acquire for their children, more interest in the children's educational experiences and more protective towards their children. These single parent fathers must also meet and accept the unique challenges associated with their new role as a single parent. Furthermore, research findings suggest that while similarities exist in single parents headed by women and those headed by men, the sex of the parent is an important factor in determining the type of family life experience in each family system.

Apart from looking after the home, the single parent father has to cope with problems in areas where there are pre-adolescent and adolescent daughters. For example, how is a man to explain menstruation to a ten or eleven year old daughter? For explaining sexuality to daughters can also present them with an almost impossible task. Even the shopping chores women do as a matter of course like buying sanitary wear can present deeply embarrassing problems for the lone father. Some single parent fathers tend to seek support and assistance from others outside their family system such as relatives, parents and teachers when they need help. Many discover that these sources are helpful in providing information and guidance about child care that improve their ability to parent their children effectively. Since all single parent fathers may not have a relative or friend next door who can be called upon to help them with these tricky situations and may have to turn to Family services, the church or even the child's school teacher for support. Many add undue stress and anxiety to their lives because they avoid discussing and sharing with other single parent's fears and concerns they may have regarding disciplining, nurturing and open communication with their children while they provide a spirit of protection and bravery in the home. Some research have shown that women and men also differ in how they handle relations with children when they become single parents In fact, it has recently be proven that some fathers are just as capable of successful single parenting as women and they bond better with the children in a single parenting situation than in a two parent set up. Women on the other hand tend to take a more authoritarian approach to children when they become single parents. They adopt more authoritarian patterns of interacting with their children which tends to promote healthier more positive adjustments among their children. Hetherington, E.M., et al.1992.

In practical terms, it was found that single fathers offer their children more space and freedom to structure their own time. They are also far more able to unwind and de-stress than single mothers which further reduce the burden on children. Be that as it may, more and more courts are giving them custody where they can and do display sufficient ability to provide for their children's needs.

In teaching the Caribbean single parent father how to handle challenges and build character a community based parenting group called Fathers Incorporated, a group was established by Jamaican men in 1991to address negative stereotypes of Jamaican fathers where workshops and awards are offered to support men in their efforts to become caring, committed and responsible parents as part of a goal to change images of fathers as merely involved providers of maternal goods. Both fathers and other men who are anticipating becoming fathers are incorporated into the organization activities. In order to carry out its mission to protect the image of fatherhood workshops, seminars and conferences are offered that addresses various aspects of fatherhood. These sessions are designed to provide information about parenting skills as well as to encourage men to play a more active role within the lives of their children. I dare say a model which can influence the model of the father/child relation throughout the Caribbean region. Despite the problems inherited by being a single parent father, it is heartening to find that a high proportion take on the burden of rearing their children instead of abandoning them to Government care.

Although life is touch for most single parent families they chose to sever the intact relationship rather than remain in an unhappy relationship. For many, they find the type of family arrangement more efficient and harmonious than a household marked by tensions and strive between the adults which can be an unhealthy environment for the wellbeing of children.

Society on the other hand makes inadequate provisions for these families and frequent display little understanding of the emotional, financial and social difficulties which they encounter. Today, especially for the Caribbean single parent family whether this family is female or male head of the household the image is no longer prominent and can hardly be viewed as a rarity. Statistics indicate that the majorities of these families are mothers who find themselves as both bread winner and caretaker with daily struggles and long term disadvantages. A sizable body of research on single parent families whether through divorce, separation widowed or by choice has demonstrated that these families face severe economic deprivation and this strain negatively affects the cognitive and emotional development of their children. Sometimes the pressures of financing the home and trying to meet the needs of the children can put heavy demands on the parents coping abilities. Some of these parents both male and female find themselves having to cope with aspects of family life which had previously been shared by two parents and which has further reduced their self confidence in trying to fulfil two roles

While the single parent must provide for all the normal needs of the family, they lack the extra physical and emotional support to help them cope with the difficulties of providing for their own and their children's physical, social, and emotional needs.

These families adjustment to the lack of being an only parent cannot be discussed without taking into consideration the altered social situation into which they find themselves. Unlike the single father who has agreed to put their children at the forefront of priority in terms of their emotional security; and seeing a new mate as inconvenient and a distraction to their relationship with their children, the single mothers had other concerns and doubts about having a partner.

A survey was carried out among some Caribbean women in single parent situations regarding their need for a male companion to buffer their loneliness and who were trying to cope singlehanded with their children. The feedback differed greatly among the women in the sample where it was felt that having a partner can at times be fraught with difficulties in fulfilling the need for new emotional involvement. Some felt that the lack of a male partner to help financially with the children cause them to result in a succession of unsatisfactory relationships while living in constant hope that the latest relationship would thrive and the men would help.

Others admitted that they end up having multiple children from multiple fathers just because they wanted a man about the house to help out financially and to assist in bringing up the children. However, at time after getting pregnant with the last child for the man things don't always work out and the men would leave. They come to realise that the men did not want any responsibility and was only interested in visiting relationships which left them disappointed and hurt. Some of these women admitted that they still felt an emotional bond for the father of their children and always had at the back of their minds that they would return They felt that the emotional frustration at times make them want to take it out on the children and saw abuse as the only way to control their frustration.

Some of these women though not unlucky in love, tend to have a propensity for choosing the wrong mate. Marsden, D. 1973.

These frequent family changes also result in frequent role changes for adults in the household leading to much confusion and stress for the entire family. Yegedis, B.L.

Research indicates that a child's chance of being physically or sexually abused whether male or female is higher when an unrelated adult usually a boyfriend lives in the home and much greater with the presence of a stepfather. In many of these situations, the children usually complain to their parent about the abuse with no satisfactory outcome. The mother may be a victim of abuse herself or do not want to lose the only source of income coming into the home. In these situations, children are more vulnerable to some form of maltreatment when the mother allows or condones physical abuse by her live in boyfriend when there are behaviour problems with the children. This usually occurs when there are tensions in the mother/boyfriend relationship. C Everet Koop MD Surgeon general-Us public health service

Many experts believe that one factor that has contributed to the mistreatment of children in the Caribbean is the secondary or minor status these children hold within these single parent dysfunctional households. Compared with children in intact families, children in one parent female households tend to have more behaviour problems and are more on their own. They tend to have more household responsibilities with less support or supervision. In many households across the Caribbean, there is a large percentage of children some as young as seven years old who often miss out on school attendance because of the responsible for parenting their younger siblings. This responsibility can at times include cooking, washing and doing major household chores especially when the mothers are out of the home all night and spend all day resting at home. Some older children in fact are expected take on the role of disciplinarian when the mother's health or confidence breakdown due to their socio-economic status and low self esteem as a result of drug or alcohol abuse. Bronstein, et al.1993.

Children in these circumstances are also expected to provide emotional support to these vulnerable parents who freely express bitterness towards the lack of child support, resulting in personal difficulties and frustration which are a result of the stresses experienced in the areas of caring for children and the lack of child maintenance and loneliness.

In the Caribbean, these female headed households need to understand the circumstances surrounding their living situations in order to meet the exciting realities of day to day living and be able to cope with both the good and bad challenges. These weaknesses and the inherent inability of such households to satisfy all its material and economic needs put them among the poorest households in society. These families, because of their severely restricted social lives, and lack of preparation for the job market, leave them isolated and with a heightened feeling of inadequacy. Those in a lower socio-economic group tend to experience prolonged living conditions, frustration and anxiety in securing an adequate income, proper accommodation and affordable day care.

Even though some of these families consider themselves independent and self sufficient, the stress of child rearing aggravated by reduced economic circumstances, the lack of child maintenance, a supporting adult to share parental burdens, and the attitude of society to their plight leave them over burdened and financially strained.

Unfortunately, when we examine statistics in relation to the number of single parents, we examine figures but do we always relate those statistics to human beings with human problems which are often always impossible to solve. Sometimes when statistics are presented the picture called to mind are those of rows of files and card indexes and not of flesh and blood victims of cruel circumstances; or of an uncaring and indifferent society. In defence of the one parent family, it isn't easy to relate cold hard facts to the desperate human problems and the actual hardship, misery and loneliness of people struggling to maintain some kind of family life within a unit that is not comparable with the family unit that most of us know.

One can relate the position of one parent families to the issue of the status and opportunities of women. After all, most one parent families are headed by women and as such receive virtually no recognition or support for the job they do as mothers and are grossly disadvantaged in the labour market in respect of job opportunities and levels of pay.

In stressing this fact, one recognises that one parent fathers have special needs and rights which need insight and sensitivity as well.

In comparing the single parent with the parent who has the support of a partner it takes little imagination to see why life is so hard and unrewarding for them especially when coupled with the problems of being the sole source of authority and affection. Most intact families have provided for their children either in a day care facility or after school supervision giving them some respite where their problems can be shared with someone to help the children with homework or to take them out while mother does her chores. The lone parent on the other hand must do the job which normally two would share. She must learn skills which women rarely have to do, like changing plugs or mowing the lawn. The kind of jobs husbands do as a matter of course though at times reluctantly after a certain amount of pressure. Still, a man about the house whom the majority of women take for granted is something the lone parent has to do without. She must learn to be both the man and the woman fulfilling both roles as best she can for the sake of the children. Many are disturbed and distressed by growing indiscipline in their children, and have great difficulty in establishing control, which hardly help their situation. Some are desperate to get out for a few hours of socialising therefore relieving some of the loneliness and frustration which their situation has forced upon them but are afraid of being condemned or reported to the authorities. Hence they are often housebound because they have difficulties finding someone to look after the children.

The Single Parent Father

In comparison with the single parent mother, there are a number of single parent fathers who struggle to raise their children alone. Given equal conditions it is generally much more difficult for a man alone to bring up his children since women are conditioned from an early age to regard the rearing of children as one of the traditions al jobs women do and can be argued as something which comes naturally and is believed to be a major feminine function. Similarly, single parent fathers have to cope with the same disadvantages as their counterparts plus other due roles which they are forced to undertake when they are launched into the double role they are forced to play.

Caribbean fathers have long been stereotyped as irresponsible in their role as care giver as they have often considered the care of children as a woman's role and are neither geared to it in practical terms nor did they see themselves in a mothering role. However, in their quest to acquire the skills to enact the steps that are necessary to realise these goals of attempting to play an active role in their children's lives many hold on to such dreams in the future. However, when the occasion arose for them to become custodians of their children they take their role very seriously and express competence as primary parents and tend to mellow in their approach to children upon assuming this status after a degree of anxiety about this new role because they do not have anything like the support network that single parent mothers have. Balky, J. 1990. Admittedly, single parent fathers do really have a tough time in a world geared for women although they generally have a more healthy economic status than their female counterparts they also find themselves filling social roles for which they are not prepared. Some fathers feel that they have lost their identity since taking on the role of a traditional mother which leaves them feeling very isolated. Others have lost their self-esteem by not being able to work or join their friends at games or socialize with the guys. Furthermore, research findings suggest that while similarities exist in single parents headed by women and those headed by men, the sex of the parent is an important factor in determining the type of family life experiences in each family system. Apart from looking after the home the single parent father have also to cope with problems in areas where there are pre-adolescent and adolescent daughters in a family system that lack sex role models normally provided by an adult woman and provide the socialization in discussing sex education, or explain the circumstances surrounding menstruation to a ten or eleven year old daughter which can also present them with an almost impossible task. Some of them who have no extended family support tend to seek support and assistance from teachers or others outside their family system when they need help. These resources can be helpful in providing information and guidance about child care that will improve their ability to parent their children effectively.

In teaching the Caribbean single parent father how to handle challenges and build character, a community based parenting group called Fathers Incorporated was established by Jamaican men in 1991. This forum intends to address negative stereotypes of Jamaican fathers where workshops were held and awards offered to support fathers in their effort to become caring, committed and responsible parents as part of a goal to change images of fathers as merely involved providers of maternal goods. Both fathers and other men who are anticipating becoming fathers are incorporated in the organization's activities. In order to carry out its mission to protect the image of fatherhood, workshops, seminars and conferences are offered that addresses various aspects of fatherhood. These sessions are designed to provide information about parenting skills as well as to encourage men to play a more active role within the lives of their children, and which can influence the model of the father/ child relationship throughout Jamaica. In practical terms throughout the Caribbean we are beginning to see a new style of parent/ child interaction emerging where fathers are becoming less traditional, more discipline oriented, more concerned with the quality of child care, more interested in the child's educational experiences and more protective towards their children. These single parent fathers also meet and accept the unique challenges associated with their new role as a lone parent.

However, many of them can add undue anxiety and stress to their lives because they avoid discussing and sharing with other single parent fathers any fears or concerns they may have regarding discipline, nurturing. Instead, they settle for open communication with their children offering them more space and freedom to structure their own time while adopting more authoritarian patterns of interacting with their children which tends to promote healthier, more positive adjustments among their children. Hetherington, E.M.et.al.1992. Despite the inherent problems experienced by these single parent fathers, they are far more able to unwind and distress than some single mothers which further reduce the burden on the children Because of their ability to effectively parent their children, it is evident that more and more courts are awarding them custody where they display sufficient ability to provide for their children's needs. There are those who take on the burden of rearing their children alone instead of abandoning them to government care.

Housing and the Single Parent Family

The problems of homelessness is very complex for many single parent families All available evidence shows that one parent families typically experience more housing difficulties than two parent families where the basic facts about housing conditions are harsh and irrefutable. Moreover the cost of land and building is high, the increase in rent is immense and the problems of buying a house or raising a mortgage are all acute problems for the single parent family. It is estimated that a large proportion of one parent families have no home of their own, and because of the situations in which they find themselves they are either sharing with relatives or friends. Undoubtedly, very many share or occupy very cramped and inadequate conditions and when they have children this is not easy. Added to this problem, of course is the trouble of finding decent housing especially when many are in the lower middle classes and have difficulty sparing the cash needed to own their own homes or afford exorbitant rent with relatively low incomes or no income at all which can force intolerable hardship especially on mothers with multiple children causing many to use extended family members for support and connectivity during difficult times.

Housing in the Caribbean show a wide range of varieties from thatch construction which provides shelter for many extremely rural families, houses of wooden construction or chattel houses which are removal to accommodated the less advantaged and a trend toward more solid concrete block construction for the more affluent working and middleclass members of the society. For example, in order to increase the housing stock and provide better accommodation for many poor, low income and working class families, the Government of Barbados has embarked on the construction of low cost and affordable government housing projects which have in most cases been successfully organised and allocated to relieve the burden of inadequate living arrangements. Many of these low income houses consist of between one to three bedrooms and are usually occupied by parents and children, and in many cases occupy up to three generation families living together under the same roof where there is often overcrowding and serious lack of privacy. In some families, there are pockets of substantial overcrowding where large families are living in houses that are too small for their needs and which are not simply inconvenient but involves such discomfort but have obvious and serious concerns for public health intervention.

Bad housing in general, is one of the root causes of most of today's social ills among families, and despite rapidly improving housing conditions throughout the Caribbean overcrowding continues to create a problem for some families. Children reared in squalid overcrowded conditions are unable to acquire high standards of good social behaviour. They grow into the problem adolescents, the vandals and the future criminals. The intention here, of course, is not to suggest that all two parent families enjoy both emotional and practical security but the stark reality is that the children of the majority of lone parents suffer by comparison with all other groups.

The housing difficulties of one parent families obviously stretch far wider than particular difficulties resulting from the breakdown of a marriage relationship. For example, with unmarried mothers the problem of getting adequate accommodation is particularly severe especially when there are multiple children. For separated and widowed parents, the problems sometimes result from failure in retaining accommodation when a marriage has ended but often are caused by wider problems of poverty. At one level, this is the result of simple prejudice against them which is difficult to quantify but some signs suggest that this kind of discrimination is due to refusal of accommodation through hostile attitude by unscrupulous private landlords. In many cases however, the policies that discriminate against one parent families in the housing arena do not affect only them adversely but are also experienced by other disadvantaged groups as well especially those on very low income.

The income of the average one parent family is considered less than half that of the average two parent family, and unless there are better social programmes this unjust evil will continue. Many of the provisions that one parent families need are necessary for other groups too, but the one parent family do have some absolute disadvantages and some relative ones which cry out for special provisions. How is a child expected to grow up into a balanced and outgoing person when it has so many extra disadvantages thrust upon it including the lack of a healthy and secure home environment? When society neglects these children they are deliberately stunting the chances of future generations so what happens to parents is of vital importance to children and affects the degree to which they can realise their potential. Of course, many perform well despite the challenges and perform better against the odds. But how about making conditions where many more perform well. For example, more money, adequate housing, a better legal system to deal with child maintenance leading to less bitterness, more practical services like affordable day care and above all acceptance by society. These are the recipes for the successful rearing of the children of one parent families if the spread of misery and even greater problems in the future are halved.

In studying the Caribbean single parent family, evidence reveal an appalling picture of poverty struggle and loneliness which suggests that these families are the fastest growing deprived group in what is supposed to be a caring society. Such a generalisation is dangerous it would seem, because most one parent Caribbean families do not regard themselves as very different from two parent families except that their need for adequate housing and other resources are more urgent. For example, in the Caribbean, many single parents manage successfully with their duel role especially the unmarried mother who is more or less used to managing single-handed and has adjusted to the dual role. It is estimated that a large proportion of Caribbean one parent families including the unmarried mothers have a deep sense of responsibility towards the children they bring up in conditions of supreme difficulty and in what amounts very often to almost obscene poverty. Many of these parents and their children are successful in their own relationships and enjoy a level of happiness that in no way differentiates them from other families. It must be recognized that despite the shabby deal that these women get in our society, their economic and social position has improved in recent years and this has led to rising expectations and lower levels of tolerance regarding unsatisfactory conditions.

According to Rutter M. 1983, the one parent home is not necessarily pathological, and the two parent family is not always a healthy environment for children. He opined that in general children grow up better adjusted when they have a good relationship with one parent than when they grow up in a two parent home that is filled with discord and discontent.

In addition, E.M. Hetherington 1980 contends that a rejecting and hostile parent is worse than an absent one.

Unfortunately, therefore, the general analysis of social factors alone has not revealed any processes through which poverty, family instability and high concentrations of disadvantaged families combine to produce high rates of abuse and neglect.

However, it cannot be overstated that anything that creates extra pressure for these vulnerable parents will reflect at once upon their children and can produce high rates of maltreatment especially when these pressures relate to the need for affordable housing and specific needs of children. Of major importance, is that for the majority of these families, however, the provision of housing does not alleviate the stigma attached to them because the provision of housing has not been accompanied by any human advancement and still leaves them in a state of poverty. And even though many of them are living in housing situations which are better than what they had to endure their problems of increased poverty remain considerable because the effect on the family's budget became more drastic. The social conditions experienced by these families will also influence the extent to which they can meet the needs of their children since the new homes are rented at a cost higher than most of them can afford, and who must do their best within the framework allowed to it in order to meet their basic necessities and expenses for food and clothing especially when there are school aged children to consider. In a recent qualitative study examining the relationship between single parenting, poverty and children's wellbeing in these diverse social circumstances found that stress unless buffered by sufficient social support and, or, mitigated by other sources of resilience is likely to be significant in the increase risk of some form of maltreatment among parents living in poverty.

In support of children and families, childcare professionals who work with and alongside families, or with children whose family fail them in one way or another must work toward the realisation that there is a range of models for family life. And that within these models, problems will be encountered some of which are insurmountable depending on the particular model because that is human nature. It is not surprising, therefore, that there is a commonality between individual families in our society, in the way tasks and functions are allocated and defined and the expectations of one member towards another.

A first step therefore, is to identify what range of alternative models of adult-adult and adult-child relationship exists in contemporary society in the Caribbean.

A second is to become more aware of the variety of ways in which the responsibilities and social expectations we have of these groups are allocated. The question for educators of family life therefore, is not what most families do once a minimum standard has been reached but which of a number of alternatives a particular family adopts. For example, how does a family, falling within the nuclear grouping cope with the conflicting expectations that are explicit in the traditions of being a good enough mother and home maker who is expected to be flexible, responsive, routine and be expected to tolerate bad behaviour in her children; or, being a good enough father and a good provider when his job necessitates his absence from home when the children are awake. Psychologists such as Bowlby, J.1953.and others in their writings have clearly demonstrated that good child care and good enough parenting are related to the type of society we live in and diversity applies equally to the way functions and tasks are allocated within families. For example, chaotic experiences can be found in a stable two-parent family as well as in other family models even though it is difficult to tolerate.

In addition to developing effective programmes career educators can be advocates for public policy designed to assist single parents in the area of employment discrimination, recognition of non-traditional roles, Government and employer support of child care, pay equality, services for potential teenage single parents and work environment alternatives. In short, policies that establish an equitable educational and economic climate for low income disadvantaged as well as recognition of single parent families as a viable family form will benefit not only these families but society as a whole.

The Problems Experienced by Teenage Mothers

There is a great deal of evidence to suggest that among the number of single parents in Caribbean society there is a high percentage of teenage mothers among the lower classes.

Research shows that teenagers are sexually experienced in their early teens, and the majority of them get pregnant before their eighteenth Birthday. Within this framework of cultural custom it is interesting to trace the sexual development of these vulnerable young people with the understanding that some of them are unable to grasp the full implications of what is happening to them.

The subject of sex and sexuality often strike fear in the hearts of parents as this is traditionally one subject that most parents find very difficult to talk about with their teenagers. For most people, sex is a normal and important part of life and for the adolescent, exploring their sexuality especially when they reach puberty is simply a part of the process of growing up. However, what every teenager must realise is that being secure and comfortable in their sexuality is a great step toward a fuller and healthier sexual appetite which demands knowledge and taking full responsibility for the possible consequences of any and all sexual acts.

Studies primarily concerning Caribbean Black teenage motherhood in low income and poor communities are an important issue to be addresses in terms of their progress because it occurs most often among the daughters of poor families and therefore tends to perpetuate poverty and lack of opportunities from generation to generation. While adolescent parenthood is not a new phenomenon of contemporary times, it has become more commonplace today than in the past. Brooks-Dunn, J. Schley, S. & Hardy, J. 2000. In a study of the Jamaican experience, as it relates to attitude and behaviour regarding teenage sexuality and reproduction among young low income adolescents found that most of them were of a poor academic calibre with little knowledge of pregnancy and sexuality. Archer, E.Y.1990 In a survey targeting teens in the twelve to sixteen age group regarding sexual activity and pregnancy, there is evidence that most of the young adolescents particularly the girls felt that they did not want to become a parent while still in their teen years. Random interviews were carried out with some teenagers between the ages fourteen to sixteen in Barbados. Many of them agree that some girls became pregnant because of being caught between male aggression and the inability to defend themselves, It was agreed also that some girls get pregnant through being coerced, seduced or even raped. In the Jamaican survey revealed that fewer than 1 in 10 girls reported that both they and their male counterparts felt that they were responsible enough to be a parent but felt however, that pregnancy a little later in their teen years may be somewhat more acceptable. It is estimated that 29% of girls and 40% of boys in the survey agreed that a girl should have a baby while she is a teenager to prove her fertility. Sobo, E.J.1996.

There is growing evidence that adolescents in the Caribbean are becoming more sexually active at an early age because family planning providers are reluctant to serve clients younger than the legal age with contraceptives which leads to the increase in the number of unwanted pregnancies, abortions and teenage pregnancies despite the provision of easily accessible birth control services and a comprehensive national sex education programme including awareness of HIV/AIDS and other sexually transmitted diseases. The dilemma faced by Caribbean Governments therefore is how they are going to protect teenagers from having babies. In today's environment, however, the solution would be abortion on demand but there are moral and ethical issues to consider. The lack of established standards, individual responsibilities and the setting of good examples raise conflict between contemporary social values over the sexuality of young people and has become an area of public scrutiny. Elizabeth Eggleton, et al 1999.

Despite the many socio-economic problems that impact the pregnancy of teenagers, with a low income status why do they choose to become pregnant only to experience the obvious difficulties of being a very young mother? Several studies have found that many of these mothers had dropped out of school prior to becoming pregnant and many of the pregnancies are a result of carelessness, thoughtlessness and by personal choice. In the general population many teen mothers chose to keep their babies although they arrived at single parenthood through a number of circumstances, motivations and different emotional reactions. Some are not ready emotionally or financially for the responsibility or sacrifice of parenthood and sees the child as a tie, a burden or an annoyance representing some interference in their personal freedom to carry out their social life. Some are uncertain about their role as a parent and may be frustrated by the constant demands of the child and are reluctant to take advice on proper child care and can be neglectful and abusive to the child. Under these circumstances, it is not hard to estimate the confusion and distress a child may experience in such situations. A teenager who chooses to have a child believes that she has little to lose and much to gain. Kristen Luker1996. Some again, may want a baby to have someone to love especially when they themselves feel unloved and uncared for and which may improve their self worth while not recognising the amount of care the baby needs. Because of this deep sense of insecurity they become very emotionally attached to the child and see it as an extension of themselves and not as a child with a personality of its own, and even though there is much bonding and attachment there may be numerous daily situations which may arouse parental ambivalence towards the child. With normal satisfactions and a positive relationship many teen parents can do well in the mother/child interaction until faced with a situation of abnormal stress.

In the Caribbean, the number of single parent households is ever present and continues to grow. Included in these statistics are unmarried teenage mothers and their children, some of whom at times find themselves locked in a cyclical pattern of dysfunction with problems that adversely affect not just the illegitimate births but also themselves and society at large since the health problems of these mothers and their babies tend to result from social and economic problems rather than medical ones. Some of these difficulties include low income or no income at all and with all the ensuing complications this may have such as the lack of emotional support when it is most needed from her family who may not be too pleased about the pregnancy, the father of her child who is either unemployed, acting irresponsibly and may deny paternity and being isolation from her peers. These young mothers also carry the stigma attached to premature pregnancies with a widely held stereotype of 'babies having babies'.

Research into teen pregnancy has found that many teenage mothers are somewhat less likely than older mothers to start prenatal care on time and are therefore more likely to have low birth weight babies and complications during the pregnancy and the birth of the child. Although these factors are associated with medical and sometimes developmental problems in their child(ren), the problems of these mothers are more social and economic when they are far more likely to physically abuse, abandon or neglect their child(ren).

Despite the negative expressions about motherhood among teenagers and its effect upon later life, having a baby as a teenager does not inevitably lead to social and economical hardship. Sometimes, these young and immature mothers, especially if they live in an extended family environment usually find that they can rely on other family members in the household when a crisis occurs, but too many crises at too young an age can have dire consequences for both mother and child.

In Caribbean culture characterized by large multi-generational households, family members usually intervene directly by assisting in the upbringing of its members where family support and close relationships are crucial to a positive and healthy family life experience with high aspirations for their educational development. However, these relationships and aspirations can become fragile with widespread confusion when a teenage member discloses her pregnancy. After this disillusionment has worn off relationships are mostly re-established after the birth of the child. During this period family support and a close relationship with the young mother are crucial to a positive experience and an emotional environment. Sometimes the child's maternal grandmother relates to the new baby as one of her own children. Some of them give up their jobs in order to become the main supporter in terms of child care and practical and emotional support while the young mother plays a passive role towards her baby's status in the home. Even when disagreements occur between the child's mother and her own mother in matters of child care while living under the same roof, the maternal grandmother stay on the fringes with varying degrees of involvement unless there is a crisis.

The adolescent mother, living in overcrowded conditions with multiple do's and don'ts in matters of child care can cause her to face poor life prospects. In absolute terms, there are dire consequences. For example, many of them are unemployed and are not actually looking for a job, and if they do find work they are likely to work in low skilled jobs. Also when they want to leave home they find that private rented accommodation has more negatives than positives. Many of these teenage mothers wanting to rent a house or apartment from a private land lord find that these are not readily available or the rent may be too high, they may be given notice if the landlord wants to sell the property. In other instances there are no children rules or they don't qualify if they are on a low income. Even if they take in the child's father or male companion to assist with the rent, he is either not earning, not earning enough, or not financially or emotionally responsible. Studies have found that some teen fathers want to help the girl he has impregnated but they themselves need assistance and support. One needs to fully aware of the fact that the picture is pretty dismal for teenagers who choose to raise children since most of them do not seek medical attention at the beginning of their pregnancy, and when they do the consequences can be detrimental considering the age, nutrition and quality care are all factors to be taken into consideration in maternal and child health of a baby. As for the mother, poor diet, lack of postnatal care can lead to health problems also. Research has shown that because these mothers are too immature to understand infants and their behaviour they has the tendency to be easily frustrated through lack of support, isolation from peers, financial pressures and societal attitudes. Many of them may develop post natal depression which can affect the parent/child relationship where they are less sensitive and less engaging with their infant therefore their interaction is less positive. Added to other socio-economic circumstances the teenage mother is more likely to suffer long term depression. Field.T.1998. With teen pregnancy there is hardly a single more productive tool for the prevention of socio-economic stress among young people than the prevention of teen pregnancies and teen parenthood. Here a distinction must be made between wanting a child and planning to have a child because surveys have shown that the majority of first born among teens are unplanned but is usually wanted after the baby is born. The fact remains that having a child at a certain time is no indication of proper understanding or readiness for parenthood. Lieberman, E.J.& Ellen Peck 1973.

Social norms regarding pregnancy and parenthood within some communities exert a powerful and negative influence on young people including their peers causing some of them to drop out of school at a staggering rate with no intention of returning because of stigma, shame and embarrassment. Research indicates however, that teen pregnancy and parenthood are not a good reason for school exclusion or for limited later educational opportunities. For them, completion of academic achievements confers economic advantages for the individual and every effort must be made to keep these young people in school and to reintegrate them as rapidly as possible back into the school system. In Jamaica for example, pregnant girls are required to leave school during their pregnancy and academic training is geared toward strengthening these participant's capabilities and prepare them academically for return to the formal school system. In general, academic achievement opportunities have rapidly improved for teenage mothers throughout the Caribbean and Education Authorities are taking renewed interest in their education by providing needed support services to reintegrate these children back into the school system while arrangements are made for the care of the child with other relatives or through the provision of a day care facility while promoting their educational goals and their long term academic success.

CHAPTER 8

CHILDREN'S NEEDS AND PARENTAL RESPONSIBILITIES

One writer, Herbert Hoover once said, "Children are our most natural resource. They are in fact our next world leaders. The love, the spirit, the zest for life, the quest for knowledge and the respect for everything they learn from us today, will govern all their tomorrows and shape their future for generations to come"

The influence of the family on a child cannot be overestimated, because it is a child's first source of information and the primary model for how a child experience relationships. It helps a child in its communication skills, and assists them in learning personal and cultural values. The family also teaches a child how to get along in a complex world while providing him with a sense of belonging and a foundation for building self esteem. Therefore, families, and particularly parents who are confident and effective in these responsibilities are more likely to raise healthy and productive children.

It appears that the development of parent child attachment is facilitated by the parent's warm, contingent responsiveness to the young child through experiences of consistent care giving and affectionate playfulness where these children are able to become attached to significant persons in their social world. Goldberg, S. 1977 also emphasises the need for balance and coordination between the mother and child. While recognising the complex interplay between parent and child, it is recommended that parents be made aware of the intricate relationships between their behaviour in their environment and that of their young child for early influences of development.

We cannot begin to improve the living conditions of disadvantaged families and vulnerable children unless we identify they and their children's needs and privileges, and provide them with a natural and profound understanding of what is happening to their lives. The effectiveness with which a child's needs are assessed will depend therefore, upon improving the living conditions of disadvantaged families and vulnerable children in every community by providing them with needed privileges and adequate resources so that they can understand what is happening to their lives. Every society has a distinct cultural awareness as to what constitutes the fundamental needs of its children, and which in itself constitutes a minimum standard of living for all children regardless of class, creed and ethnicity. Any discussion about children having a voice and an opinion always call to mind their relative powerlessness and the strong influence adults have had in regulating their livelihood., The turn of the nineteenth century saw considerable changes in the way children are treated and continues to do so. In absolute terms, the general position of most children has improved internationally. However, though the plight of maltreated children has gained a lot of attention and intervention, many of the abuse practices remain in the home and in society as a whole.

In the acquisition of their needs, and in defending their rights, children need a fair and equal opportunity to grow and develop. But before this can happen there must be a commitment to do what must be done to realise those rights. The Convention on the Rights of the Child intends to improve the lives of children worldwide by seeking to establish a set of principles which are reflected in the provisions made for all children. In recent years, Caribbean countries have taken the initiative and adopted those principles that are inherent in the Declaration of children's rights 1959. These include access to health and social services, education, love and understanding while in the care of, and under the responsibility of their parents or parent substitute. This should occur whenever possible in an atmosphere of affection and security, and be protected from all forms of neglect, cruelty and exploitation. In committing themselves to pursue these goals, Caribbean leaders agree to be guided by the fully articulated principle that the essential needs of children should be given high priority in the allocation of resources at all times and at national, international and family level.

Caribbean countries adoption of these rights is evident in the many organisations, Government and Private agencies that have developed programmes dedicated to the prevention and detection of child abuse and neglect, as well as providing for the abused child and his family. While there is no denying that enormous strides have been made in trying to eradicate the scourge of child abuse in the region, adequate protection of its children from abusive acts still remains somewhat of an unfilled promise.

In spite of the increasing involvement of social service agencies, law enforcement personnel and our court systems, it remains evident that access to safeguards for our children and their families remain difficult and discouraging. Another factor worthy of consideration is the widely held belief throughout the Caribbean that the way parents treat their children is nobody else's business. If we agree that children have rights, then we must agree that how children are treated within families is everybody's business. This has brought with it the recognition that children must be protected at all costs and can have far reaching implications for the concept of proper growth, development and survival. As Katz so aptly point out," Children are no longer classified as property, but as persons." This implies that children's rights to medical, physical and educational care and protection against gross maltreatment and exploitation have gradually been recognised. In addition, parents are now expected to provide children with a nurturing environment, and to ensure that they develop socially, emotionally and intellectually as well as physically. By the year 1993, all Caribbean countries have ratified the Convention on the Rights of the child which obligates these Governments to protect and promote children's rights with a commitment to intervene on their behalf to ensure that these rights are addressed.

Concern with children must also involve recognition that they have needs which are to be met to ensure their optimum growth and development. In too many walks of life children's needs are not being taken seriously, and sometimes, even ignored.

Research has shown that until children can meet their own needs they require many things from their parents. A universal truth held by many specialists in child care and development are of the view that the greatest challenge to child rearing is their emotional requirements in terms of their fundamental needs which should be met in any society if they are to enjoy life, develop their full potential and grow into participating and contributing adults in order to ensure their complete and healthy psychological growth. These can be identified as security, praise, proper nourishment, adequate rest, a comfortable and secure home environment and the need for new experiences which should be conveyed through a stable, continuous, dependable loving relationship with parents or significant parent figures, recognising that basic psychological needs are the same for all children which when fulfilled can promote personalities that are satisfying to the individual and his society. These can be identified as lack of proper nourishment, inadequate rest, an uncomfortable and insecure home and lack of proper health care. As Dr. Kelmer Pringle 1974 puts it children are not just objects of concern and recognises that basic psychological needs are the same for all children, and she identifies four basic needs which when fulfilled can promote personalities that are satisfying to the individual and his society. She identifies these as love and security; praise and recognition; the need for new experiences, and the need for responsibility, which are conveyed through a stable, continuous, dependable and loving relationship with parents or significant parent figures. Stevens and Matters 1978 argue that the strength and character of warm long lasting emotional attachments is likely to influence the quality of the parent-child relationship and help the child to develop a secure base of trust and confidence. It should not be taken for granted therefore, that children enjoy much comfort or emotional security in interaction with parents or parent figures that ill-treat them or are unkind to them. As Naylor, A.K. 1970 puts it: *"One cannot expect mature behaviour from a parent whose own nurturing was poor, and whose development was full of conflict."*

It can be argued, therefore, that in order to help children we must first help families. This can only be achieved through helping them to recognise their own need for fulfilment and the need to promote the development of their children through understanding their basic needs, and serving as models of appropriate behaviour. Many parents whose power it is to protect and provide for their offspring has been eroded by sickness, poverty, disability and a lack of essential social services. It is essential therefore, that early intervention strategies be put in place to support children and disadvantaged families before problems either from within the family or as a result of external factors escalate into crises or abuse, and which can impact negatively on parenting capacities.

Being a parent is a very important job. It is intended to be a time of great joy and responsibility. It is rewarding and fulfilling, and occasionally very frustrating. Every day as a parent is important, and every day seems to bring new possibilities and new challenges. Perhaps, more than anything parenting is a time to share and prepare, a time of getting a child ready to face the world alone. Psychological facts of course inform us that all this takes place in steps and stages, But to be truly successful in parenting means ultimately letting go after helping children become self-sufficient and good decision makers. During these years, there is much for children to learn from basic facts about the world around them to the difference between right and wrong It is also a very tough job and carries a responsibility that demands knowledge, energy, patience, wisdom and self sacrifice among many other skills, all of which have the potential to tax our capabilities in the act of child rearing. One of the most challenging tasks in life is that of taking on full responsibility of raising a totally helpless infant into a self-disciplined, productive member of society. Even so, nature is not very selective when it comes to choosing a parent. Individuals with all types of temperaments and personalities have the opportunity to be productive. Producing a child does not require any test, licence or specific qualifications. There are those parents who stumble through their child-rearing practices having had no training in the principles of parenthood, and rely on the same methods used by their parents. More often, these methods are violent, abusive and neglectful.

Bringing up children to become good citizens of a community to which they belong is fraught with many difficulties, and parents will always make mistakes regardless of how well intended because perfection in parenting is an unattainable goal. However, there are those parents who do not have the capacity to parent their children, and look on their children's behaviour as the source of their problem.

They often do not see that their own emotional instability produces a rippling effect on their children's behaviour and subsequently on the way they are treated.

In order for these parents to carry out these tasks efficiently and effectively, they need to be healthy, mature and be able to handle the new and intricate situations that come with children. Whether there are two parents or only one parent, love and respect among family members help make a happier home and positive relationships. Parenting is influenced therefore by the personality of the parent, the family and the home environment taking into account the individuality of the child.

It is widely accepted that the early years of childhood are the formative ones when attitudes and beliefs, and understanding about others and the world around them are formed, and where young children learn a lot from the adults around them. Parents are therefore expected to mediate their children's understanding of the world from the perception of their first environment that is the home. From there, the extent to which parents provide meaningful experiences for children largely determines the children's ability to discover meaning and values and a range of behaviours and attitudes. It is crucial, therefore, for parents to have a clear understanding of how best they can support the healthy development of their children if they are to give to society human beings who are able to interact with, and function within the norms of this complex society.

As one begin to explore the considerable variation in child-rearing beliefs and behaviours across the English speaking Caribbean, it becomes clear that there is not a universal standard for raising children, neither must we accept any form of inhumane treatment of children in the name of culture. Culture, no matter whose it is, must never be an excuse for hurting children. However, we must try to understand what is normal or acceptable in our child-rearing practices.

There has been much research and books written about child-rearing, and so there are many different theories and schools of thought on the subject.

In order to get a better understanding of the strategies used in raising children in present day Caribbean cultures, it is necessary to investigate the child-rearing practices of Caribbean people, by understanding the attitude and beliefs of care takers and other adults of the society towards children. Also to discover how culture influences the way they interact with them in the socialisation process. Children are completely dependent upon the care given to them by their caregivers, and any study of the conditions of their environment must take into account the child rearing habits of his caregivers.

CHAPTER 9

PARENTAL GUIDANCE AND DISCIPLINE

The reality of being consciously willing to be a mother takes a willing heart to have a child where ambivalence has no place in the thought, but becoming a parent is a process which demands a series of behavioural adaptations as the child develops.

It is one of those essential facts of life that raising good children demands time and attention and while carrying out this activity involves doing what comes naturally, being a good parent is much more complicated especially in trying to understand his behaviour from infancy through adolescents which is likely to have a significant influence on his distinct behaviour variations.

According to psychological theory, children in all parts of the world mature in roughly the same sequence. For example, some tend to race toward developmental milestones, while others move at a more leisurely pace. Still the genetic inheritance of all human infants ensures that the sequence of development will be much the same which proceeds in an orderly fashion throughout life. Kathy Silva and Ingrid Lunt, 1982.

In studying child development and the orderly progression of the maturation process, we have agreed that it is both measurable and demonstrable in relation to psychosocial and reciprocal interaction without being subjected to grave frustration while assisting the child in meeting the demands and challenges of his progress through these developmental processes. Findings from new studies about the nature of infant development depict an infant as showing highly competent behaviour and being actively involved in learning to master his or her interactions with the environment Messer, D.J. et.al 1986.

One important aspect of control of the negative characteristics of pro-social behaviours in their children is for parents to understand these children's development problems and be able to exercise effective controls over their behaviour.

Theorists and researchers have acknowledged that child development as an area of study encompasses four major aspects of human growth from birth to adolescents which comprises the development of the body, the progressive elaboration of intellectual skills and the complex interaction between psycho-social factors, physical maturation and socialization which are all processes by which children adjust to the expectations of society. Gesell, Arnold 1929. But what kind of interaction between parents and children might be expected to contribute to children's positive orientation towards others when they do not get such developmental support whether it is their heredity endowment or the environment they are raised in? The opinion that this development is due mainly to environmental factors that cannot be changed, but never the less makes an impact on the child. Critics of behavioural genetics research say that these studies dismissed the influence of parenting practices and direct intervention that seem to foster effective parenting. Such studies offer evidence that parental influence contributes greatly to developmental outcomes independent of hereditary effects. Collins, et.al. 2000. Certainly most parents have some conception of what behaviours they want to promote in their children but because children are individual beings with their own innate personalities and genetic differences, not only will their abilities develop differently but their social lives will be different also as they develop despite certain similarities that they share with each other. Clearly, the views of parents on how children should behave are seldom in agreement with their children's own views. However, if there is to be social interaction and positive behaviour attitude, between parents and children there are a number of issues which are relevant to their understanding of their role as a socializing agent for their children.

In contemporary society within the Caribbean context, parents require more than providing love and nurturance as a basis for proper guidance and discipline in their children. They need to find more effective ways to perform their task in interacting with their children and attain goals for their child rearing efforts, providing proper guidance through communication, changing their attitudes toward their children, help them in developing their personality and self-esteem, imposing family values conducive to the family environment and preparing them for an uncertain future in a rapidly changing society Research has shown that the strength and character of a warm long lasting emotional attachment is likely to influence the quality of the parent/child relationship and will help the child to develop a secure base of trust and confidence.

The teaching and guiding aspects of parenting are perhaps the greatest concern that care givers have in adequately performing their duties. The issue of how to provide adequate and appropriate discipline in guiding children's growth and development is of primary concern to parents and other who provide care for children. Sometimes there is so much emphasis on understanding and responding to the needs of children that parents own need for personal gratification and development is obscured. For instance, they need understanding of themselves as parents and people with their own needs values and self worth and of how the lack of these can affect the way they rear their children. They have to learn the capacity not only to provide their own self—preservation, but also to place a high value on their very existence. Unless we care about our own lives and our own worth as parents we cannot very well express much interest or concern about the wellbeing of anyone else. But how does being who we are affect our relationship with our children?

It allows us the ability to love and understand relationships,

To be flexible of mind and thought,

To communicate effectively,

To be consistent in our attitudes and behaviours

To make decisions and accept responsibility,

To cope in stressful situations, deal with conflict, and most importantly, to be able to say "I love you. Or "I am sorry". Unfortunately, for some parents these are very painful words if throughout their lives they were hardly used and will have little or no meaning. Despite these parental misgivings, the family is still accountable for providing the basis for bringing up succeeding generations of children, and it is incumbent on parents to help children develop into complete adults by ensuring that the nurture they offer is indeed the training that will accompany this.

Research indicates that a family where there are two parents tend to produce well—adjusted children, but there are those who will challenge this notion. However, whether there are two parents or only one parent, the amount of love and respect among family members can help make a happier home and positive relationships.

In order to understand Caribbean family life and its inherent concerns, one needs to consider their points of view which in turn require an acknowledgement of the culture from which the family comes, with special reference to its child-rearing practices and its influence on their physical and psycho-social development. One must likewise have an understanding of existing child-rearing practices taking into account a study of the conditions in his environment and its impact on the care given to him by his caregivers, since Caribbean culture has its own particular child rearing customs as well as its own beliefs, attitudes and idiosyncratic ideas and beliefs. It is helpful however, for parents to adopt a consistent plan of action for appropriate discipline to be administered and function effectively for the benefit of all family members.

Psycho-Social Development of the Child

In studying child development and the orderly progression of the maturation process, is both measurable and demonstrable in relation to the reciprocal interaction without being subjected to grave frustrations while assisting the child in meeting the demands and challenges of his progress through these developmental stages. In fact, child development as an area of study encompasses four major aspects of human growth from birth to adolescents which comprises the development of the body, the progressive elaboration of intellectual skills, and the complex interactions between psychosocial factors physical maturation and socialization which are all processes by which children adjust to the expectations of society Gesell Arnold 1929.

It is well established that Language is the key to learning. Without language a child cannot understand other people and therefore cannot communicate with others. The rate at which a child progresses will depend upon his own ability, the encouragement given by his parents and whether or not there are siblings in the home. His contact with external stimulus means that the child is exposed to influences that lead it into a course of development the aim is which to make it a social being except, for instance if the child is slow to develop language because of psychological problems, he has a physical defect, is mentally retarded or has other language deficits. Based on a study by Arnold Gesell 1945 who has studied child development to age sixteen years, there is one aspect of his study which demonstrates how the child attains a particular level of functional ability is his intellectual development. This process of socializing the child makes possible the achievement of a certain pattern of behaviour. It is well known by psychological means that the rate at which a child progresses proceeds intellectually, emotionally and physically according to tables of maturation and according to how the child reacts to other people and his adjustments to ways of communicating with other people. Below, is the approximate stage of intellectual development at various stages that will help the child to progress to the next stage of development.

0-7 weeks   the child cries, makes cooing noises and responds to noises and voices.

2-4 months   the child starts to produce the simpler vowel sounds and some Consonants.

4-6 months   the child can vocalize and begin word formations such as mama and dada can be distinguished.

6-9 months   babbling continues, but with more meaning. The child will be joining- up more and more syllables which implies a big step forward toward real speech.

9-12 months the child will be able to say two or three words and understand some simple commands, reacts to its own name and will say the words that are important to him such as "cup", "dada" and "no"

18 months the child's linguistic ability has developed. He chatters a lot, can say six to twenty identifiable words and has good comprehension

**18 months-
2 years** the child's language has improved considerably and he is able to form two-word phrases and short sentences such as wanting to go to the bathroom or other needs which may include wanting a cookie, etc.

3 years the child has a deep understanding of words and chatters incessantly. He has a vocabulary of at least two hundred words and understands many more. The child now can classify, identify and compare by asking many questions.

It is important that one understands that children are not taught how to speak their own language. Remember they are surrounded by people speaking it in the home, the nursery, in the street and on the television and radio. Because of this new language opportunity, the child's curiosity is aroused, and with increasing physical development he sees a need to communicate. Therefore, the adults around him should listen to him, answer his questions and give him encouragement which all contributes to his social skills.

But what can be done to help children who do not get such developmental support? The concept is closely connected with the intricate problems of bringing up children to become good citizens of the community to which they belong, and since it is the interaction between himself and his surroundings that makes him adopt forms of behaviours that are not in accordance with the norms and values of the adult environment the aim is to create conditions for the development of a well integrated individual by providing therapeutic and educational services to families that need help in meeting children's psycho-social and developmental needs.

Cultural socialization influences child rearing practices and the way that parents and other adults interact with children in verbal and non-verbal communication. These practices help to form and shape the child's view of himself and how he/she fits in the world.

In Caribbean societies, children are raised as a source of love and satisfaction. Mothers are concerned about their children's development. They get them to behave by developing in them respect fixed on moral values and the ability and strength of character to distinguish between right and wrong. There is general agreement among behavioural scientists that parents and early experiences within the family are among the most important influences that shapes the personality and affects the behaviour of the child. The child-rearing practices of any society must take into consideration shaping the development of the child so that he will become a well—adjusted adult with the abilities and skills necessary to function in the social environment of his society and the world as a whole. Equally important is his immediate physical environment which has a direct impact on certain child-rearing practices, and where the daily routine that takes place primarily in the social setting of the home environment teaches appropriate social behaviour from interaction with his community and in the parent-child relationships.

In the traditional Caribbean society, children were provided with much sensorial stimulation in the home by mimicking his older siblings or by being cared for by an older relative. However, the observation has often been made that the traditional childrearing practices did not consciously encourage curiosity and exploration. The reason being that "he likes too much playing" and is expected to help around the home. Mothers and other adults did not make a conscious effort to speak often to their young child with the intent of teaching them how to communicate. This was not the same awareness in western societies of encouraging a child to express himself. This lack of verbal interaction between the Caribbean mother and child has sometimes been used as an explanation for the extreme timidity and inability to perform well which requires them to relate or communicate with adults. In this case, the child may not receive the intellectual stimulation necessary to help him develop certain skills required for successful adaptation in today's world. These parents did not endorse play as a beneficial pastime for their children, and therefore there was not the positive reinforcement or verbal encouragement of intellectual curiosity that one has come to expect in most modern societies. Early nurturing of the child involves helping him learn how to manage and control his body and how to observe, distinguish between and communicate about his inner and external experiences even before he speaks. It entails furnishing him appropriate stimulus experiences and learning opportunities. Parents must understand that play is the young child's work The importance of these nurturing functions in the child's early life has been recognised clearly only in recent times, and has provided opportunities for the child to acquire verbal competence and increase his capacity to invest in peer and adult relationships. When these nurturing tasks are not adequately fulfilled, the potential damage to personality development, social adjustment and educational capabilities become unrealistic. Sandstrom C.I. 1968. As the child got older, his curiosity developed and his need for exploration is manifested.

In present day Caribbean society however, with expectations and goals undergoing rapid change, and social groups being radically refine, the Caribbean family have also made radical changes in the way their children are socialised in the home and in the wider society. In keeping with western culture, the Caribbean culture is now being influenced by social mobility and high achievement goals for their children. They have become involved in the basic obligations of ensuring that their children receive proper and appropriate social and intellectual development by acquiring the proper parenting and childrearing skills needed to prepare them for school, also by teaching and guiding them at each level of social development that create positive home conditions that support learning and develop more flexible childrearing attitudes. The characteristics of many young parents today hold high aspirations for their children's intellectual orientation, so that eventually they will inculcate the dominant views of society and at the same time value the importance of these nurturing functions in the early life of the child. In short, it is in this way that the child learns social customs and norms and be socially integrated into his family and his society.

According to Sandstrom C.I 1968, Socialisation is a lifelong process by which a young person adopts forms of behaviour that are in accordance with the norms and values of the adult environment. The concept is closely connected with the intricate problems of bringing up children to become good citizens of the community to which they belong. This general concept, includes helping children learn to control their impulses and to acquire the social skills that will allow them to participate actively and fully in family life, work roles and in interaction with other people, the emphasis is upon getting the family functioning as a satisfactory social unit, and so providing an environment conducive to a better standard of physical and mental health.

Jean Jacques Rousseau French philosopher believed that the development of the child occurs naturally in a series of predestined internally regulated stages that are born good and become warped only by repressive environments.

In his gospel of man's return to nature, Rousseau dreamt of the "noble savage" he imagined him as a highly developed and enviable type of man who had in his upbringing been influenced as little as possible by grownups. The inherent goodness of man would ensure that development would lead to ideal human goals. He maintained that these ideas are found in modern views of upbringing when it is claimed that the child for its self-realisation must enjoy a measure of freedom to prevent its becoming impeded or misdirected in its development the child must also be allowed a positive and creative role in the interaction between himself and the world. Studies have shown that cultural environments can also influence children's acquisition of developmental achievements related to their socio-cultural orientation. For example, it is well known that a child imitates what others say or do that stimulates his thirst for knowledge and understanding according to the more experiences he is provided with in the socializing process. This also affects various developmental areas he is exposed to such as verbal and emotional concepts and other cognitive areas including his physical development. As children become socialized they learn how to fit into and function as protective members of their society. Studies have also shown that children perform better when they feel good about themselves whether at home school or with peers. Assuming that children feel loved provide them with a solid foundation that will facilitate their psycho-social development.

The child rearing practices of any well functioning society are directed toward shaping the development of the child so that he/she will become well adjusted adults. Depending on the nature of a particular family system certain standards may be promoted more than others. This brings into question the methods of child rearing practices and how effective are they? A central goal of Caribbean parents like most parents is to manage their child behaviour along with the added task of preparing them for positive concepts.

Long established cultural patterns among Afro-Caribbean people witnessed a trend toward beliefs and practices in the socialization of young children as they challenge areas of intellectual concern and its effects upon the unique Afro-Caribbean cultural values are already involved in profound processes of social change, some of the present trends promise to be favourable to child care and training practices as alternative lifestyles have become part of Caribbean culture, attempts to shape social attitudes, competencies and behaviours of children in new ways have emerged.

In the meantime, however, there have been some notable additions to our knowledge and understanding about how parental responsiveness is associated with optimal cognitive development for their children's achievements and aspirations. Since societies are undergoing rapid change in how children are socialized and the avenues that are open to it for social mobility, and social groups are being radically refined, their children's higher educational achievements are often seen by them as a prerequisite to early childhood education programmes which can have a great impact on later cognitive development of their children.

A number of researchers into the socialization of the Caribbean child have looked at the contribution of parents and the home environment which have had a great impact on the study of child rearing and its psycho-social development.

Some of special attitudes and techniques required by parents to enhance these harmonious relationships are based on knowledge of the developmental process, and on those characteristics of the parent that will stimulate the child to accelerate its social, cognitive and emotional development.

When discussing the customs used by the family in raising and taking care of their children, these customs are in fact strategies for encouraging their psycho-social development to coincide with diverse factors such as education and occupation given parents goals and aspirations for what constitutes a properly socialized child.

Having looked at a series of traditional habits and attitudes involved in what is considered a well brought up child, most areas in which the socialization places great emphasis will be examined.

A child growing up in the traditional Caribbean Society is trained to recognise the importance of knowing his place in the family and must behave as a responsible member of the community in which he lives. For example, it is considered bad manners or a lack of respect to address older individuals by their first name. Family friends are referred to as "auntie" or "uncle" and elders as "Mr." or "Mrs." Children are not allowed to speak or take part in adult conversation. They are admonished to "take their place" or "be seen and not heard", it is considered lack of respect to make eye to eye contact when being spoken to, and this gesture implies that the child is rude and challenging. The word "please" is used for greeting and responding and is considered being polite and respectful. For example, children are expected to say "yes please" when called and "yes please "or "no please "when a response is required. These parents hold high aspirations for their children and often have predetermined goals and expectations for them with the hope that they will grow up healthy and well adjusted, and who can in due course become happy, healthy and well adjusted adults. However, it has been observed that in the traditional Caribbean culture mothers and other adults from lower socio-economic status did not engage their children in meaningful conversation with the intent of teaching them how to communicate or express themselves. This has often times been used as an explanation that the child is extremely timid and unable to perform well both in school and when speaking to adults. However, when traditional child-rearing practices no longer efficiently corresponds to modern realities, or when there is a breakdown in the social structure of the family, the effects can lead to harsh and excessive parental behaviour. It must be emphasized, though, that these attitudes do not mean that all Caribbean children are disadvantaged in the acquisition of language or productive competence.

When Discipline Becomes Abuse

Over the years, a number of social scientists and mental health practitioners have engaged themselves in exploring the connection between physical abuse, discipline and culture and have found that many rules are violated worldwide. In the Caribbean, for example, child rearing is highly influenced by ethnic culture where what children need to learn and the method considered best for teaching them are passed down from one generation to another. These patterns of parental discipline and socializing appear to range from very strict to more relax as a cultural tradition and according to the parent's mood where some children are at times beaten with whatever object is available at hand within the appropriate age range. Other differences may include being slapped in the face, punched in the back or the occasional scalding with hot liquid especially for giving "back chat". These methods of discipline seem to be widespread thus leaving the children quite confused especially when these children are not aware of their parent's mood swing or temperament.

It is well established that instilling discipline in a child is an essential part of teaching children what is right or wrong and what types of behaviour is considered acceptable. We also need to recognise that children were not born knowing behaviours or actions that are appropriate and should be guided along these lines through parental expression and interpretation.

A review of the research literature on parental disciplinary practices suggest that parents must deal with these issues of young children who have wills and minds of their own but who still have a lot to learn in terms of what kinds of behaviour works well in a civilized society. Inconsistencies in parental behaviour may cause children to become afraid and paranoid when these parents lose control thereby undermining their ability to influence their children's behaviour. Grusec, J.E & Goodnow, J.J 1994. During the seventeenth century, the methods parents used to discipline their children instituted such measures as locking them in their room for many hours, or shut them away in dark cupboards or in animal pens rather than inflicting physical punishment on them to correct misbehaviours. Although these forms of discipline have gradually decrease due to their compliance with rules and behaviours according to social standard, the intrusive methods used by parents never the less required steady pressure by parents to maintain proper discipline in their children. By the nineteenth century, however, many parents no longer needed to terrorize or beat their children, as more gentle and psychological means began to be used to socialize children. The fact is that more acceptable and conventional methods of discipline are still the main model of upbringing in western nations featuring the mother as trainer and the father as protector and provider. In western cultures, this type of training is referred to as discipline which is part of proper child rearing, and, depending on how it is enforced can have negative or positive effects upon a child's social and psychological wellbeing.

When comparing abuse and discipline in the Caribbean context what is the parent trying to achieve? In trying to understand the characteristics of these two parental actions some would argue that any physical force imposed upon a child constitutes abuse, others maintain that spanking a child falls under the category of reasonable discipline, while there are those who felt that culturally everything they did were simply imposing discipline to socialize the child.

From a functional approach, there are a number of factors that may cause caregivers to misuse discipline. However, to get a better understanding of why it is termed misuse, it is necessary to at least in a concise manner explain discipline as it should be genuinely administered, and its positive effects and achievements when appropriately applied; in addition to view the factors based on the definition of discipline. According to the Oxford English Dictionary, discipline is training that enforces obedience, develops self—control, and assists in character building. Discipline is also described as the act of instilling the above behaviours to a person or persons with the intention of preserving a value system that can stem deviant behaviour. In the Caribbean, the way some parents behave toward children in carrying out their responsibility of guiding and disciplining is widely varied. Some believe that children should accept parental authority without question. They are of the view that the standard of discipline today is contributing significantly to the rapid decline of the society and are of the opinion that the use of corporal punishment has brought up a society of highly intelligent and civil minded leaders. They argue that the children of today have too much of their own way and corporal punishment is not being served on them enough. They believe that the essence of good discipline is to produce good citizens. And that any correction for a child is only constructive within the context of the biblical notion of sparing the rod and spoiling the child when the child is doing something they wish to stop while maintaining a meaningful relationship with their children. The other rationale is that within the Caribbean, however, there are those parents who, because of their cultural beliefs naturally enjoy the customary sense of power and control and cannot resist the urge to use corporal punishment as a method of controlling and giving direction to children. There is a considerable body of evidence that supports the notion that in the Caribbean, parents, especially those less fortunate members of the society continue to inflict harsh discipline on their children because they were badly brought up, raised in a hostile environment and the notion that it is culturally accepted by their society. In most cases these parents are not educated enough about children at different stages of development and as a result can inflict severe punishment as a means to control, restrict taunt and hurt deliberately. Juliette Barry 1972 is of the opinion that a balance should be found between when a parent should be friendly or firm in exercising discipline to a child. She argues that the experience can exert extreme harm and stress to the child even if it is intended for his own goodwill. In absolute terms, discipline is only but a small part of effective guidance that should be used when necessary and only in specific situations. Furthermore, discipline does not mean making children act by adult standards or using harsh and inappropriate discipline. For example, a child of two years old cannot be expected to behave as a child of eleven years old. Thus the punishment must be age appropriate and fit the severity of the behaviour. When parents combine firmness with understanding, children can learn to control their actions. Effective discipline can help children learn to get along with others and to deal with their own emotions.

Since harshly punished children are temporarily obedient, these parents conclude that their method of discipline is effective, but there is evidence that these children store up their frustration and later vent itself at school or toward parents in later years.

This raises the argument that parents should consider the use of alternative methods of discipline as a conventional child-rearing effort as an adjunct to the generally accepted idea that withholding of privileges or setting of limits is the best method of controlling behaviour in children.

CHAPTER 10

STANDARD DEFINITIONS AND INDICATORS OF CHILD ABUSE AND NEGLECT IN THE ENGLISH SPEAKING CARIBBEAN

Physical abuse, sexual abuse, neglect and emotional or psychological abuse have become a widespread problem in Caribbean society, and as such, a child of any age, sex, race or economic background can fall victim to this scourge. In order to prevent and treat child abuse and neglect effectively, there must be a common understanding of the definition. It is also important to understand how these categories of abuse, are defined in practice. It is vital that everyone who is concerned with children of all ages be alert to the first signs physical child abuse or non-accidental injury. Although these may be very slight in some cases, suspicion is aroused by the character and distribution of the injuries, by the history of the injury, by inquiry into the personality of the parents, by the social circumstances of the family and by the history of the child. Sometimes, it is difficult to determine immediately whether the injury was accidental, whether it was carelessness on the part of the caregiver, whether it was neglect or whether it was inflicted. Whichever the case may be, it must be emphasized that minor injuries are as important to recognise as having been inflicted as severe ones because of the risk that severe injury will follow if the first was unrecognised. Remember that most cases of physical abuse represent the result of sudden loss of control by a desperate parent or guardian.

Physical Abuse

Physical abuse generally refers to the use of inappropriate physical harm inflicted on a child by a parent or caregiver which is caused by more than accidental means. Inflicted injuries most often represent unreasonable severe corporal punishment or unjustifiable punishment. In a majority of the cases, the harm is not intentionally inflicted but is the end result of harsh disciplinary methods or corporal punishment that have escalated to a point of physical injury or a substantial risk of physical injury, and occurs when a frustrated or angry parent strikes or otherwise harm a child. While injuries to a child can occur accidentally while a child is playing, physical abuse should be suspected if the explanations given do not fit the injury or if there appears to be a pattern of frequency.

Physical abuse is the most visible form of child abuse because the physical indicators are the first to be noticed. The longer the abuse continues, the more serious the injuries are and can result in risks of serious physical or emotional harm to a child.

Child care practitioners must always be alert to why and in what circumstances child abuse is suspected from a family dysfunctional theory. For Example, if there is a known history of previous unexplained injury, or of previously known child abuse of one child or other children in the family. Previous injuries known to have occurred are not mentioned to the worker. Unexplained, or recurrent injuries of which conflicting explanations are given. Inconsistencies in the history are apparent. There is a delay in seeking help. There is a complaint of irrelevant problems unrelated to the injury. The parent or guardian is reluctant to give information. Consent is refused for further diagnostic studies. Cause of the injury is projected onto a sibling or third party. There has been a frequent change of Doctors or Hospitals seeking medical attention for the child's injuries. The parents cannot be found. The adult accompanying the child is violent. Once suspicion is aroused, the behaviour of the parents is always a factor to consider, and attention should be paid to the condition of any other children and to the general situation in the home.

Indicators of Physical Abuse

Deliberate acts of violence that would be considered abusive to the point of endangerment to a child by Caribbean standards include: Bruises on any infant, especially facial bruises, bruises in unusual patterns that might reflect the pattern of the instrument used, unexplained bruises, broken bones, abrasions, lacerations, fractures, belt and buckle marks, human bite marks, burns from being branded with a hot object such as a clothes iron, cigarette burns on various parts of the body, usually in clusters and at different stages of healing, immersion of hand in hot water as a punishment for stealing, dousing with hot liquid, rope burns that may indicate confinement, dry burns indicating that a child has been forced to sit upon a hot surface, any lacerations or abrasions to external genitalia, metaphyseal or corner fracture of long bones caused by twisting or pulling, head injuries, subdural haematomas which is haemorrhaging beneath the outer covering of the brain due to violent shaking or hitting around the head, knee scars as a result of making the child kneel for long periods on rough objects, using a clothes peg to hold the child's lips together, combing the child's hair in a vigorous manner to cause pain, giving of alcohol, cough medicine or other non-prescription drugs to sedate young children.

Internal injuries include Duodenal or jejuna haematomas which are blood clots of the duodenum, injuries to the small intestines due to hitting or kicking in the midline of the abdomen, fractured ribs due to hitting or kicking.

Children who are abused physically or emotionally display certain types of behaviour. Practitioners should be aware that injuries that are considered to be indicators of physical abuse should be viewed in light of consistent medical histories or the developmental ability of a child to injure himself. For example, there are several factors to be considered in raising the question of possible physical abuse.

Firstly, is acknowledging that child abuse does occur.

Secondly, in recognizing any signs and symptoms of injuries in order to determine if a child is being abused.

Thirdly, it is important to consider the nature and extent of the injury, i.e. does the injury fit with the explanation given. Or, is the child's age or developmental stage consistent with the type of injury.

Situation Warranting Referral:

A 7 year old boy arrived at school with several marks about his body and was very withdrawn. He informed the teacher that his father gave him a lashing for constantly wetting his bed and then sent him to sit in a bath of cold water before getting ready for school.

Sexual Abuse

One of the difficulties encountered in any discussion of child sexual abuse involves the terms of the definition. The term sexual abuse brings to the minds of many people an image of sexual violence and physical molestation. While such incidents do occur and periodically capture the public's attention, from a sensationalistic approach they represent only a small proportion of the reported incidence of child sexual abuse. The fact is that sexual abuse of children takes many forms and is likely to become part of a troubling cycle of dysfunctional family.

Any attempt to define sexual abuse is problematic because it is described according to the culture of the individual and is based on the values and beliefs of society at large. In the Caribbean for example, sexual abuse is frequently interchanged by victims as "interfered with me, or "troubled me." This may mean anything from genital manipulation to intercourse. Cunnilingus or oral sex is referred to as "spitting in the vagina." These cultural descriptions regarding the wide range of adult/child experiences have not been thoroughly understood within a legal framework of reference, makes it difficult for the legal and, or medical profession to give consideration to the interactive aspect of the sexual experience. In this case, the professional social worker whose primary interest in helping the child need to focus on the incident that has occurred between the child and the abuser in order to gain an understanding and be able to interpret the legitimate terms used by victims in the abuse experience.

One of the most widely referenced definitions in referring to sexual abuse of children is given by Schecter, M.D.and Roberge, L.1976 who refer to this illegal sexual experience as, "the involvement of dependent, developmentally immature children and adolescents in sexual activity that they do not fully comprehend and are unable to give informed consent to; and that violates the social taboos of family roles."[

According to psychologist Sigmund Freud 1905 in his theory of children's sexuality and the Oedipus complex, "a child's sexuality is influenced by a recognition of his unconscious as well as conscious feelings and their controls which shape the development of their personality and sexual relationships in early parent/child relationships". Dr. Fine, in his Thesis on Freud 's theory held the belief that although an infinitely modified but inescapable fact, it does not figure prominently in the characteristics of parent/child incest because research findings show that sexual arousal is more evoked by the parent rather than the child, and include a rudimentary theory that infancy was the period when sexual differentiation takes place but is not yet complete; further, that the prohibition of childhood sexuality must therefore be formed in a socially acceptable manner by repressing or sublimating the character trait of sexual predators by restrictive measures embedded in the handling of the problems of child rearing and sexual influences by puritan parents. Fine. R. 1962.

While there has been throughout history an extensive literature concerning sexual relations of adults toward children, one may ascribe to the fact that infant sexuality is never found in a purely natural form but is always defined in relation to socialization Constantine, Larry and Floyd Martinson 1981. The strongest arguments for the sexual rights of the child constitutes an understanding that sexual feelings must be felt, understood and controlled as part of lifelong psycho-sexual maturation. Therefore, learning about child sexuality must be more structured and non-accidental since it is claimed from many sides that sexual abuse in childhood is occurring on a hitherto unknown scale and that a great deal of mental suffering is caused by early sexual abuse. The idea that an adult has sexual relations with a child is more difficult to accept than when a parent strikes out and hurts a child which is a more acceptable norm in Caribbean society. It is essential therefore, that therapists planning to work with sexually abused children must first spend adequate time exploring their own attitudes and ideas regarding the various issues of sexuality, and to understand why families behave the way they do and at the same time be alert to their own responses. Public opinion is that lack of sex education is an important component of the sexual abuse problem. They are inclined to believe that many parents teach their children about the hazards of playing with matches, of how to cross the road or even how to avoid strangers, but unfortunately children are not taught to be empowered against sexual molestation. The rational is that these parents do not know how to talk to their children about sexual abuse or they do not see the need to do so. In my own experience of working with abused children, I do believe that many children could be saved from the inappropriateness of the abuser's behaviour if they had been well informed and protected.

The Prevalence of Sexual Abuse in the Caribbean

In the Caribbean region within recent times there has been much concern about the ordeal of prosecution of child victims of sexual abuse. Unfortunately, national statistics are not reliable because many jurisdictions do not have proper systems in place for gathering such information. Sexual abuse in the Caribbean is not a new problem. Despite the incidence rate those cases that are reported to individual agencies and departments throughout the region indicate that it is not as rare a phenomenon as many would like to believe. Like rape, child sexual abuse is one of the least reported crimes in Caribbean society. Although estimates of its frequency vary from region to region, those cases that are officially reported to the appropriate authorities clearly represent only a fraction of incidents that actually occur, hence the phrase 'the tip of the iceberg'. Although there are a high number of reported cases among the lower socio-economic classes it is not known whether this reflects the greater visibility of this group to social service departments and the police department, or whether the true incidence is actually higher among other groups that are not known to any Agency. Since there seems to be a class bias against the poor in the reporting of child abuse cases, Doctors, teachers and the police are less likely to accuse affluent families of molesting their children even when the evidence is clear. Children in the Caribbean are seen as vulnerable targets of sexual abuse for a number of reasons. They are conditioned to comply with authority, they are in subordinate positions they are susceptible to bribes, threats and promises of rewards which by their own nature make them ideal victims of sexual exploitation. The recognition of sexual abuse of children as a social problem is a lengthy and difficult battle to solve in any country. However, in the Caribbean context avoidance and denial are widespread among the general public and is characterised by fear, denial and reluctance on the part of family members and professionals alike to bring the problem out in the open. According to the World Health Organisation, sexual abuse in the Caribbean is grossly surrounded by a culture of silence and stigma. For example, it states that 1 in 10 children are abused in the Caribbean. Of these, 40% by parents or step parents, 25% by other relatives and 10% by strangers. This data, however well articulated in research did not identify the mean age of the children who are the subject of the research nor the referral source in the target years. It is likely, therefore, that child sexual abuse is even more common in the Caribbean than these figures indicate. It is interesting to note that certain groups of professionals do not seem to refer cases of suspected sexual abuse to other professionals or agencies. This may be that they are concerned about preserving the reputation of the family in question, or, they were not aware of any existing disturbance in the family.

While there are attempts to enlighten professionals within the region regarding the need for adequate intervention and treatment of physical abuse and neglect, there requires a greater shift in orientation towards quick and decisive intervention into the prevention of sexual abuse if we are to see children as having rights to be protected from unscrupulous predators within Caribbean society.

Indicators of Sexual Abuse

Sexual abuse generally refers to interactions between a child and an adult when the child is being used for the sexual stimulation of another person. The abuser may use physical abuse, bribery, threats or take advantage of a child's lack of knowledge. Acts constituting sexual abuse are not limited to: fondling a child's genitals or breast, getting the child to fondle their genitals, mouth to genital contact, the abuser rubbing his genitals on a child, penetrating a child's vagina or anus, caressing, and, or kissing the child inappropriately, showing the child pornographic or video movies, filming or photographing children for the sexual stimulation of others.

Because the circumstances, reactions and dynamics of child sexual abuse appear to differ depending on whether the perpetrator is a stranger or someone with whom the child is closely acquainted it is useful to examine the two situations separately. In cases of assault by a stranger, the behaviour of the perpetrator is more likely to be an expression of deviant or abnormal sexual preference than is that found within the family grouping where normal or appropriate sexual preference may have become perverse, disoriented, or inappropriately directed toward the child Even so, most persons who sexually abuse children, whether they are strangers or known to the child, do not fit the usual stereotype of a child molester. Peters 1976 is of the view that many child molesters have extremely poor self-concepts and dysfunctional personal relationships, but the majority are not considered to be "sick" as society has traditionally held. Peters.J.J 1973.

While aggressive sexual offences do not always involve penetration, contraction of sexually transmitted diseases, or infliction of serious injury, exhibitionism and fondling by strangers are often compulsive and habitual forms of behaviour, and are rarely violent and may have minimal impact on their victims depending upon how the situation is subsequently handled. Paedophiles on the other hand are those who receive their primary sexual gratification from minor children and are only a small percentage of sexual abusers. The vast majority of known sexual abusers are heterosexual in their sexual orientation.

Sexual abuse by strangers is usually a single episode and occurs more frequently out of the child's home. In contrast, sexual abuse by family members or family acquaintances is more likely to occur in the home of the victim or the perpetrator, and occurs repeatedly over a period of time. DeFrancis, 1969. DeFrancis in his research also found that while there are cases of sexual abuse by adult women on children, the overwhelming majority of perpetrators are men. Thus in speaking of sexual abuse the primary conclusion is talking about sexual encounters between adults and children.

How would you know that a child is being sexually abused?

Many parents expect that their child will tell them if he/she is being sexually abused. However, because abusers often threaten the child or convince him/her not to tell anyone about it, the child will not tell. There is also the belief on the child's part that if someone finds out he will be punished because he sees the act as his fault. Parents, caregivers and health care workers should be aware of the following behaviour changes in a child that may be symptoms of sexual abuse:

Noticeable new fear of a parent, other adults or a certain environment, unusual or unexpected response from a child when asked if someone touched him, abrupt change in behaviour i.e.(aggressive or disruptive) overly submissive behaviour, truancy or running away from home.

Physical signs of sexual abuse may include the following: anal or genital pain or bleeding, unusual discharge from the anus or vagina, blood stained underwear, sexual transmitted diseases including HIV and AIDS, repeated urinary tract infections in females, pregnancy in older females.

The sexual exploitation of a child by a parent, trusted family member or someone the child knows and trusts is perhaps the most unrecognised form of trauma inflicted upon children.

Unlike physical abuse, sexual abuse typically occurs in secret leaving no visible scars and results in the child feeling as though he is at fault. It is the most concealed, most distressful and most controversial form of child abuse occurring far more often than is generally believed. Although studies indicate that most victims are female and most perpetrators are male, boy victims are relatively common and are likely to suffer more from lack of effective treatment than female victims. In the Caribbean, boys tend to have more freedom of action and thought than girls and as a result they are not afforded the protection or empowerment necessary to protect them from sexual predators. Sexual abuse of children is now recognised to be far more prevalent than once imagined, and it is only in recent times that the Caribbean has realised the vast number of its children who are affected by this type of abuse. Significant data on the subject is hardly available on a national scale but much media information and public awareness indicate that it is a problem which is more widespread, more seriously distressing and more difficult to discuss than other areas of child maltreatment.

Child sexual abuse can also be recognised as a fundamental betrayal of childhood trust and an affirmation of the powerlessness of being young and vulnerable in a society where victimization is often recognised and protection is not guaranteed in an environment where they are expected to be protected, nurtured and most importantly be able to feel safe. However, because of their vulnerability and lack of maturity they are unable to resist or avoid the abuse.

Researchers into reported incidences of child abuse have indicated that race, ethnicity or economic boundaries on the part of the victim or the perpetrator do not limit sexual abuse of children. Akin to the abuser, sexually abused children are not special children with special qualities or characteristics. In most cases they are normal children with average abilities and intellectual capacities. Nevertheless, there are a number of factors that are of critical importance in determining how a child will react to the experience. These factors include the child's age and development, the child's relationship to the abuser, the amount of force applied, the degree of shame or guilt and most importantly the reaction of the child's parents. In some cases, when sexual abuse is disclosed, the reaction of the child's parents usually the mother would rally in support of the child and her anger and feelings of retribution are usually directed toward the abuser. However, there are occasions when the mother would blame the child for condoning the abuse or not informing her that such abuse is taking place.

Most victims of child sexual abuse are for the most part abused by persons whom they know and trust. The once familiar image of the dirty old man or the shady character that children are warned to keep away from are no longer an adequate portrayal of the majority of persons who are responsible for the sexual exploitation of children. Studies have found that persons who commit the majority of sexual offences against children are family acquaintances, family members and relatives such as natural fathers, step-fathers, older male siblings or other familiar adults such as the mothers' boy friend, neighbours, teachers, the clergy and youth leaders. Mzarek. P.M, and Kempe, C.H 1981. In the Caribbean, while there is no statistical data to indicate that females are perpetrators of sexual abuse to children this must not be discounted even though the overwhelming majority of perpetrators are men. Caribbean fathers and step-fathers who commit intra-familial sexual assault on children are of the opinion that because they raise and support these children it is their given right and privilege to have a prior right over their sexuality without interference from outside forces. Some mothers also allow their children, some of whom are in their early teen years to be involved in pornographic or sexual activity in order to supplement the family's income

When a child is sexually assaulted by an adult, it constitutes a gross encroachment upon his immaturity and innocence and robs him of the right to mature unmolested towards sexual self-determination without interference.

1n the culture of contemporary society, a child's capacity for consent is not recognised legally for any contract sexually or otherwise even if the child is seductive or provocative. Frequently, girls, particularly adolescents are often accused of being provocative and of encouraging sexual acts, but however much a child actively participates in sexual activity; it is the adult who must bear total responsibility for it is the abuser who wields the power.

In the Caribbean, the problem of sexual assault on children receives slow negative responses; it is either denied or avoided by some communities and some professionals because of the uneasiness it evokes as well as its management.

Most people find the idea of children being sexually abused very distressing and would prefer to imagine that such acts are committed outside their homes, but in reality, almost every society contains cultural taboos against sexual abuse and incest of its children. It is a problem surrounded by myth and misconception and by ideas we must dispel in favour of a less disturbing reality if we are to move toward the protection of our Caribbean children.

Case study

Laura is an only child from a middle class elite family. Her mother assumes a dominant role in the family and would leave the responsibility of Laura's care to her father when he is at home. Her mother is home maker and her father works at an engineering firm. The family have a history of separation. When her parents were divorced, Laura's mother was awarded full custody with visitation rights to her father. Laura resented her mother and did not have a good relationship with her father. Laura was sexually assaulted over a period of time and subsequently raped by a neighbour who is a friend of the family. This traumatic experience precipitated a crisis of withdrawal, moodiness and occasionally running away from home because she was not able to disclose the abuse. At aged thirteen, her exasperated mother sent her to stay with her father in another part of the country for a period of time. In the home, Laura was further sexually assaulted by her father and continued to hold the secret of the abuse. She was later united with her mother where there continued to be much conflict in the mother/daughter relationship.

At aged fourteen Laura finally ran away from home and subsequently became a high priced prostitute who gained nothing from this experience except grief and further disgust. Laura was soon admitted to Hospital after a drug overdose and was later discharged to a group home as a temporary ward of the State. At the home, Laura entered a very withdrawn phase refusing to co-operate with anyone. Her reluctance to talk about the abuse prompted the social worker and other professional staff in the home to conclude that Laura seemed to have blanked out her traumatic past. At aged eighteen, Laura returned to live with her mother since the home no longer held any legal responsibility for her. It was not clear what transpired between Laura and her mother during this period but she was soon to be admitted to a psychiatric hospital after a serious suicide attempt where she was diagnosed as borderline psychotic. Laura remained in the hospital where she was treated with drugs. Laura continued to be in a permanent state of acute distress where attempts were being made to offer her a therapeutic programme which might help to remove the terrible ghost from her past.

This case study is an attempt to describe some of the most serious repercussions that have been observed, and to identify a number of important variables that operate in determining a child's reaction to a sexual abuse situation. It is clear that Laura desperately needed therapeutic intervention to enable her to overcome the long term effects of the abuse. Consequently she has experienced a high level of mental health problems because the system has not served her well.

It is impossible to make a general statement about the effects of sexual abuse on children. Besides the fact that there has been little research on the effects of sexual abuse, children react differently to different situations depending on a number of variables that may be operating at the time of the occurrence. While it is not possible to generalize across the population of abused children, children who are sexually abused are not special children with special characteristics; they are not of one age, one sex, one race or one social class. Their role in the abusive situation, their disclosure of the incident, their relationship to the perpetrators, and their reactions both long and short-term all differ. DeVine 1977. Nevertheless, a number of key factors are commonly believed to be of critical importance in determining the ways in which a child reacts to the experience. These include the child's age and development, the relationship of the child to the abuser, the degree of shame or guilt evoked in the child for his/her participation, and, perhaps most importantly, the reactions of the child's parents and those professionals who become involved in the case.

If the sexual behaviour between adult and child has occurred over a long period of time, if it has involved a series of progressively intimate incidents, or if the child is old enough to understand the meaning and cultural taboo of what has occurred, then the effects may be more profound. Extreme feelings of guilt are a common consequence of intra-familial sexual abuse and cause many victims a great deal of anguish. With children for whom the experience the experience was totally repugnant and upsetting, guilt may stem from the fact that they allow the situation to continue because they felt too fearful and powerless to take any action to stop it. They are in turn predominated by responses characterized by fear of being harmed by fear and anxiety, and frequently include such specific symptoms as aggressive behaviour, anger, guilt, running away and inappropriate sexual behaviour. Studies of clinical and non-clinical population of children confirm that in many cases these effects can persist over long periods of time and in turn can produce progressive deterioration in functioning that becomes a precursor for more serious complications such as personality disorder and impaired functioning. Browne, A. and Finklehor, D. 1986. Children with poor ego-strengths and impaired self-concept are probably most likely to be victims and are easily coerced into silence because they do not have the ego-strength to resist seductive approaches from an adult male as well as the ability to reveal the abuse immediately. With older children and adolescents for whom the experience was extremely repugnant and upsetting, guilt may stem from the fact that they allowed the situation to continue. Accounts from victims often stress the degree to which they believe that they are the only person who has had this experience and that others will reject them if they discover the secret. Courtois, C.1979. As a result they may withdraw from all social contacts with their friends in school and in their social environment.

Sexual abuse of children within a family context whether biological parent or close family friend can have devastating consequences for the child whose mental health and adjustment can be permanently impaired if treatment is absent or inadequate. The reaction of the child's family can do much to either lessen or enhance her guilt feelings once the child has disclosed. However, in the case of Laura there is no clear evidence that the mother knew of the abuse and failed to intervene. We need to be cautious, therefore, in accepting the hypothesis that all mothers should be aware that their child's behaviour problem is a manifestation of sexual abuse. Child sexual abuse can be disguised as, and be mistaken for a wide range of disorders including behaviour problems which could result from the negative parent/child relationship. If the mother mistakes the erratic behaviour or deliberately ignores it to avoid getting involved, or feels that the mother/daughter relationship is too stressful, it can spell tragedy for the child. The error of attributing clinical findings to sexual abuse when there are in fact manifestations of serious social conditions in the child's environment can be a source of distress. For example, how the mother saw her maternal role can have a significant influence on the daughter's behaviour. There is research evidence that even a relatively brief interaction with a person who relates to a child in a warm fashion, in contrast to a person who relates to a child in a relatively impersonal way, has different effects on behaviour. In this case, if the mother has a low level of social perception in her care giving role, it would be difficult for her to recognise the need to seek professional help for her daughter when she recognised that the significance of the behaviour was uncertain.

In intra-familial sexual abuse, evidence was found to indicate that there were several situations in which sexual abuse took place for several years without parent's knowledge because children refuse to disclose for fear of being accused of initiating the contact. Also, children are strongly influenced by family values and morals and so they fear that they may be punished for engaging in behaviour that is not acceptable to the family.

Evidence points to a society unconcerned with its children which cares little about, and neglects specifically those children who become its responsibility.

Children in the community requiring child guidance or psychiatric care often suffer from faulty or misguided rearing, and in the hospital setting they also suffer from therapeutic neglect and unsatisfactory living conditions frequently found in public institutions. So the questions remain. What kinds of services are offered to child victims of sexual abuse to reduce long term effects of emotional responses? And how do we make people hear what children are saying?

Sexual Abuse Carried Out By Young Offenders

Young sexual offenders are described as young persons from prepubescent to adolescents, who commit any sexual act with a person younger or older than themselves where there is no consent, or consent is not possible; or by another child who has power over the victim without equality or as a result of coercion. This form of abuse can have the same damaging and long lasting effects on its victims as crime committed by adults. Shaw, J.A. et al. 2000. This form of abuse includes teasing in a sexual manner, sexually harassing, threatening, through coercion or actual penetration. Unlike father/daughter incest, power and control is not necessarily a motivation in sibling incest. If the intent is exploratory rather than a means to exploit the victim may continue to maintain a trusting relationship with the abuser with no traumatic effects. Child sexual abuse committed by another child is very difficult to define because the incidences are not known with any certainty because it is not widely known by the public; it often occurs outside of adult supervision and frequently goes unreported. Even if known by adults it is sometimes dismissed as harmless by those who do not understand the implications. Loseke, et al. 2005. While an adult having contact with a child is easily defined as abuse especially if the abuser is related to the child, more difficult issues come into play when the abuser is another child in the family who may be a sibling, a cousin or sometimes an unrelated child.

Historically, sibling incest has been unrecognized, disregarded, under-discussed, minimized or dismissed as normal childhood curiosity and is labelled as sex curiosity, experimentation or mutual exploration rather than sexual abuse. Despite this lack of awareness, sibling incest is thought to be more prevalent than parent/child incest. Finklehor 1979. While it is widely accepted that sexual exploration occurs as a normal part of a child's sexual development, confusion remains as to what extent it is normal and when it becomes abusive. Sibling incest is especially difficult for parents who have a tough time defining it and therefore refuse to acknowledge that it exist in their home and is even more traumatized if both the victim and the abuser are their children, and although they may feel ashamed about what has occurred they often feel that they have to choose which child to support.

Smith and Israel 1987 noted that sibling sexual abuse is the result of fragmenting and dysfunctional family processes rather than a case of the family's dysfunction. The assumption is that the family's overall dynamics seem not to influence the occurrence of sibling incest but where there are multi-problems in these families they will obviously affects all the siblings including those that offend.

In a Caribbean context, there are several factors that can lead to cousin or sibling sexual abuse. These usually arise in an environment that fails to protect the child through poor supervision, lack of knowledge about their activities in and out of the home and failure to set appropriate boundaries through inappropriate sleeping arrangements. In some instances, the perpetrating child was exposed to pornography, or witnessed sexual activity of adults at an early age, allowing opposite sex siblings to share the same sleeping arrangements, lack of privacy in the family, inappropriate parental interest in the child's sexual development and extremely relaxed views of sex. Absence of the father in particular has been found to be a significant element of most cases of sexual abuse of female children by a brother. Jane M Rudd; Sharon D Herzberger. 1999. Others are those children who are reacting to some abuse they had experienced at an early age by acting out against another child. Caffaro, J and Conncaffaro A. 2005 noted that in response to the inadequacies of the family, a stronger and inappropriate close sibling bond may develop to compensate for the parents dysfunction, or an abusive bond may develop and replicate the parent's dysfunction thus creating a disintegration of the family structure and an increase in anxiety in the siblings which could promote a sexual relationship between them in an attempt to nurture each other.

Case Study (a)

Mrs H. visited the Social Service Department in her District, appearing very tense and troubled requesting to see a social worker. At the interview she explained to the social worker that she is having problems with her two children, a son who is 14 years old and a daughter who is 10 years old. The social worker suggested that the mother say something about the situation. Mrs H. explained that she is a single parent having separated from her husband when the children were 7 and 3 years old. She is employed full time and the children are expected to prepare themselves for school because she has to leave home early. She received a report from the school's Attendance Officer that both children are often late or absent from lesson periods. The school further reported that the children often appear unhappy and keep to themselves during break periods. Mrs. H. further explained that she discussed this information with the children and found it difficult to get a response to the school's report.

Mrs H. told the social worker that she became suspicious about the children's behaviour and returned home unexpectedly to discover that the siblings were involved in sexual intimacy with each other. When confronted about this behaviour the children admitted that it was not the first time. She told the social worker that she realise that the children may be unhappy that their father does not keep in touch with them and questioned why they would resort to such behaviour. She now feels at a loss as to how to handle the situation which makes it all the more disturbing to her and especially the relationship between her and the children which has become very strained. During the course of the interview, Mrs. H. Constantly compared the two children by blaming the daughter for initiating the abuse stating that she is always difficult to control, can be very unapproachable and her interest in boys is very unwholesome. She admits that she hardly has any trouble with her son and her daughter only gets along with him as long as she can boss him. She however accused him for letting the abuse happen thereby subjecting the children to much emotional abuse. This attitude toward the children has caused them to seek comfort from each other and the abuse continued whenever the opportunity presented itself. Consequently, mother and children were referred for therapy.

Sexual abusive adolescents are persons searching for sexual identity and as such must be understood in the social and developmental context of their lives. There is a growing body of research that aim to identify certain characteristics that set them apart from the general population. Some of the main characteristics that are thought to be important in addressing the problem are gender where the vast majority are male, and behaviour where poor impulse control may be a factor in young offenders which may contribute to their being discovered rather than having any causal significance for the abusive behaviour. Epps, K. and Fisher, D. 2004.

Studies have found that when sexual abuse is the presenting problem within the family this tends to be left behind and there is concentration on other family difficulties because the emotional trauma of the sexual impulse is too strong for the family to cope with. And if the therapist does not normally deal with matters involving sexual deviance the problem can be ignored resulting in denial and chaos within the family.

Case Study (b)

Miss M. is a single mother with two children, a boy 13 years old and a girl who is 5 years old. She visited family services with her daughter requesting to see a social worker. At the interview, she appeared very agitated and spoke seriously and in a concerned manner. As she related her story, she became very nervous and at times lacking in verbalizing her concern. Responding to the interviewer's concern, Miss. M. Explained that her daughter complains to her that whenever she visits the school's wash room she is being sexually molested by other pupils there She continued to explain that she discussed this with the teacher, the Principal and subsequently the Education Authority with no satisfactory resolution to her daughters safety at the school. The daughter was later brought into the interview to give her side of the story in the presence of her mother. She was alert and vivacious in her manner and appeared very confident. She informed the social worker that no one ever "interfered" with her in a sexual manner at school but that her brother was always trying to touch her private parts when they are alone. When she tells her mother about this she would approach her brother with the words" you better leave my girl child alone" At the child's explanation, the mother became very surprised and dumbfounded. When she regained her composure she expressed remorse for her lack of responsibility in dealing appropriately with the situation. She then admitted that the child did tell her about her son's behaviour towards his sister but she did not want him involved in any sexual scandal because he was preparing for secondary school examination and she did not want him distracted by his sister's allegation. The family has been referred for therapy with the need for strong parental involvement.

When responding to young people who sexually abuse, in particular where there is an allegation of sexual abuse, the question remains what kind of behaviour should be considered abusive. There is a common perception that a young person who has sexually abused a female child will only present a risk to other female children. However, research studies on the subject has indicated that victims tend to be chosen based on factors of vulnerability and accessibility rather than anything related to the abusers sexual arousal or interest. Further studies have concluded that in the case of sexual abuse by perpetrating minors, legal action is not an issue if the abusing child is under twelve years of age. In this regard, child sex offenders must be seen as a health issue rather than a moral one requiring psychological intervention where there is possibly a better chance of changing sexually inappropriate behaviour which can be viewed as a means toward ending the intergenerational trauma of sexual abuse.

Sibling Incest Treatment

In any treatment programme, the victim's safety becomes a clinical concern where the child's safety should be the priority of the family and the professionals involved. In sibling incest, whether or not the offending child remains at home is dependent on the parents ability to ensure the physical and emotional safety of the victimized child. In some cases where the parents are acting protectively alternative care may not be necessary. Where the perpetrating minor is not a family member it is recommended that both families should, as a matter of course attend joint therapy sessions because whether the perpetrating minor is a family member or not, these families frequently react with shock and disbelief followed by intense feelings of shame, anger, guilt and depression. It is crucial therefore, that there is parental accountability to both the victim and the perpetrating minor by providing adequate supervision in the long term interest of all concerned. For most treatment providers, working with abusing minors for as long as required is likely to reduce their likelihood of reoffending. This means ensuring that the key messages are consistent and that they reach the stage of accepting responsibility for the abuse.

Neglect

Child neglect can be defined as a condition in which a caretaker who is responsible for a child either deliberately or by extra-ordinary inattentiveness permits the child to experience avoidable suffering, and/or, fails to provide one or more of the ingredients generally deemed essential for developing a person's physical, intellectual and emotional capacity Norman, A. Polansky 1972. Child neglect is usually a chronic failure to provide necessary physical and emotional support for a child. It is the most common form of child maltreatment and the most frequently identified unlike physical and sexual abuse, it is usually typified by an ongoing pattern of inattentive or dangerous child rearing practices and is readily observed by individuals in close contact with the child.

Some families with a history of neglect usually tend to have multiple problems often requiring long term child protection services, while other families may only require short term intervention depending on the extent of their vulnerability to cope with certain stresses in their environment. Relieving stress in the life of some abusing families can help the parent and child to interact favourably and therefore prevent the recurrence of child neglect. While it remains a debatable subject on what constitutes child neglect, there is no doubt that child neglect is widespread not only among the poor and disadvantaged but also those parents whose psychological imbalances might be a contributing factor.

In examining the plight of these children, where will the real guilt lie since community concerns about neglectful families do not take pride of place in the evaluation of child maltreatment? Will it lie with the less than adequate parent any more than with child protection services that are there to protect children and rescue families which, if not addressed are likely to constitute a neglectful section of Caribbean society. In varying degrees, the neglectful family is a victim of society because if parents' needs are not fulfilled they will lack the capacity to fulfil the needs of their children.

Indicators of Child Neglect

When considering the possibility of neglect, it is important to note the consistency of indicators. For example, do they occur frequently and are they chronic or episodic; or is this culturally accepted child rearing or genuine neglect.

The general indicators of child neglect are defined in the following terms:

Lack of supervision, when very young children are left unattended or in the care of siblings who are not at the legal age to baby sit for long periods of time. Children at times die in house fires as a result of this practice. Other indicators include.

The refusal or extreme delay in seeking necessary health care for the child

Total abandonment of children or for a long period of time

Rejection of the child

Failing to adequately provide for the child's safety and physical and emotional needs

The child who fails to reach its developmental milestones

Lack of adequate nutrition, where there is insufficient quantity or quality of food and where the child consistently complains of being hungry, and is constantly begging or rummaging for food.

Non-school attendance at mandatory school age

Refusal or failure to provide the child with needed psychological care

Constantly withholding of affection

Leaving children alone with elderly caregivers who are unable to provide appropriate care for them; when the parent fails to maintain physical or emotional contact with them. For example, the migration of parents where support for children in the form of financial remittance is not forthcoming

Failure to provide appropriate health care for the child although financially able to do so

Failure of the parent to protect the child from unwholesome or demoralizing conditions such as the state of the parent due to alcohol abuse, drug addiction, prostitution or criminal activity

Unsafe and unsanitary housing conditions with exposed wiring and exposed to dangerous or poisonous substances.

Refusing to seek medical treatment in order to save a child's life

Failure to provide needed age appropriate care such as food, shelter, clothing, education and other basic necessities needed for the developmental, physical, intellectual and emotional capacity of the child.

Situation Warranting Referral:

A 12 year old boy is forced to live in a sheep pen in his parent's back yard for staying out late despite scolding from his parents. They say his behaviour is unacceptable and his release from such punishment will be at their discretion.

Failure to Thrive

Failure to thrive is a manifestation of child neglect which is a delay in a child's growth and development. It is usually referred to infants and children up to two years old who do not gain or maintain weight as they should. Children who suffer this form of neglect are said to be among the smallest of children for their age and fail to develop appropriately both mentally and emotionally although they do not have a detectable illness to account for the slow growth. In some cases, these children tend to increase growth rate rapidly when separated from their parents. A good working definition of growth failure related to unacceptable standard of care giving is the failure to maintain an established pattern of growth and development that responds to the provision of adequate nutritional and emotional needs of the child. Most cases of failure to thrive are not related to neglectful care giving although it may be a sign of maltreatment and should be considered during an evaluation of growth failure [Bremmer, J. Gavin, et al 2004. Research into child development has identified the risk factors in Failure to Thrive that should alert paediatricians as a possibility of neglect include:

- Parental depression
- Stress factors
- Marital conflict
- Parental history of abuse as a child
- Mental retardation and psychological abnormalities in the parent(s)
- Young and single mothers without support
- Alcohol or other substance abuse
- Social isolation
- Poverty

- Parents with inadequate adaptive and social skills
- Career oriented parents who are actively away from home
- Failure to adhere to medical regimes
- Parental lack of knowledge of normal growth and development
- An infant with low birth weight or prolonged hospitalisation.

Concerns of abuse or neglect should be raised during the course of intervention and should be monitored if the following becomes evident:

- Intentional withholding of food
- A parent with strong belief in health or nutrition that jeopardises the child's wellbeing
- The family that is resistant to recommended interventions despite the multi-disciplinary team approach

In young toddlers and infants, failure to thrive must always be considered an emergency as it is a common problem in infancy and childhood and is almost always multi-factorial in origin. Inadequate nutrition and disturbed social interaction can contribute to poor weight gain, delayed development and abnormal behaviour. The syndrome is known to develop in a significant number of children as a consequence of neglect Zenel, J.A. Failure to Thrive needs to be considered a chronic process with long term aggressive multidisciplinary intervention either in the hospital or community setting. With nutritional failure to thrive most children can be managed in the community with close medical follow-up. However, for infants or children with extreme failure to thrive hospital care is justified to implement a structured feeding regimen and documented weight gain. In order to promote a successful outcome, close monitoring of the family and the child's growth is imperative to ensure the safety of the child on an ongoing basis through appropriate at home visits by the community nurse to monitor feeding style interactions in order to differentiate between organic failure to thrive and inorganic aetiology.

Situation Warranting Referral

A 2 month old infant spends most of the day in its crib. At feed time his bottle is propped up in his mouth. The mother says she has other young children to take care of and does not have time to pick the child up. Since his discharge from hospital he has lost a tremendous amount of weight. A medical examination indicates a drop from the 30 percentile to the 20 percentile.

Emotional or Psychological Abuse

A child learns to be kind, considerate and helpful to others and respond appropriately to the demands of his society through a positive and healthy interaction with his parents or caregivers. Among the most obvious is the need for warm nurturing affectionate relationships if growth and personality development are to take place. Unlike the young species in the animal kingdom, human infants need constant care and attention and in all cultures it is the responsibility of parents to assume ultimate protection and upbringing to help them feel satisfied and secure. For a parent's warmth and affection have several positive consequences which can create an atmosphere within the home in which children are more likely to learn what parents teach them verbally or through their examples. An affectionate warm relationship with a parent is likely to make children want to be like their parents and adapt their values and behaviours to a greater degree. Having the experience of a benevolent environment that treats them well, children are likely to be benevolently oriented towards their environment and the people in it, and to assume that other people are kind rather than unkind and to desire contact with others rather than to avoid them.

Emotional or psychological abuse is a pattern of ongoing behaviour by the parent or guardian that can seriously affect the healthy development or emotional functioning of a child. It happens for many of the same reasons that physical abuse occurs and can be more devastating psychologically. Emotional abuse includes acts or omissions by the parents or other persons responsible for the child's care that have or could cause serious behavioural, cognitive, emotional or mental disorders. For example, the parent or caretaker use extreme or bizarre forms of punishment such as torture, rejection, criticism, blaming or belittling a child, beating a child in the presence of school mates, telling a child in a variety of ways that he is not wanted, blaming the child for all the family's problems, lack of attachment and nurturance, being emotionally unavailable to the child, the child who is singled out for criticism, have expectations far beyond the child's normal abilities, would not allow older children to be involved in extra-curricular activities, the child not being exposed to stimulation, threats to the child to do well in the eleven plus examination by parents and teachers, yelling at children while calling them bad, stupid, useless and troublemakers and negatively comparing the child with the other parent. Research has indicated that less severe forms of early emotional deprivation may produce babies who grow into anxious and insecure children who are slow to develop. Emotional abuse is the least visible form of child abuse and is very difficult to identify because it carries no visible scars or visible signs to observe or to make a judgement. Behavioural signs and symptoms may often be the only outward indicators that a child is being emotionally or psychologically abused. To effectively identify and confirm emotional abuse, it is necessary to observe the interaction between the abuser and the child on varied and repeated occasions.

Situation Warranting Referral

A 9 year old child is persistently being blamed for the family problems and is constantly accused of being wicked and a troublemaker.

CHAPTER 11

THE INCEST TABOO

To put it in a nutshell, incest is when parental love is sought in an atmosphere of acceptance of sexual practices between family members and children across all races and socio-economic classes, and where the surface action of the family does not meet the needs of its members for nurturance and care in an appropriate way relative to the maturity of those individuals. de Moise L. 1974. It has been argued that even though some incestuous families display characteristics that are different on the surface, their underlying family dynamics are remarkably multi-factorial. The word "parent" is used here as opposed to "male" or "father" because researchers have found that mothers and aunts also sexually abuse children although there is no documented evidence within the Caribbean. In most cases of incest, the parent abuses the parental role in order to exercise power over the child. For many, the abuse begins in early childhood and continues throughout adulthood.

The act of incest is generally not a unique or novel event but is often an early indication of indirect sexual advances. The child is sometimes prepared for a full sexual relationship through a lengthy period of "courting" this process appears in such acts as a parent bathing an older child and towelling him/her down, inappropriate kissing, exhibiting themselves naked or scantily dressed in the presence of the child or interrupting the child while she is having a bath. In most instances of incest, a trusted and loved family member tells a child that the proposed or actual sexual activity between them is good and beautiful, but it is "our secret" This secrecy and collusion may generate closeness and excitement. In short, the sexual abuse of a child is a case of trust versus manipulation.

How widespread is Incest?

In the Caribbean, there is even less knowledge about the incidence of incest than there is about other forms of child abuse. The situations of incest which surface to the attention of the authorities tend to arise from conditions of obvious conflict within the family such as:

- Disruptive marital relationships
- A working spouse or partner
- The power control of the perpetrator
- The disgruntled child
- Over-crowded sleeping arrangements
- Loose moral standards in the home
- Paedophilia, where an adult is recurrently driven to seek a child for sexual; arousal or release of sexual tension
- Psychopathic disorders

How Does Incest Present?

Cases of incest are usually reported to the authorities in basically the following ways:

- Medical and law-enforcement referrals, when suspicion is aroused after a child has been treated for recurrent genital infections.
- By a concerned or suspicious neighbour, or other extended family member.

In most instances, when the father becomes very possessive and restrictive or jealous by refusing to allow the child to attend extra-curricular activities or form positive peer relationships the child may try to free herself from the incestuous relationship by telling someone outside of the home such as a friend, school teacher or school counsellor when he/she experiences pain, fear, guilt, depression, physical harm, jealousy or pregnancy. In some cases, of incest, the child may tell a parent or guardian about the first incest contact only to be met with disbelief.

Where the parent disbelieves the child, he/she is likely to remain silent and reluctantly continue to be an incest partner unless the child is resourceful enough to protect himself by telling someone outside the family.

Child victims of incest are usually under tremendous pressure not to tell. They fear that if they tell no one will believe them or that in some way they are to be blamed for the activity. This fear is not ill-founded because adults are likely to believe another adult than a child, and often there is no corroborating evidence.

A parent may avoid telling or letting out the family secret for a variety of reasons, that is, they may be ashamed, protecting the family unit, financial concern if the partner is accused or arrested and fear of retaliation to the child or themselves are all possible barriers. There may also be ignorance of the Laws of incest or the demoralising long drawn out and stressful repetitive cross questioning by the bureaucracy.

Researchers have revealed that children who are victims of incest very rarely accidentally tell other people about the abuse. The truth is revealed deliberately however confused the actual statement of the abuse might be even though the precipitating factor may be something else such as an incident of violence or some major family squabble. If children are expected to tell when they are sexually assaulted or molested, parents, social workers and counsellors need to convince them that they are not to be blamed in any way for the sexual encounter. It is therefore vital for children to feel able to communicate their experiences to adults who really believe them and can assure them that there are other children in similar situations and with similar problems.

Case Study

Mr. X is a 56 years old and his wife is in her late 40's. Mrs X met Mr X when her first two children from a previous relationship were a boy aged 4 years and girl aged 2 years. The current union produced 5 girls and 1 boy whose ages range from 19 years to 7 years. The coupled had a common law union for 10 years and married 10 years later. The husband became very restrictive in terms of control over the children but otherwise played a passive role in the home where major decisions were made by his wife and the children were able to manipulate situations to their advantage. The father, in his efforts to gain control over his family, would monitor their every movement within and outside of the home. He would attend to all their ailments and also monitor their menstrual cycle with approval from their mother.

Mrs. X is a rather obese woman who spends most of her spare time resting when not at her part time job. She admitted that she no longer enjoys sexual intercourse with her husband because she is often too tired to participate.

Mr. X administered physical punishment to his oldest natural daughter then 14 years old for an alleged association with a male neighbour. This incident resulted in the daughter reporting her father to the police for having sexual intercourse with her from the age of 12 years. Consequently, a case was brought against the father for having unlawful sexual activity with his daughter. However, the case was dismissed because the mother refused to testify against her husband. The daughter continued reluctantly to comply with her father's demands but would complain to her mother who made no stand to protect her daughter. Consequently, the daughter attempted suicide and was removed from the home environment. Attempts at therapy with the family proved futile due to lack of cooperation from the rest of the family.

Four years later, two of the daughters aged 13 and 15 years ran away from home because the father had threatened to beat them for being disobedient. During this time, the 13 year old told a friend that she was being sexually abused by her father; she was then accompanied to the police Department to make a report. The matter was referred to the Child Care Authority for investigation into the pathology of the family.

From intervention and investigation into the dynamics of the family, it came to light that the father had been sexually assaulting all of his daughters from aged 12 years old except the last two who were ages 7 and 10 years old. The mother admitted to the social worker that the girls had made several complaints to her but denied that she willingly encouraged the incest. Although the girls were somewhat hostile toward their father, they projected a lot of anger toward their mother for not protecting them from the abuse. In one therapy session, the girls all confronted their father accusingly yet he continued to deny the incest while the brother remained passive throughout the investigation and therapy sessions. The girls were removed to a more caring environment and the rest of the family have reluctantly accepted therapy.

As the preceding case illustrated, the father's future was not a critical factor in this case. The family was reluctant to make an internal adjustment to the situation thus the legal consequences became less prominent. While it was desirable for the father to be interviewed, it was evident that he was defensive and reluctant to become involved in the therapy. Similarly, the mother was quite ambivalent about the course of the evaluation with the possibility that the husband will be separated from the family.

In assessing incestuous families, an important consideration is the issue of family loyalty, where, in an attempt to keep the incestuous relationship the family secret, the children are placed under intense pressure especially if the incestuous relationship is well established.

In intra-familial sexual abuse, there is still no clear evidence to suggest that any one particular type of therapy is specifically indicated in the treatment of child sexual abuse. However, it is of great importance that the whole family be involved in the therapeutic process. For example, when sexual abuse is revealed, family members are quick to blame one member while refusing to look at the contributory role played by the rest of the family.

The main message here based on clinical research is that like the physical abuse of children, sexual abuse is an expression of severe relationship problems in the family and can lead to both physical and psychological damage to a child.

Denial, disbelief and minimizing the occurrence of sexual abuse to children may represent attempts by society to deal with its own feelings, but these occurrences have powerful damaging effects on the victims and their family. Still evident although weakening is the reality that in almost every society there are cultural taboos against incest and sexual abuse f its children. It is a problem surrounded by myth and misconception and by ideas we must dispel in favour of a less disturbing reality if we are to move toward the protection of our Caribbean children

Treatment of Incest

Before addressing the issue of what constitutes an effective treatment programme, we must examine what is ineffective about the way in which we intervene with this population. Unfortunately, solving the problem of sexual abuse of children is not a simple task. It is okay to empower children against sexual abuse by telling them not to take sweets, money, and other gifts or accept rides from strangers. But how can a child be told that it is normal behaviour not to accept an appropriate kiss or affectionate hug from his or her parent, or, that the kindly neighbour who at times offer moral support to the family must be shied away from or ignored.

It is an accepted fact that child sexual abuse is a vicious crime. However, sanctions against perpetrators of child sexual abuse within the family should be considered from a more therapeutic than punitive stance where the focus of treatment in most cases will be the family as a whole. In many cases, culpability for incest may never be clearly established. However, if an admission of guilt is made by the perpetrator, this may be the first and most important step in keeping the perpetrator and the family in treatment. Giarretto H. 1976.

The Therapeutic Approach

All children who have been involved in an incestuous relationship should not be denied the opportunity to deal with current observable psychological distress. It is surely a mistake to minimize the emotional impact of this experience. In planning a programme of therapy for families where sexual abuse of children is presented, the approach can be based on the following pre-suppositions that:

The removal of a child from its family without therapeutic help often means an escalation of some aspects of the original traumatic experience. For example: The child loses contact with its social environment, family and friends and ultimately feels guilty and responsible for the abuse.

That the imprisonment of the perpetrator without the therapeutic input leads to a danger of repetition of the abuse, either on returning to the family or by abusing another child in a newly "created" family.

That in describing the various approaches to understanding sexual abuse of children we recognise that the process is similar whether the victim is a girl or a boy.

The Goals of Therapy

Disclosure of child sexual abuse within the family leads to an intense crisis for all members, and the nature of this crisis poses some dilemma for those professionals concerned about treatment and prevention. Therefore, in any attempt at treatment, primary attention must be given to the child through therapeutic intervention. Likewise, to enable this professional component to work effectively in treating abusive families, these professionals must agree on a consistent treatment approach which will not come about by chance.

Therapeutic intervention in child sexual abuse is aimed at the following objectives:

- Providing children with a safe environment in which to express anger, grief and other emotions, and teaches constructive strategies for handling them.
- Encourage the perpetrator to take sole responsibility for the sexual act.
- Provide both parents with the opportunity to accept responsibility for the emotional care and well-being of the child
- Working on the mother/daughter relationship to enable the mother to become a more central and emotionally—caring parent for the child
- In the case of incest, dealing with the sexual and emotional conflict in the parental relationship had allowed the sexual relationship between the father and daughter to develop.

- Dealing with the special relationship that exists between the child and the perpetrator in order to allow the child future ability to relate appropriately to male relationships.
- The Therapeutic process can range from verbal statements to re-enactment in play therapy. They can be encouraged to put their feelings into words using poems, stories and songs or into pictures and drawings.

In a primary therapeutic approach, police action and prosecution of the perpetrator may be necessary as a way of initiating therapy for the family rather than as a means to facilitate incarceration. For example, Finklehor 1985 in his research into the sexual abuse of children noted that most sexual abusers are men who are much more resistant to offers of help. They characteristically rationalize their behaviour and tend to be amenable to change only when under substantial pressure. Certainly, the single, most important feature of a successful treatment programme for victims of incest is group therapy. It is recognised by many therapists that peer group counselling is the most effective method of giving support to abused children. The advantage here is that treatment gives the children the opportunity to:-

- See that there are other children with the same experience
- Increase awareness and self-esteem
- Increase their ability to make decisions about themselves.
- For most a relief from presenting symptoms.

A practical consideration in organising the therapeutic evaluation is that the therapist must have adequate time with the involved members of the family in order to elicit sufficient information with which to make the required judgement.

There is no doubt that the success of direct intervention into incestuous families by individuals of the helping profession, depends on how they view their role and how they view the problem. In this respect, the therapist has several issues to face not only in the treatment process, but also with himself as a responsive human being with a whole set of emotions. It is their responsibility to be aware of their own attitudes and reactions to the incest taboo in order to maintain objectivity and be free from any emotional involvement with those families they intend to help in the treatment process.

CHAPTER 12

THE EFFECTS OF ABUSE ON CHILDREN

Children who are abused physically and emotionally display certain types of behaviours. More than reactions to abuse itself these behaviours tend to reflect the child's response to the dynamics of the family and especially to disturbed parent-child interactions.

The behaviours which characterise abused children include being overly compliant, passive, behaviours aimed at maintaining a low profile, avoiding any possible confrontation with a parent which could lead to abuse, aggression, attention seeking behaviour, destructive anti-social behaviour, reluctance to go home, inability to react with emotion, scared of failure, shows anxiety, fear or depression, have learning difficulties, sleep problems, low self-esteem, bed wetting, cry for no apparent reason, frozen watchfulness, role-reversal behaviour or extremely dependent in response to parental emotional and even physical needs. Abusive parents have been unable to satisfy certain of their own needs appropriately and turn to their children for fulfilment. Their failure can produce such behaviour in a child where the child may be expected to assume this task and become inappropriately adult and be responsible. This type of abuse leaves hidden scars that manifest themselves in different ways.

Children who are forced to exude energy normally channelled towards growth into protecting themselves from abusive parents may fall behind the norm for their age in socialization and language development. This lag in development may also be the result of central nervous system damage caused by physical abuse, medical or nutritional neglect or inadequate stimulation. Some abused children live in an uncertain environment where requirements for behaviour are inconsistent and unclear. In some families abuse is frequent and severe enough to be emotionally and physically harmful but insufficient to threaten the child's physical development.

Research has shown that the most likely physical abuser of a young child is the mother, especially if the mother is not emotionally attached to the child. This lack of attachment can result in lifelong damage to the child's emotional life and the capacity for developing social relations. There is further evidence to show that the longer the child experiences abuse the more likely he or she is to become an adult abuser, and the more varied the forms of abuse and the younger the child is when the abuse starts the deeper the effects will be. In addition, intense but unpredictable episodes can cause a greater increase in long lasting fear and anxiety. Aator,R. 1994.

When children are physically abused they are affected in different ways depending on the severity of the abuse, the frequency of the abuse and the child's ability to cope with the conflict. Other aspects of the severity of physical abuse on a child depend on how hard the child is struck, the instrument with which the child is struck and the age of the child. Many child psychologists believe that a child between the ages of 3-5 years who is swatted on the gluteus maximums with a flat object such as a slipper or a ruler produces less effect or harm than the older child who is beaten about the body with such objects as a piece of stick, the heel of a shoe, the buckle end of a belt or inflicted with other serious body injuries. Harm done to a child as a result of physical abuse is measured both by the harmful effects of the physical injury and the trauma of the emotional effects of the injury. These include the ability to trust, fear of physical contact, cower and cringe when in close contact with the abuser, difficulty in concentrating and are easily startled. As the child gets older these signs are more serious where there are weakening social relationships with peers, spouse and offspring over a lifespan period. Karen Roberts 1994. Research has shown that boys who experience recurring physical abuse suffer more by dealing with their problems by being aggressive, fighting, being cruel to others, truanting from school, lying, stealing, social withdrawal, being destructive, displaying deviant behaviour, associating themselves with undesirable peer groups, drug taking, low level of social skills, other anti-social behaviours and more prone to suicidal tendencies. Jaffe, P. Wilson, S. Wolfe, D. and. Zak. L. 1986. Other Research on the effects of maltreatment to both boys and girls has sighted neurological, intellectual and cognitive behavioural, emotional and personality consequences where they become passive and withdrawn or active and aggressive. It is also noteworthy that teenage boys and girls who were abused younger may react by running away for self protection and end up at most being involved in drugs or alcohol.

It is impossible to make a general statement about the effects of sexual abuse on children. Aside from the fact that there has been little Research on the effects of sexual abuse, it is not possible to generalize across the population of abused children. What is of even greater significance is the fact that children who are abused do not provoke the abuse but rather is the recipient of concern and support from family and friends; therefore, the degree of violence or physical coercion by the abuser is, of course, another important factor in cases of sexual assault on children. In the case of sexual abuse, the effects on children and adolescents has numerous and possibly some of the most debilitating social effects which can be evident in emotional, physical and behavioural ways and includes depression, anxiety, poor self-esteem, have poor relationships with family members, poor performance at school and drug abuse. Boudewyn Arnie C and Joan, H. Liem: 1995. These effects can be just as devastating whether there was one occurrence or repeated occurrences. It is difficult to compare the effects of the different occurrences because the abuse experience is hardly ever the same. There needs to be increased awareness that children are vulnerable to sexual abuse because of their age and innocence.

Overtime, there has been numerous studies and clinical reports of the short and long term effects of early sexual experiences of children with adults in that if a child has been raped or otherwise physically hurt by an outsider, both the short and long term effects can be expected to be far more serious than if, as is usually the case the assault has been non-violent. The problem however, in assessing the long-term effects are that not nearly enough is known about them. The prognosis therefore, is that many cases of non-violent sexual assault on children by a stranger can be treated with short-term crisis intervention techniques that emphasize putting the incident in perspective and returning the family to its former state of functionality. It is believed that the closer the emotional ties between the child and the abuser the more emotionally traumatic the situation is likely to be for the child. Nonetheless, the degree of emotional impact will vary greatly depending on the nature of the individual relationship. Sgroi, S.M. 1975.

The later effects of child sexual abuse cannot be simplistically related to the sexual nature of the abuse. In truth and in fact, the manner in which the child perceives her role in the sexual relationship can have a strong influence on the way she reacts to the situation once it has been disclosed. For instance, very young children often have difficulty separating fact from fantasy and may have a very different and less distressing image of what occurred than older siblings in the family because their view of the world may provide what can be described as a layer of unconscious self-protection that enables them to react only to what it is they imagined has happened to them.

If the sexual behaviour between adult and child has occurred over a long period of time, and if it has involved a series of progressive intimate incidents, or if the child is old enough to understand the meaning of what has occurred then the effects may be more profound. Research has revealed that children who experience intra-familial sexual abuse may experience extreme feelings of guilt as a common consequence and cause many victims a great deal of anguish. It is further argued that these guilt feelings may be intensified by a number of factors such as whether the child was an active participant, whether she encouraged the sexual contact or whether she experienced any pleasure at all from it. However, whenever there is serious harm regardless of the perpetrator's relationship to the child, or whether her pleasure of the experience stems from acceptance and approval, or from a normal physical reaction to sexual stimulation, there is yet some painful source of shame for many children. Conversely, for those children where the sexual experience was totally upsetting their guilt may stem from the fact that they allow the situation to continue due to fear and a lack of power to take any action to prevent it.

Despite the growing interest of the effects on Caribbean children, it continues to a complex problem and a serious public health and social service problem in its definition, identification and prevention and treatment. It is a term used to encompass many situations ranging from a parent or care givers momentary inattention to wilful deprivation. Most commonly, gross neglect not only compromises the immediate health of our nation's children but also threatens their growth and intellectual development, their long term physical and mental health outcomes, their prosperity for pro-social behaviour, their future parenting practices and their economic productivity as eventual wage earners. Research has shown that neglected children are at risk for a number of behavioural, social, academic and medical problems. These include low self-esteem, attachment problems, anger, malnutrition, lifelong poor health, impaired cognitive development, low academic development and a risk for delinquent behaviour. Egeland, B. 1988. Wallace, H. 1966 concluded that children with non-organic failure to thrive who were once within the normal height and weight for their development became below the normal distribution. His research further indicated that there is no medical or organic evidence for the child's condition except for the fact that it is attributed to an inability of the parent to physically care for the child. The widely held view which is still considered today from Caribbean studies is that most children are and will continue to be resilient to certain stimuli within their particular environment whether it is perceived as harmful or pleasant. In practice, however, while the potential for severe negative consequences from childhood neglect exists it is difficult to say which causes of stress as it relates to this type of abuse has the most catastrophic effect upon the child because deprivation both of affection and security must be particularly hard for these children to withstand. In general, the research has looked at such factors that can have an impact upon the effects of neglect so that the child is able to maintain healthy functioning in spite of the inherent difficulties. Prilleltensky, I. & Pierson, L. 1999. Whatever the predisposing factors for child neglect, it is difficult to say which causes of stress as it relates to this type of abuse has the most catastrophic effect upon the child because deprivation both of affection and security must be particularly hard for these children to withstand. Conversely, there are those children who were victims of severe neglect and were able to overcome any serious deficiencies or disasters, and were less traumatized because of certain protective factors according to their individual characteristics such as their inherited considerable resilience to negative social and emotional stimuli in their home environment, their self determination, their self confidence, their intelligence and independence or external factors such as access to good health care and a good social support system by other relatives, neighbours or a caring community.

Emotional or psychological abuse has been studied less extensively in the Caribbean than other forms of child abuse and has so far provided little insight about its prevalence precisely because it can exist independently of other forms of abuse. Preliminary evidence suggest that there are similar consequences associated with other forms of abuse but emotional abuse is more harmful and destructive to the child's psyche than other forms of abuse because it is deemed to be the most difficult form of child abuse to identify and prevent. Research has found that the effects of emotional abuse is also more debilitating for the child than physical abuse because professionals who work with children and families are not able to intervene and diagnose the risk factors that can cause such mistreatment to children. The difficulty in not detecting emotional abuse is that unlike physical abuse, there is no evidence of bruises, no cuts and no physical scars which makes it a significant risk factor. Danya Glaser 2002 finds that emotional abuse can be more strongly predictive of subsequent impairments in the children's development than the severity of physical abuse.

There is growing consensus among professionals that emotional maltreatment appears to be an integral part of all forms of abuse. There is also the opinion that the characteristics of the child may in part contribute to the parent's abusive behaviour because it is likely to occur when the children are overactive and disruptive especially if the parent has insufficient or no moral support.

In an analysis of the psychological effects of emotional abuse on children, reference is made between two types of children and their characteristics in emotional abuse situations. Studies have found that some victims display numerous symptoms while others demonstrate fewer psychological symptoms or a complete absence of symptoms depending on the specific characteristics of the child in terms of his own personality and disposition and the severity of the abuse. In contrast, some children may experience lifelong patterns of depression, fear, anxiety, withdrawal, low self-esteem, troubled relationships or lack of empathy (Jantz, 1995). It was further contended that as adults, these victims may have trouble recognising or appreciating the needs and feelings of their own children and emotionally abuse them as well. These children, who realise that they cannot have a fair and equal opportunity to grow and prosper, sadly resign themselves to this kind of unloved, uncaring and un-nurturing behaviour, and as a consequence they lose all sense of self-esteem and purpose in life. At the end of the spectrum, there is the child who feels that he is unable to please, is ignored or despised will fight for attention even though provocative and offensive behaviour brings on further disapproval and punishment. The distressing effects of this type of ambivalence is the way it influences the child, and if the child decides to stay in this type of environment because it is the only environment he is familiar with even though it is distorted, it is virtually impossible for them to become decent members of their community. Since they have become accustomed to receiving disapproval they then behave in a self-fulfilling predictive manner at home, at school and finally in society. However, for these children all is not lost because when given the right environment, encouragement and understanding, this negative attitude and behaviour can be overcome and be replaced by confidence through the attitudes of clinical treatment which will do most to help and relieve the insurmountable distress.

For the caseworker, one of their greatest skills lie in knowing when and how to evaluate and interpret the risk factors associated with emotional and psychological abuse with the purpose not of treatment but as an aid to diagnosis through observation combined with some features of play for the younger child and collateral study which will show the importance of treatment. It is, for instance, commonly suggested that the social worker as therapist, in assessing the ambiguity inherent in defining emotional abuse should take into consideration the following factors. For example, can the way the parents behave create an emotionally harmful environment for the child easily observed? Do the child's actions or physical health show observable or measurable effects related to the parents' behaviour, and will these effects if any create or lead to serious future harm if not treated? And is treatment available to the family that would relieve the child of the emotional harm. The main lessen to be learnt here is that close vigilance by concerned and responsible people who are charged with meeting the needs of children in this present time followed by determined action to increase self—confidence and social adaptability is the recipe which will work provided that the attitude to the children is one of deep concern.

CHAPTER 13

CARIBBEAN SOCIETY'S ATTITUDE TOWARD SEXUAL ABUSE OF CHILDREN

Sexual abuse of children in the Caribbean has gradually been recognised and is now far more prevalent than once imagined. Like rape, child sexual abuse is one of the least reported crimes in Caribbean society. Although estimates of its frequency vary from region to region and those cases that are officially reported to the appropriate authorities clearly represent only a fraction of incidents that actually occur. Hence significant data on the subject is hardly available. Many signs including public awareness indicate that it is a problem which is more widespread, more serious, more distressing and more difficult to discuss than any other area of child maltreatment. Hence, many people, though concerned about the plight of sexually abused children tend to bury their heads in the sand to issues involving the sexual abuse of children.

In the Caribbean context, although most members of society react with predictable horror at what is done to children by perpetrators of sexual abuse, many are not aware of what often happens to them subsequently at the hands of most Law enforcement personnel who are either not trained to work with sexually abused children or are unsympathetic toward these victims. For example, an adolescent female who is being interviewed during the preliminary investigation, and is unable to articulate the facts of the abuse through fear may find herself being strongly admonished by the Law enforcement officer for not being able to relate the details of the incident and is of the view that she was an active participant. In Caribbean culture, the differential and complex way society treat children who report sexual abuse little allowance is given to the child's ability to comprehend or compete with adult offenders. Stevens, D. and Berlinger, L.1976. In many instances when an incident of sexual abuse is brought to light victimization of the victim is often recognized and protection is hardly guaranteed because society is so quick to pass judgement. Too often, in such situations the protection of the child is sacrificed in the process bearing in mind that for a child, going to court has a number of negative aspects Aside from the most obvious problems and procedural complexity the effect that facing the court can have on the child must also be weighed in the balance. The stark reality is that the victim is usually not protected from the defence Attorney's attempt to attack her credibility as the main witness, a factor that can literally put the child's wellbeing in jeopardy, especially so if charges are pressed against the perpetrator and there is a successful prosecution which can lead to the breakup of the family with little or no concern about the impact this may have on the child.

Society has traditionally look to the machinery of the criminal justice system and protective services to provide the best available assistance to victims of sexual abuse and their families but the process has often and sadly meant additional trauma for all persons involved. In situations where there is already a high degree of family disruption, the threat of further trauma to the family may take on much greater significance to family members than anything that has previously disrupted the family in the past.

Although research has consistently shown that children rarely make up stories about having been sexually abused, and false accusations continue to be rare, the potential for false accusation continue to be an area of great concern in sexual abuse cases. The child who falsely accuses a family member of sexual abuse without any emotional trauma could deem to be acting with malice or spite as an inappropriate motive with the intention to disrupt the family relationship. Unfortunately, these are rare circumstances that must be viewed with some credibility as the potential is always there and is guided by a state of mind that is hard to prove. Sadly, society, no matter how well intentioned is the cruellest assailant of all. In the Caribbean for instance, when circumstances of intra-familial sexual abuse has occurred, it is not uncommon to learn that a child has gone to the parent or other family member or teacher to report what has happened only to find that the victim is either not believed or accused of being wicked or trying to destroy the family's income. Such expressions can cause a child to feel guilty for causing emotional distress in the home. More often than not, the mother herself becomes a victim of her circumstances immobilized by a situation in which she feels powerless and ineffectual that she can take no action to protect her child. Research findings indicate that in the area of sexual abuse, few people are aware of the true status of this hidden crime instead their beliefs have been shaped by misconceptions and popular myths. It is regrettable to say the least, that although society claims that all children should have equal care and opportunity the evidence points to a society unconcerned with its children when their actions and attitudes assists sexual abusers by silencing the victim and thereby encouraging public denial about the true nature of sexual assault against children. Some are too quick to believe that the abuser is innocent even though there may be plenty of supporting evidence. Salter, A.C. 2003.This unfortunate situation could be because no disturbance existed in these families before the incident, or, alternatively no disturbance was expected and therefore not sought. In the midst of such vulnerability the court may descend upon a child and its family with such a devastating impact that they are left with feelings of remorse and guilt. For instance, persons who are aware that sexual abuse is suspected might be willing to report their concern if they could be confident that the effect of their action would not add to the trauma the child was already experiencing.

CHAPTER 14

CHILD ABUSE AND THE LAW, A CARIBBEAN PERSPECTIVE

Children today need the same things they always needed such as, and not exclusively stability, security, ongoing warm nurturing relationships, physical protection, safety and regulation and a bright secure future for their optimal development. These essentials do not need Government programmes or even high paying jobs for parents. In fact, most success stories from poor families come not because the children were given material things but because they were given these fundamental elements for healthy development. They had stable parent-child relationships, they were taught standards of right and wrong and they were given hope and guidance to become successful citizens of their country. They also had intellectual stimulation and personal sacrifice which is best cultivated through a loving and nurturing relationship. The question is, whether we as adults are willing to make these sacrifices for our children's needs or whether we are content to hand our responsibilities over to someone else.

In an ideal world all parents would make sure that their children would receive just what they need in the way of nurturance and love and none would be victims of abuse and neglect. However, in a not so ideal world, abuse and neglect might exist but when they were recognised all efforts would be made to solve the problem in a humane and effective manner where professionals involved in human and family services would work together in understanding and recognising the problems of child abuse and neglect and in a unanimous agreement of the measures necessary to correct it.

Abuse and neglect, however, do not exist as clear-cut alternatives to nurturance and love in this far from ideal world. Rather, they are one in a continuum made up of ways of behaving toward children. In the worst of circumstances when children are disfigured, become a victim of permanent emotional damage or even die as a result, then people easily see the harm clearly and denounce it. However, the further from this extreme we go unfortunately, the more difficult is the judgement is to whether abuse or neglect is occurring and what must be done to prevent it and protect the children. From a more realistic perspective the world is real and not ideal. Therefore, respect for individual privacy, strong emotions such as fear and love, cultural childrearing differences, family stress, rights of parents and children, important legal issues, ambiguous legal codes, provisions for emergency custody and the biases of observers all conspire to make the task of recognising and rectifying child abuse and neglect very complex and challenging for the social worker so much so that the laws and legal procedures connected with child abuse and neglect might seem unreasonable demanding.

Child abuse and neglect is prevented first, through awareness then early detection and intervention. Consequently, protecting children from abuse and neglect must be the first and foremost concern of law enforcement and family service agencies who must work collaboratively in situations involving suspected physical or sexual abuse and to take the appropriate action to protect children by the way of child protection proceedings through civil laws administered through a family court.

A child in need of protection is one whose life, health or emotional wellbeing is endangered by the actions or omissions of a person Children are also protected under criminal proceedings when the offence is punishable. These include criminal negligence, assault, sexual assault and sexual offences against children.

It is generally agreed that parents are given the rights of care, custody and control of their children. However, when a parent grossly abuses these rights the law may intervene to ensure that the child's health safety and welfare will be protected through laws that are legislated to:

- Make parents or guardians who are guilty of abusive physical conduct towards children be subjected to the normal criminal penalties.
- Use of the Family Court Act which establish procedures for the processing of child abuse cases on a civil basis
- Identifying abused children and setting in motion legal procedures to investigate the child's situation and either to provide protective services for them in their own home
- Remove them to a safe environment either in foster care, residential care, in hospital or a satisfactory caring relative.

Civil Procedures in Child Protection

Within the Caribbean, the usual manner of dealing with child abuse and neglect through a family court, a juvenile court and a magistrate's court where the focus is upon the welfare of the child in the total context of the family. Following this first concern, the law usually requires that a child protection agency receives and investigates any reports of child abuse and cases involving serious neglect and must determine if a child's injuries or the parent's behaviour can be classified as abusive under the law. Legal intervention begins only when the risk of serious harm is unacceptable great. A case then begins with the filing of a petition alleging abuse or serious neglect. If the report is substantiated, or if the child is already removed to a place of safety by a police officer or a social worker. In the consideration of law and best practice, reasonable efforts are to be made to prevent removal of children from their home giving consideration to the health and safety of the child. Protection of the child to a place of safety is a major consideration if the child's safety is threatened by the giving of evidence against the abuser

Generally, court action should be considered to remove a child temporarily or permanently from the home or to seek adequate treatment based on the following criteria:

- The child is in immediate danger of harm because conditions in the home are dangerous to his or her physical, moral, mental or emotional wellbeing.
- Attempts at treatment have failed because the parents have not made progress towards providing adequate care for the child or live up to their responsibilities.

In the case where permanent placement away from home is recommended, emergency custody should be considered by way of a Court Order, bearing in mind that these decisions can differ significantly from region to region within the Caribbean depending upon the type of legal structure in each jurisdiction. This protection is offered whether the offender is a parent or a stranger.

The Court Room Setting: Cases Held 'In Camera'

In Barbados, criminal court cases involving child abuse are held in a more friendly court room atmosphere and in the absence of the general public and arranged in a way to make the child feel as comfortable as possible. The social worker assigned to the child is present during the child's testimony generally to give them support and encouragement. The rule of law in criminal prosecution for child abuse and neglect cases are not held 'in camera' but behind closed doors where only such persons as the child parent (s) and representatives of authorized agencies who have an interest in the case.

In a fact finding hearing, where the victim has to give evidence, there are a set of criteria to be considered by the court.

1. There are reservations to videotaping the interviews of children because their use is conditional upon the child being available and age appropriate for cross examination because the tape alone cannot be put forward as evidence.

2. The child should be able to understand the difference between the truth and a lie. This criterion penalizes young children or those with special needs who are aware of the difference but may have difficulty explaining it

3. Before a fact finding statement about abuse and neglect is admissible by the child relating to any allegation be admissible as evidence, both the child and the defendant have a right to face to face contact to afford the child proof of evidence against the perpetrator beyond a reasonable doubt. The difficulty arises, however, when the child who feels threatened by the perpetrator has to stand before him and accuse him of the abuse. This makes the child fearful of any reprisal by the perpetrator and would rather not give evidence against the person especially if that person is a parent. Unfortunately, situations do occur where cases are known to be dismissed by the court under such circumstances.

Other areas of concern is the delay in presenting cases involving abused children which can be unnecessarily painful and places tremendous pressure on these children, their families and the social worker who usually has her work cut out in court related cases. In some cases, the attorney for the abuser comes across less sensitive while interrogating the abused child. The length of time they have to wait for a case to be heard further contributes to the trauma experienced by the child and family.

Unfortunately, cases do get caught up in the slow judicial process, and as a result cases get dragged on for years. Some cases at times are repeatedly postponed due to tampered evidence or the unavailability of the perpetrator's legal representative. Under circumstances such as these, the child who is the main witness cannot remember pertinent details of the abuse and the accused is acquitted of the charge.

Sexual Abuse and the 'Age Of Consent' Rule

While the phrase 'age of consent' typically does not appear in legal statutes, when used in relation to sexual abuse, the age of consent is the minimum age at which a person is considered to be legally competent of consenting to sexual acts according to the legal age which differs between jurisdictions, and whose ages range between 14 to 16 years.

Sexual abuse of children can be described as any sexual activity with a child age 16 and under committed by a person who is 16 years or older from less threatening acts to more serious activities as described according to the law.

One of the most widely referred definitions when referring to the sexual abuse of children is given by Schecter, M.D. and Roberge, L. 1976 who refer to this sexual experience as 'the involvement of dependent, developmentally immature children and adolescents in sexual activity that they do not fully comprehend and are unable to give informed consent to; and that violates the social taboos of family roles.

According to Forde, N.M 1989, in reference to the consent rule, she opined that careful consideration must be given to rationalize and bring into harmony child abuse laws in the region where a child of 12 years in one territory may make a positive decision on sexual intercourse while the age of consent is 13 or 14 years in another.

Several countries have since reformed the laws relating to sexual activity which are intended to alleviate these discrepancies. This allows for laws to set an upper age limit for childhood but equally will allow for exceptions for some territories where the age of maturity is set lower. For example, the Criminal Code does not now criminalize consensual sexual activity with or between persons 14 years or over. Furthermore, consensual activity with those under 14 but over 12 may not be an offence because of cultural norms and practices.

Child Marriage under The Rule Of Consent

Marriageable age is the age at which a person is allowed to marry either as of right or subject to parental or other forms of consent. While globally the age distribution of marriage is increasing, child marriages are still a common occurrence in parts of Africa, India and parts of Latin America and the Caribbean. Although the age and other requirements vary between countries, the marriage age should not be confused with the age of majority or the age of consent. Against such a background, the marriage age in a country may be below the age of majority and the age of consent that applies in the country.

Additionally, the age at which sexual activity occurs may be below the legal age of marriage.

The following extract is from the book 'Elements of child Law in the Commonwealth Caribbean' by Zanifer Mc. Dowell 2000.

"The need to protect children from entering marriage too early is reflected in the legislation of various territories. For example, under the Laws of Guyana marriage shall be void if one or both of the parties is under the age of 16 in the case of a male and under 14 in the case of a female. It further states that if a female under the age of 14 becomes pregnant or is delivered of a child she may apply by petition to a judge of the high court for permission to be married under that age to a person not being a person under the age of 16; or if under that age he admits to being the putative father of the child whether yet delivered or not ; or is adjudged by a court of competent jurisdiction to be the father of the child, shall judicially declare by order in writing that the marriage may be solemnized under the authority or direction of that Order shall be good, valid and effectual to all intense and purposes as if both parties had been above the age of 18. However, the Equal Rights Act 1990, made the minimum age 16 for both sexes making any purported marriage to be void below the age of 16 except in cases where a female below the stipulated age is pregnant and has successfully petition the court for permission to marry."

Statutory Protection

Generally, there are three main areas of the law which affects the general field of child protection.

Laws that mandate the reporting of suspected cases of child abuse and neglect through the establishment of various protective services and designate the public and private agencies to deal with the problem.

1. The traditional provision of the penal law which makes the parent or guardian who are guilty of abusive physical conduct towards children, amenable to the normal criminal penalties.

2. The juvenile and Family Court Act which establish comprehensive procedures for the processing of child abuse and neglect cases on a civil or criminal basis.

In the English Speaking Caribbean, the Domestic Violence Protection Law is designed to establish procedures to help protect children from injury or mistreatment and to safeguard their physical, mental, and emotional wellbeing. It is set up to provide a due process of law through its juvenile and family court to intervene against the wishes of a parent or guardian on behalf of a child so that his needs are properly met.

When used in this title, and unless the specific context indicates otherwise, an 'abused child' means a child under the age of 18 years whose parents or other person legally responsible for his care:

1. Inflict or cause to be inflicted upon a child physical injury by other than accidental means which causes or creates a substantial risk of death or serious protracted disfigurement or protracted impairment of physical or emotional health

2. Commits or allows to be committed a sexual offence against a child as defined by law.

3. Neglects a child under the age of 18 years whose mental, physical or emotional condition has been impaired or is in imminent danger of becoming impaired as a result of his parent or other person who is legally responsible for his care to exercise a minimum degree of care in supplying the child with adequate food, clothing, shelter or education, medical, dental, optometric, or surgical care though financially able to do so; or in providing the child with proper supervision or guardianship by unreasonably inflicting or allowing to be inflicted harm, or a substantial risk including the infliction of excessive corporal punishment, or by using drugs or alcoholic beverages to the extent that he loses control of his actions, or who has been abandoned in accordance with the definition by his parents or other person who is legally responsible for his care.

In the Caribbean, Child protection is guided by civil proceedings either in a magistrate's court or a juvenile court which intend to guide the safety of children in child abuse matters and to determine whether child abuse and neglect has taken place. This task is carried out by specially trained social workers in the area of child abuse and neglect whose responsibility is to investigate every report by following established criteria to determine which situations are the most urgent and what needs to be done to assess any risk to the child. The less serious cases may warrant treatment and prevention services only, however, the more extreme cases are referred to court for criminal investigation to determine the need for prosecution and incarceration.

Child Protection Court Orders

This section looks at the way in which the child care and protection will affect child protection work in the context of the Acts overall philosophy and objectives. Much of the Acts philosophy is equally applicable in most Caribbean territories, but before examining the provisions relating to child protection work, it is important to place the Act in context and to have an understanding of its purpose.

A child in need of protection means any child under the age of 18 years who is subjected to any form of gross maltreatment requiring social and legal intervention. If legal intervention is a requirement, the court may make a protection Order which sets forth reasonable conditions of behaviour to be observed for a specific time by a person who is legally responsible for the child's care since there is legitimate concern that in abuse cases it is often difficult to prove that injuries to a child were caused by non-accidental means.

Since there are no mandatory laws in the Caribbean, in order to address this problem, some Caribbean Islands have introduced certain protocols to deal with this issue. For example, in Belize, there is the enactment and wide dissemination of the Family and Children's Act which incorporates the mandatory reporting of child abuse regulations. In Jamaica, there is the Child Care and Protection Act. In Guyana there is the finalization of a Children's Bill, and the recent commencement of consultation for revision of the Sexual Offences

Act. In Grenada there is the development of National Child Abuse Reporting and Management protocol. Dominica, St. Vincent and the Grenadines and St. Kitts and Nevis are undertaking similar processes which are all steps in a positive direction towards the protection of children. UNICEF in Latin America and the Caribbean 2007

Child protection cannot simply be remedied by child care services alone. The question then becomes what forms of intervention are likely to enable parents to care for their children in ways that are acceptable to themselves and society? The issue that must be addressed concerns the proper legal mandate which is required in situations where there are risks to children The decision to exercise this authority seeks to bring children the protection and jurisdiction of the court based upon the recognition that there is a constructive goal to be achieved vis-à-vis the protection and safety of children and to provide and strengthen family ties whenever possible.

In conformity with the vigorous set of objectives set out to improve the protection of children, a most comprehensive piece of legislation was enacted as a framework in the Caribbean for the protection of children from gross abuse and neglect through Acts of Parliament which have entrusted the legal protection of abused and neglected children in either a juvenile court, a family court or a civil court process. These courts are bound by all the rules, regulations and constitution as place of settings and procedures of a magistrate's court except in as far as they are modified. This Bill sets up the mechanism for providing protection to children under the Domestic Violence Protection Act, and introduced several important concepts which have been preserved in the current legislation. In recent times, several countries in the Caribbean region have introduced laws against Domestic violence to children. Until then, most children of the Caribbean had limited protection from abuse and were further abused by being removed from the sanctity of their home while the perpetrator was able to enjoy the comfort of the home to the detriment of the child who is left with the feeling of guilt and psychological trauma as they considered their removal as a punishment.

Mc. Dowell in her research into child protection and Domestic Violence in the Commonwealth Caribbean offer a review of the current Acts pertaining to children's rights and the welfare of children although one must be careful in assuming that the law offers protection in all or most of these situations. These Acts differ significantly from country to country in their mandate but all of them describe precisely how they operate in practice. For example, In Jamaica, the Domestic Violence Act 1995 allows the court to grant a Protection Order where the respondent's conduct threatens a child. The application may be made by a parent or guardian, a parent approved by the Minister responsible for Social Services or a constable. The application may be made to the Magistrate's court or the Family court. This order is deemed necessary for the protection of the child.

In Trinidad and Tobago, the Domestic Violence Act 1991, offers protection to a child faced with Domestic violence by a person against a child of the person. Applications are made to the Magistrate's court, and the persons who may bring the application include a parent or guardian, a social worker or a public officer upon the approval of the Minister for Social Services, a police officer, a probation officer or a medical social worker. Other Jurisdictions have established a "Child Protection Service" to perform those functions assigned by this title. For example:

- In Antigua and Barbuda, here is the Domestic Violence Protection Act of 1999.
- In the Bahamas, the Sexual Offences and Domestic Violence Act 1991.
- In Barbados, the Domestic Violence Protection Order of 1992
- In Belize, the Domestic Violence Act in 1992
- In St. Lucia, the Domestic Violence (summary proceedings) Act amended 1997.
- In St. Vincent the Domestic Violence (summary proceedings) Act in 1995.

Emergency Custody With or Without A Court Order

In reviewing the current child care legislation as it relates to the Caribbean, it is not only the laws that are controversial but the interpretation of concepts such as the way the courts and the social services agencies deal with the welfare of the child, the parent—and—child constitutional rights, and how existing laws within each territory promote the welfare of children and improve their current protection. Traditionally, the underlying presumption has been that of the family which asserts that children are the possession of their parents and that parents rights must not be violated. As is often the case, however, most of the arguments take place around the exceptions to the general rule. Children are highly vulnerable, and because of their dependence they are powerless to prevent abuse by their parents hence the need for protective legislation where the laws relating to child protection and safety must remain a flexible tool capable of sensitive application according to the age and circumstances of the child. The most pressing need at the present time, however, is not so much for new legislation but for the implementation of appropriate laws which are already on the statute books

Most countries in the Caribbean have laws in place permitting the removal of children from abusive situations in their home some of which may differ from country to country. For instance, in Barbados, the Prevention of Cruelty to Children Act 1904, amended 1981, and the Child Care Board Act 1981 provide improved measures for children in need of care and protection with provisions for the prosecution of parents or guardians who abuse children in their care.

Also applicable to Barbados, are general guidelines for the emergency removal of children to a "Place of Safety" without parental consent and which can be executed with or without a Care Order. A child may be detained in a Place of Safety by order of a Magistrate if he/she is suspected of being a victim of gross abuse or neglect or is in other ways 'at risk'. The responsibility for investigation and seeking a suitable Place of Safety will rest with the social worker who sought the Place of Safety Order, or a police officer with a warrant to search for and remove a child. The investigation must involve any necessary enquiries to enable the Director of Public Prosecution to decide whether or not there is sufficient evidence for a case to be brought. According to the rules governing the care and safety of the child, any suitable placement is considered a safe place such as a hospital, a children's home, a foster home or a caring relative who has been evaluated, and for a period not exceeding 28 days in the first instance. Although the Social Service Agency has responsibility toward children who are subjects of a Place of Safety, such children are not subjected to a Care Order. The fact that the court is satisfied that the child has suffered significant harm does not mean that a Care Order will automatically be made. Roche Jeremy, Rogers W.S 1992. In this process, the court has to apply certain principles which govern its decision making in all proceedings including the use of a guardian-ad-litem who play a full and active role in providing independent social work advice to the court aimed at safeguarding and promoting the welfare of the child, and to ensure that relevant evidence is brought before the court in care and related proceedings. Depending on the severity of the offence, the court might decide not to make a Care Order and instead make an Order enabling the child to live with relatives.(Roche J. and Rogers W.S. 1992.

In the case of a Care Order, continuance of custody needs to be validated through a petition filed in the Supreme Court by a child care agency provided that the child is in the care and custody of that agency. In such events the petition should state facts sufficient to establish that the child is in such circumstances that it is necessary for the court to assume immediate jurisdiction over the child. The social worker or a person on the courts discretion is the responsible person who will remove the child from a place of safety to a child care residential home while a decision is made by the Supreme Court judge for long term placement or the assumption of parental rights.

Rights of Parents

Before a child can be removed from his parents it is necessary to show that abuse has actually occurred. It is not enough to assume that parental standards have, or are likely to fall beneath an acceptable level, or that a child would be better off placed from the parental home. For example, there are those who will argue that parents can be abusive and appropriate action must be taken to safeguard "at risk" children. On the other hand, there are those who argue that parents have rights. Naturally, the discussion will focus on how best to protect children taking into account parents roles and responsibilities. The other question which looms large is whether promoting the rights of children is the best way of promoting children's interests without the consideration of parental rights in rearing children as they see fit subject to the child's general welfare.

The legal protection of children is based on the intention that the child's needs come first and paramount consideration must be given if these needs are to be met. There will always be those parents, who, despite their ambivalence towards, and ill-treatment to their children still have certain rights and privileges which must be taken into consideration whether or not permanency placement away from home is being planned.

Parental rights provide the framework in which parental obligations can be responsibly exercised. It provides the framework also in which the child's right to his own family can be met, and whether a parent is or is not responsible for the ill-treatment of a child, he or she remains the parent and every effort should be made to encourage the natural desire to do what is best for one's child. Parents, like their children need clear explanations of what is going on and what is likely to happen. They should be treated with courtesy, openness and honesty even when it is necessary to question them about the abuse or to exercise statutory powers. It is possible to help them to understand and respect professional concerns even when these lead to the removal of the child. They must be kept informed, consulted about their children's needs and encouraged to play as full a part as possible in any plans made for their child.

Evaluating the Effectiveness of the Child Protection System

Beginning in the 60's, child abuse and neglect laws were focussed on identifying abused children and protecting them from abusive treatment by removing them from unsafe situations. However, while there are laws that offer children some protection they may not be sufficiently well known, understood or supported by professionals whose work bring them in contact with children, and more precisely with the legislation aimed at protecting their short and long term interests; or with the provision of treatment where appropriate.

The Convention on the Rights of the Child emphasizes the wishes of children in their protection with the condition that the child is a human person and not an object. This includes involvement in decisions about their future which is an important principle guiding their protection. Based on this premise, what kind of service are children offered in court proceedings? Due to the negative experiences children have to endure as child witnesses in abuse cases, and the feeling that they are being re-abused one cannot help but agree that in court proceedings children are seen as second class citizens who receive a second class service from the legal system. At present, there needs to be put in place systems which will prevent further abuse and suffering by not having the child recant the trauma of the abuse which they would already have done through investigative interviews by several people including the social worker and the police who in most instances are not equipped with the appropriate skills essential for interviewing victims of abuse and neglect and in particular sexual abuse. In most instances, the child may well have become ashamed and guilt ridden by the barrage of questions and constant prodding for answers which the child at times is unable to give along with the lack of preparation for the court environment.

In addressing the need for protection of children from abuse and neglect, the legal system is based on the premise that the welfare of the child is given paramount consideration in any court proceedings with the premise that the task of child protection is already overloaded with procedures, guidelines and systems of accountability. Yet, while there is the need to address the court procedural defects and injustices in our child care system, careful consideration must be given to the social reality of the psychological damage inflicted upon the child involved in court proceedings. It follows, therefore, that however valuable procedures and guidelines may be, the complex reality is that there is need for radical changes in the current system of court procedural hearings involving child witnesses.

As child abuse and neglect is so topical, child care practitioners should adopt a high profile and use every opportunity available to speak and act on behalf of these children and amidst their own unique statutory responsibilities plan for the protection of children based on their value judgement and the determination of the court.

So what is wrong with the current legal system of child protection in the Caribbean?

Existing child protection laws in the Caribbean come from several Acts in several territories which were implemented over the years by varying degrees, and have, through its legislative provisions demonstrated that its main objective is the rights and protection of children who are subjects of gross neglect and abuse. However, research studies have indicated that child care laws as they relate to abused children in the Caribbean are in a mess and need to be seriously addressed. It is imperative therefore, that a system be introduced where a society which claims to care for children should cease to discriminate against them, and should introduce a fair and just legal system while acknowledging the need for change. Caribbean Governments need to reform child care legislation at inter-regional level by consolidating and simplifying existing laws to suit the Caribbean on a whole. Against this background, will be the eradication of the continuing victimization and lack of sensitivity towards the most vulnerable members of our society who have no voice of their own. It is a travesty, to say the least, how the present judicial system within the Caribbean and the wider society continually acts against the best interest of the child and appears to protect only the perpetrator.

Other considerations point to the desirability for each Island state to have some uniformity of proceedings through the use of a family court to escape the personal and professional brutality of the current adversarial system and which would provide an atmosphere more conducive to putting the protection of children uppermost while being cognizant of the concerns of their parents. All in all, there needs to be child protection laws which are administered equitably and humanely.

It is to be expected that any child appearing before a Magistrate's court and particularly in cases of abuse and neglect are to be given a degree of special consideration where they are protected from publicity, and where the child's parents alone are required to attend. Most importantly, all courts are required to take into account the welfare of any child appearing before it.

On what grounds, therefore, can the use of the family court be justified? A family case worker hoping to improve the emotional climate of children who are subject to abuse and neglect cannot completely counteract any damage done by parents or care givers who express their negative feelings directly to their children, or to follow this with advice on better child care. Their other recourse, therefore, is to invoke court intervention in determining what is in the child's best interest. Under these circumstances, the use of the family court can only be a step in the right direction where the family's situation can be looked at comprehensively, and where social workers can feel comfortable in putting over the views of the family in an atmosphere more conducive to a thoughtful yet legal consideration of the child's best interest. One big problem as agreed by research, is that as far as child protection and the court go the law is seen as one sided!!!!!

CHAPTER 15

TREATMENT AND PREVENTION MEASURES

Treatment Options

Every child has a right to be well and safely born as well as the right to be born in a nurturing and emotionally supportive environment. As a general rule, acknowledgement of the development needs of the child will provide a framework for the caretaking requirements which can be facilitated by anticipatory guidance and parent child bonding first to the child's existence and later to his full mental and physical wellbeing. In looking at parental ambivalence towards children, Pearlman 1968 stresses the point that parenthood requires a basic, consistent, continuous willingness to give or lend oneself to the nurture and protection of children. It is suggested that the causes which appear to be behind some of the violent, destructive and anti-social behaviour towards children in Caribbean society at times, lie in the root causes of the family and in the unsatisfactory family situations which are stressful to the growing child and is primarily both competitive and materialistic. Fortunately, nations of the world have recognised the need to stem these negative consequences and are addressing the issues relating to child abuse and neglect while instilling a sense of responsibility in the care of children with greater determination.

Education programmes play a critical role in the overall fight to reverse the trend of child abuse and neglect. Proper education provides a pathway to successful intervention and treatment by increasing community awareness of the damage to children and families. Education is also critical in helping parents and care professionals understand the nature of the problem and consider how best to respond to a particular situation.

Collaboratively, a wide range of community workers and agencies such as social workers, medical practitioners, public health nurses, welfare agencies, mental health clinics and hospital emergency personnel are dedicated to providing appropriate human services to those high risk families so that they will not be limited to a future of dependency; and reduce the incidence of several childhood conditions.

As increased knowledge of the aetiology and treatment of child abuse and neglect is gained, these community personnel are asked to provide specific psychological treatment along with medical follow up and social support. Of course, many researchers and service providers alike have agreed that work with these high—risk families often does not always alleviate the problem. Understandably, a caseworker is not able to give realistic guidance to parents, nor is he/she in a position to modify their expectations of their children unless he/she is appropriately trained to observe patterns of childrearing and social work practices. In some cases, this is because resources are too limited or intervention begins too late; but in many cases it is the lack of adequate training and support for workers that hamper the delivery of care. He opined that work with this client group is particularly difficult because of the highly charged feelings aroused by such work. Timms, N.1968 It may well be a truism that these feelings often prevent social workers and therapists from making proper decisions and mitigate against good case management even when the cases are adequately understood. In examining all the factors including shortage of manpower and other resources, one important concept in treatment for distressed families and their children deals with the cumulative effects of stress. However, if only some of the stress situations can be relieved through treatment across a broad spectrum of education, social and family situations, the effects can be less far reaching for the whole family.

Whatever general statements can be made about the effectiveness of various kinds of treatment for abused and neglected children, they cannot sensibly be used to determine the response to particular cases in which decisions have to be made. Studies of effective social work intervention in families at risk within the Caribbean have shown that little research exist on the relatively effectiveness of short term and long term treatment because some problems are not sufficiently recognised and the ability to tackle family problems is often perceived as makeshift and merely scratching the surface. At the same time, it is recognised that social workers in the Caribbean clearly possess considerable professional and personal autonomy giving their clients the opportunity to experience positive and friendly worker/client relationships. Cohn A.H. and Daro D.1987 concluded that successful intervention with at risk families require a comprehensive package of services which must address both the interpersonal and concrete needs of all family members.

Interventions for physically abusive and neglectful parents, target parenting skills, anger management and stress management. Family systems approaches for sexual abuse are also used and include comprehensive programmes that use a sequence of therapies such as individual therapy for each family member as well as family and marital counselling. For sexually abused children, interventions often target the negative feelings associated with this type of abuse such as guilt, shame, anxiety, anger, depression and stigmatization. Group therapy is also often helpful for children who were sexually abused to confront issues of secrecy where they are afraid to disclose the abuse and issues of empowerment. Sexual abuse empowerment programmes help children to avoid predators and to report any victimization. These programmes generally teach children the knowledge and skills necessary for protecting themselves from a variety of dangerous situations, and emphasize two main goals. These are, keeping the abuse from reoccurring and encourage children to report past and current abuse.

The fact remains that for many people a good material standard of living is their chief concern in life, but what is really needed if we are to build a generation of people who have physical health, a sense of purpose and civilized goals are basic preventive work and treatment options.

Putting into practice the concept of treatment are several forms of therapeutic interventions that are available for families affected by child abuse. These interventions may take a variety of forms including various combinations of the following: individual counselling, group therapy for older children which may be activity based or discussion of problems and experiences shared in common, play therapy for present incidences of abuse.

Since community intervention facilitates the provision of necessary prerequisite or supporting programmes, they commonly serve as adjunct to some of the other intervention methods previously mentioned. Such programmes attempt to address situational and social factors that might contribute to child abuse and neglect, and can be addressed through a variety of services such as home visits, the use of a hotline and other support groups.

Prevention Strategies

Preventing child abuse begins when people recognise its existence and are willing to get involved in reporting their concerns or suspicions. Failing to act means that a child may be killed, irreparably damaged or forced to endure suffering that will affect his or her entire life. Some abused children will grow up to abuse their own children because it is the only form of child rearing they know. And the cycle continues.

Preliminary studies indicate that many of societies violent criminals were seriously abused neglected or deprived as children. A study by Silverman I.J. 1993 identifies an important link between child abuse and neglect, and delinquency. Prevention of child abuse, therefore, can mean a reduction in violence in society generally.

The old adage, an ounce of prevention is worth a pound of cure is an obvious truth in the fight against child abuse and neglect. Child abuse and neglect prevention is recognised as a crucial; element in the long range goals of breaking the cycle through world-wide activities aimed at reaching every nation, every society and every community. The goals of prevention are to bring awareness to everyone and motivate them to get involved in the fight against this scourge. Many experts believed that the prevention of child abuse and neglect hinge on the ability to provide guidance and support to families at risk for abuse and neglect. Though it was generally accepted in earlier times we are becoming more aware that no matter how involved people become in working with children, families and various support systems it is obvious that casualties will occur within the endeavour. Of course, one must be cautious in making moral judgements about parental competence and help in relieving their stresses. These programmes operate on the assumption that methods which are focussed on teaching at risk parents how to be effective in their child rearing practices should reduce incidences of child abuse and neglect. Many of these programmes attempt to identify at risk parents and intervene at an early stage. Hence, many family violence professionals across the Caribbean are demonstrating their concerns for the growing problems of child abuse by establishing community wide prevention programmes. The general goals of prevention are:

1. Increasing parent's knowledge in the basics of parenting and child development with post, prenatal and early childhood education.
2. Improve overall child rearing skills
3. Improve parent/child communication skills
4. Increase parents knowledge about the triggers of abuse, and increase their use of non-violent approaches to child discipline
5. Training or counselling for parents to help them face their responsibilities and develop more satisfying relations with their children
6. The provision of short-term foster care to provide much needed respite for vulnerable parents who at times may be more isolated from relatives both in terms of geographical location and emotionally dependent within the community and
7. Subsidized day care provision which represents the ideal environment for a small child to find healthy emotional outlets in a supportive tolerant and stimulating setting.

Child abuse and neglect prevention programmes should be involved in a range of community outreach education programmes and professional training activities and projects which should include the distribution of training materials to hospitals, social service agencies, universities and colleges, the distribution of pamphlets to the public to make them aware of the problems of child abuse and neglect, the funding of seminars and training workshops for professionals such as Doctors, nurses, teachers, the law enforcement personnel, social workers, Judges and Lawyers and programmes to foster co-operation among local agencies, other professional personnel and the general public, lectures and public talk discussions to the print and electronic media, school groups, parent/ teacher associations and other organisations and individuals involved in the study of child abuse and neglect.

While the specific focus of these individual programmes may differ according to the needs and resources in each individual territory, the primary purpose of the programmes is always prevention of all forms of child abuse and neglect. In spite of the resulting enormous needs for societal and community intervention, social scientists have turned their attention to the tragic phenomenon of child abuse by fostering awareness of programmes in light of the emotional and physical destructiveness. Such assumptions since any project with regards to the prevention of child abuse and neglect must form the basis of a theoretical foundation. Experts in this area of prevention have now begun to recommend approaches that emphasize a truly moral definition of child abuse. Bloom, B.L 1968 makes a detailed and analytical contribution to child abuse and neglect by identifying other commonly used methods to define and describe prevention in working with abusing individuals. He describes these manoeuvres as Primary, Secondary and Tertiary prevention. According to Bloom, these three main kinds of prevention programmes are:

1. Primary prevention which is a broad program aim at the general population. This type of prevention includes, public awareness, education for children and professional training and advocacy. These activities are intended to reach a large population including those at high risk for abuse or those who are victims of abuse. The intended goal is to help people cope in their own lives and eliminate the potential for child abuse and neglect in a general population.

2. Secondary prevention which attempts to identify and treat a smaller population such as those at high risk for child abuse and

neglect. These attempt to provide early diagnoses and prompt treatment for parents and children at high risk of abuse, and

3. Tertiary prevention which focuses specifically on victims and perpetrators in an attempt to stop and prevent recidivism of chronic child abuse and neglect. Here, help is provided for victims including abusers through family therapy and residential programmes for children.

These interventions undertaken by concerned, responsible and professional people are indicative of ways of meeting the needs of children and troubled parents in the present time. However, considerable work still needs to be done especially in evaluating the relative effectiveness of the different models of intervention, because successful treatment and prevention of child abuse and neglect do not happen spontaneously. There is considerable thought behind the scenes at every stage. For example, there must be constructive use of the resources available and the process of planned intervention which must be centred on the dynamic functions of the family as a unit.

In general, the efficacy of child abuse and neglect prevention provides some clear and simple messages for strengthening the preventive aspects children being of child good about themselves and parents to respond positively to parenthood. However, with limited funds being available for human service programmes it becomes increasingly important to establish the value of preventing child abuse and neglect in financial terms where accurate information on costs and outcomes can help agencies and professionals make their case to funding sources, sponsoring organizations and policy administrators.

Child abuse and neglect prevention programmes need not be expensive. However, for them to be effective in achieving their intended outcomes, it is necessary for child abuse and neglect prevention and family support programmes to conduct evaluation activities such as observing what is currently practiced, thinking what needs to be done and adjusting the current practice if necessary as part of the ongoing quality assurance efforts because too many children are being victims of child abuse and neglect care through inadequate services. The objectives being, that those children should be able to feel competent, happy and accepted.

CHAPTER 16

CONCLUSION

Finally, it would seem that present policies towards the problems experienced by the disadvantaged family implies a weakening of their family life, and any failure to tackle social deprivation among these families means that only a percentage of parents are able to provide for their children. Any reluctance to improve social work preventive services serves to perpetuate emotional deprivation and the need for statutory intervention. Further, the attitudes conveyed by these trends towards the parents who are deemed unloving and irresponsible will only intensify their sense of defeat and increase their ambivalence toward their children and destroying their family life. The question then becomes, what forms of social intervention are likely to enable such parents to care for their children in ways that are acceptable to themselves and society.

During the past two decades or thereabouts, available statistics and the amount of literature on the incidence of child abuse and neglect by parents or parent substitutes in Caribbean society is quite alarming and devastatingly widespread. One can argue, therefore, that child abuse and neglect is considered a grave social problem, and as such warrants special attention almost by its perceived definition. There can be little doubt that one would wish to drastically reduce the incidence, but if this line were taken, one ought to be careful not to assume that such deficits in parental attitudes, behaviours and lack of essential resources do not warrant an explanation since its impact and in some cases its very existence can be determined by the operation of certain social processes such as environmental factors, social pressures and personality traits which can be found in any society. The description and explanation of these processes must form just as important a part of the social and psychological concern to which it gives rise, and it must always be borne in mind that these deplorable circumstances and the entirely new phenomenon whose manifestations are not readily evident to the general public can have implications for lack of emotion, recognition or even participation in the fight against child abuse and neglect. However, once they are brought to the attention of the general public and their implications explained, there may be general agreement upon defining them as social problems and upon the need to take urgent steps to deal with them.

The ability to offset and understand the causes of child abuse and neglect in the English speaking Caribbean is crucially dependent on the extent to which the nature of those problems are understood and the effectiveness of different policy approaches to alleviate them. It is well documented that the ability of some parents to meet the needs of their children is associated with the socially depriving circumstances in which they find themselves. This issue is equally central to the argument that child deprivation and child protection policy must be seen in the context of social policy where the objective is to promote the social conditions and societal attitudes which would allow parents to raise their children with love, security and stimulation. Entailed in this is the need for radical change in income distribution, housing provision, subsidised day care for children and access to educational and job opportunities. Only then, can we accept the premise that disadvantaged families will have opportunities to enjoy normal family life. Whether this policy reform would radically reduce poverty and deprivation would depend on the extent to which they would narrow the relative distance between those who have and those who wished they had.

Overtime, there has been much debate by child care advocates and family service agencies alike over how much Government within our Caribbean region should do to support the needs of families and their children. We need further to recognise that work with children and families cannot be seen as an alternative approach to policy aimed at a redistribution of resources alone, but is highly relevant to the issue of child deprivation and protection. While social administrators and policy makers may appear inefficient and lacking insight in their consideration of the plight of disadvantaged families, it is somewhat naïve to consider their interest as merely being spontaneous reactions to incoming data on child abuse and neglect. And even if they occasionally appear relatively insensitive in their reactions to the phenomenon, one can still investigate assumptions about child abuse and neglect and how it should be treated as it is incorporated into the day to day administration of social services departments. Here, research is needed, but one needs to wonder whether they are merely recording statistics or dispensing judgments in court.

In addressing the need for the delivery of intervention services which would give priority in defence of extensive social deprivation among the less fortunate in Caribbean society, it is noted through research that there is enough information within the Region which indicates that the current range and degree of community and child care resources do not strengthen effective prevention work with troubled families or even respond to the limited definition of child abuse and neglect. It behoves Governments within the Caribbean Territories therefore, to state explicitly the kind of society they wish to create for these socially deprived families, and the extent to which they desire to rearrange resource differences which will improve their vulnerability within their environment, and ensure optimum care for their children with minimal disturbance of lifestyle and development because many families lack access to resources which are available to the majority. Objectives concerning such policy decisions have partially determined the extent to which child abuse and neglect intervention in the Caribbean can be measured. In response, individual Governments need to make significant improvements towards a greater equality in the provision of services which will enable more families to cope, and give them the opportunity to attain the child care standards set by the norms of society. I believe that it is timely for Governments to tackle social deprivation as it confronts Caribbean families by undertaking an extensive review of current problems and programmes in the delivery of social service provisions as an objective of social reform with an emphasis on competence, enhancement and restoration.

If the link between deprivation and child abuse are not recognised by Government policy, then obviously the socially disadvantaged members of their society are more likely than other groups to experience such conditions which involve the intervention of social service agencies.

In addressing the issue of social policy without a proper framework for social action, it may well follow that the responsibility for deprivation problems, child maltreatment and the task of child protection are placed on the personal social services which are already top heavy with case load management.

There is nothing wrong with ideals of good practice in caseload management, but when these ideals are not in line with practice situations unfair standards of expectations and judgement will inevitably follow.

Given the service orientation in social work and its direct involvement in human relations guidelines for child protection work a level of working together inter-professionally towards a common goal in child abuse treatment and prevention often simply doesn't exist. It is imperative, therefore, that an interdisciplinary approach be part of casework intervention in child abuse and neglect if the necessary treatment objectives are to be achieved.

What is being argued, is that no one profession has a monopoly on caring to the needs of children because they have a multiplicity of needs in terms of promoting their continued growth and development and a healthy wellbeing. Implicit in this therefore, is generally the need for such significant interventions drawn from the fields of psychiatry, psychology, nursing, social work, education and social administration. These practitioners provide the necessary interventions in different contexts and amid varying concerns and responsibilities. In accordance with these causal chains for strengthening aspects of the child care networks, how effective is social casework intervention in the treatment of child abuse and neglect, and providing interventions to parents and parent figures aimed at the prevention of anti-social behaviour? A convincing argument is that there is the need for all aspects of the support systems including social casework because they are valid and necessary depending on specific circumstances, but before any attempt to give a detailed analysis of the basic methods or processes involved in social casework intervention, there must be clarity as to the nature of the casework phenomenon.

In the past, social casework was seen as the almost exclusive method of working directly with children or helping families in crisis situations. The shift tended to be in favour of concern with families and their social circumstances with relatively little interest in wider measures aimed at social change with the tendency for some social workers to see their role as little more than goodwill, commonsense and kind-heartedness Weightman, K. 1988. This conception of social work intervention carried with it a marked reluctance to credit professional social workers with any special or additional expertise, and reduced it to a routine activity where the need for urgent consideration or attention was not seen as the most important aspect of a human situation. Furthermore, interventions aim at treatment and prevention of child abuse and neglect poses great questions, what happens when social workers are asked to process clients at a rate and in circumstances which make such an approach to treatment impossible? What place did social work hold as an agent of both social caring and social control, and more precisely, what were the implications for society and social work of its forcible expanding functions. Richmond Mary,E. 1922, A pioneer of the social welfare movement, came up with several definitions of social casework, but the one most preferred by her students, was that "social casework may be defined as the art of doing different things for and with different people by co-operating with them to achieve at one and the same time their own and society's betterment" The main emphasis in this model is as an extension of the process of ordinary living.

A more recent definition of social casework stressing functions is that of De Schweinitz1939 where he stated that, "Social casework consists of those processes involved in giving services, financial assistance or personal counsel to individuals by representatives of social agencies according to policies established and with consideration of an individual's need." In fact, De Schweinitz's emphasis on social casework as a means of fulfilling agency function is open to being misinterpreted as denying social caseworkers any autonomy, but sees it merely as an instrument for merely carrying out agency policy, which is by no mean s the exclusive prerogative of social work.

More recently, where much emphasis is placed on professionalism in the provision of personal social services, the pendulum has swung in the opposite direction where there are far reaching changes with a redefinition and re-adaptation of much in social casework. Its purpose was to assist social practitioners in recognising that they are to fulfil their functions of concern for the wellbeing of individuals, and to promote and enhance the lives of children and families through a careful and appropriate balance between aspects of caring and the promotion of social change. In realistic terms, these basic principles would allow for constructive action and public accountability with a clarification of what is social work and what are its functions in terms of social service provisions.

Since social work practice became 'generic' rather than 'specific' the two fields of function are not separate and distinct, they complement each other and are interdependent. They have particular implications for social work practice where social workers are expected to provide services to a broad range of clientele maintaining a wide scope of knowledge, and practice a great diversity of skills.

To validate the opinion that social work intervention is a critical factor in accomplishing the goals of child and family preservation and various intervention modalities, Hopps June and Pauline Collins 1995 have given some deeper and contemporary insights into the nature of social casework through direct service and individual change. They contend that the profession of social work responds to wider historical change and have describes casework as, "any of various professional activities or methods concerned with providing social services to disadvantaged, distressed or vulnerable persons or groups such as investigatory and treatment services or material aid."

According to Gordon Hamilton1940," Social work and social casework are not coextensive since casework like group work is indispensable as a foundation for social planning and social action with the same philosophy but not the same techniques." In light of this philosophical concept, and its possible influence on conventional social work, how can social casework organise itself to play a professional role in forwarding the objectives of addressing problems associated with the social needs of families and proper child care objectives? The concept of social casework like any other part of social work provides social workers with its basic terms of reference in relation to its broad objectives perhaps the most relevant, which is the acquisition of knowledge, skills and values which forms the basis for social work practice to be effective. To put it all in a nutshell, social casework must utilise knowledge derived from other profession, notably the social aspects of medicine, law and psychiatry and must draw heavily on the social sciences including politics, economics, psychology and anthropology, but with its own specialization in order to add to the content of knowledge and the ability to solve problems as they relate to family dysfunction and child abuse and neglect. It must take into account social changes of society and the family with a greater concern for the growing number of children in distress, and policy efforts to increase support for social programmes to assist children and families and an effective provision of services in the community. I believe that it is only by acknowledging the reality that the primary goals of casework management is to optimize the clients functioning by providing quality service in the most efficient and effective manner to individuals and families in distress. What I am trying to say is that the effectiveness of interventions in the decision making process as a concept and a practice in pursuit of their goals, rests on the acceptance by policy makers and programme directors where bureaucratic controls within their statutory roles limit what social caseworkers can achieve and what they must strive to overcome in terms of providing therapy or in tackling poverty and inequality; and an effective provision of services to the community.

While it is not possible to draw a rigid line of demarcation between professional knowledge and technical knowledge, in contrast, the former is primarily concerned with knowledge which can be transferred and with the ability to identify both similarities and differences in situations; and furthermore to know what is applicable to bring to a new situation from past experience and what new knowledge is required. For example, Bartlett 1970 theorises that "For a profession like social work to be effective in today's society, it must identify an area of central concern that is meaningful in terms of the profession's values and goals, practical in terms of available and attainable knowledge and techniques, sufficiently distinctive so that it does not duplicate what other professions are doing and common to the social work profession as a whole."

No one can deny that social casework is a common body of knowledge and skill within the framework of social work which is integrated within working with families and communities. Since social casework is composed of hereditary or environmental factors, a social case cannot be determined by the type of client but by person and situation of objective reality, and the meaning of this reality because no matter how well—prescribed procedures are and how sophisticated in allowing professionals the exercise of discretion in complex situations, the ultimate goal is to develop services which can respond to the needs and wishes of children, and families who fail through a lack of those basic resources necessary for meeting the needs of their children.

APPENDICES

Appendix 1—Inter-Agency Management Procedures

Child Protection Service Agencies are legally required to respond to concerns about the protection of children who should be entitled to interventions that protects them from abuse and neglect and other exploitations. Wherever possible, children should be brought up and cared for within their own families and offered a service to meet each child's identified needs. Help should be offered as a service drawing upon effective representations and complaints procedures with effective collaboration between Government agencies and those from private and voluntary sectors.

The principles underpinning child protection in relation to agency responsibilities and systems that provide services to children and families are guided by a framework of Intake, Investigation and Assessment.

The Intake System

Intake is the first of the child protective service process and is one of the most important decision-making points in the child protection service. It is the point at which reports of child abuse and neglect are received. It involves gathering and screening information to determine whether services are necessary or appropriate. The Intake process applies when there is a request for service or a report that a child is or, might be in need of protection. Reports or referrals of possible child abuse and neglect are generally received by Child Protection Services intake team. This team uses criteria to determine if a report should be accepted for investigation or assessment. Reports that do not meet the criteria are screened out at intake and referred to other services or agencies for appropriate community resources. The Intake team through its agency must develop good practices and clear procedures for deciding when and how reports are to be made screened and investigated, and to ensure better handling of reported cases and follow-up responses.

Intake workers should be trained social workers with special skills to listen to concerns and ask questions before deciding how urgent the situation is and what type of intervention is needed. In face to face reporting the intake worker must structure the interview to gather all available and pertinent information from the reporter.

Case Study

This is a situation of a mother and her boyfriend both in their mid 30's. There are 4 children in the family. The first two children—a girl 10 years and a boy 9 years from a previous relationship; a girl 2 years and a boy 4 years from the present relationship. The mother works at night and the boyfriend is responsible for maintaining the household. The mother presented at the child care agency in a very distressed state and related problems ranging from an unhappy relationship with the boyfriend to financial difficulties. She stated that she works during the night and wondered whether the worker could help her in getting a day job so that she could be with her children at night because she misses being with them during the night. She further explained that there is a positive relationship between her the children and the boyfriend because he is a good provider and assists with the care of the children. She further commented that he even minds the children while she is at work. She is also in receipt of welfare benefit for the first two children.

The intake worker was concerned why the mother appeared so distressed yet her problem did not appear unduly stressful and told her that she must be feeling very frustrated and anxious about not being there for the children and queried if there were further problems or concerns which are causing the distress. At this point of the interview, the mother became very tearful while playing nervously with her handkerchief and wavered between wanting to talk and holding back. She then explained that her daughter informed her that the boyfriend had been "interfering" with her since she was 8 years old. She had not discussed this with anyone and instructed her daughter to do likewise. She further explained that her daughter only told her about one incident because she had threatened the boyfriend that she would kill him if he attempted to molest her daughter again and she did not want her mother to go to prison. The mother in the interview informed the worker that when the boyfriend beat the child it reminded her of her own childhood experience when her father would beat her to exert his authority over her so that she would submit to his sexual demands. She was adamant that she did not want the police involved in view of her dependence on the boyfriend.

When interviewing a reporter face-to-face, it is important that the intake worker must have well trained eyes and ears, and a keen sense of observation to achieve the most significant case data. Hurrying an interview can cause the worker to lose salient information and can put a client at a disadvantage by not gathering or recording pertinent information to plan or direct the investigation.

Types of Abuse Referrals

Referrals may come from different sources including members of the public, those working with children and from regularly involved professionals such as teachers, paediatricians and psychologists. Referrals can be made via the telephone, face-to-face walk-ins and anonymously. Upon receiving a report, the intake worker attempts to gather as much information as possible about the family as a whole and the nature and extent of severity. The intake team supervisor prioritises the investigation response time based on a number of factors including the nature of the allegation and the age of the child. The intake worker needs to record and review the information given and with the team supervisor decide on disposition of report by either referring it to the police if certain types of abuse are alleged, refer for investigation or closure.

When a report is made, all information given and the identity of the reporter should remain confidential where possible.

The Initial Investigation

Investigation is a highly involved process of gathering detailed information. It is the first step to ensuring the safety of the child who is reported as being abused or neglected. Its focus is on assessing the validity of a report and subsequently any risk or harm to the child. All case decisions are made within the agency with the intake team members in collaboration with the team supervisor who must prioritise any action to be taken.

When a report of suspected child abuse and neglect is received, it is reviewed by the intake team supervisor and assigned to a qualified case worker who will conduct an investigative assessment of the referral based on the following:

- A review of the facts of the case
- Determine the appropriate method for first contact with the family. i.e. visit or invite
- Determine the appropriate method of initiating the first contact based on the subject of the report
- Interview the parent and the child separately and jointly
- Assess the home environment to define any problems or stresses in the family
- Determine the need for in-home treatment or removal
- Initiate appropriate action that will ultimately lead to treatment, prevention and termination

The investigation must involve any necessary enquiries to enable the child protection service to decide whether they should take any action to safeguard or promote the child's welfare. This should be seen as a first step when a question of child protection arises. In an initial assessment, the investigating officer investigates the referral by visiting the child at school, at home or other location. He/she will assess the safety of the child by interviewing the family and others involved with the child.

Individual circumstances and level of risk for the child involved determine the response time. For example, if a child is in immediate danger a contact worker will respond immediately. If the worker determines that the child is not in immediate danger or risk of harm, investigation response can be made within 24 hours or 7 days, and reassigned using the agency's comprehensive guidelines to determine the risk in each situation. In most cases the child and family will be offered supportive counselling to keep the child safe at home. If the report is unsubstantiated the case will be closed.

One of the primary activities of investigation into an allegation of child abuse and neglect involves interviewing the child, parent and others who may have knowledge that can assist in the investigation. Interviews are conducted to gather information for assessment or to gather evidence. Remember that the interview is only one aspect of a complete investigation and should not include open-ended questions, direct questions or coercion.

Before the interview, the investigating worker must begin by introducing him/herself, explaining their job, their agency and the reason for the visit. He/she must approach the abusive situation in an objective manner while remaining professional at all times. He/she must:

- Make a careful note of any injuries or circumstances which caused concern.
- If an injury is observed, ask the child to describe how this happened.
- Ask the parent / caregiver if present to describe how the injury occurred and make careful note of the explanation given.
- Inform the parent/ caregiver of your concern and any action you will be taking.

In the case of an in home visit, the worker should under no circumstances leave the home without being able to see a child where there is a report of suspected abuse.

If in the course of investigation access to the child or information as to his/her where about is refused or denied, the police have important powers in protecting children under these circumstances, and when there is cause to believe that a child would otherwise be likely to suffer significant harm the court may issue a warrant authorising the police to assist in this exercise. Normally, a social worker will accompany the police officer in executing the warrant to place the child in suitable accommodation. Alternatively, they may take reasonable steps to ensure that the child's removal from such accommodation is prevented. For example, it is known that there are abusing parents/caregivers who wilfully refuse to disclose the child's whereabouts when there is evidence of injury or other noticeable forms of abuse.

A child who has been the subject of removal by warrant is referred to as having been taken into protective custody which is usually referred to as a place of safety which can be residential care, foster care or an approved relative. Where in the case of these investigations, the child is assessed to be not at immediate risk, reasonable steps must be taken to prevent such children from suffering abuse and neglect and to reduce the need to bring proceedings which may result in the need for emergency protection.

If the interview is conducted out of home, any other interesting person/s in the room should be introduced and the child informed that the reason for their presence is to assist in his/her protection.

The child should be interviewed first and alone taking into consideration his/her age and developmental level, using specialized child oriented interviewing techniques that can relax the child and help him/her describe the situation and sequence of events with the least amount of trauma and embarrassment. Working in this way can be a most rewarding clinical experience as it enables the worker to get first hand information regarding any indicators of abuse and to begin assessing the risk of future harm. While the primary purpose of seeing the child first is to determine risk, this also helps lessen the likelihood that they will change or recant their story in response to possible parental threats

Before concluding the investigative interview, explain to the parent what will happen next allowing for either negative or positive expressions of emotions. In this respect, consideration must be given to protecting the child from retaliation and punishment by parents for having disclosed the abuse. These principles apply to all stages of the investigation to the point of closure.

On-Going Services

Once an investigation assessment is completed and it is determined that on-going treatment services are needed to reduce the risk of abuse or neglect, a family service long term plan is developed with the on-going caseworker. These plans involve working with families to establish goals that focus on maximizing children's safety and minimizing their risk of harm. This caseworker provide service to meet needs identified in the assessment, monitor progress towards achieving goals and closing cases when goals have been reached. He/she facilitates change through continual assessment, case management activities and referrals to services in the community as well as sometimes being the primary service provider or key worker.

This type of work with children and families is usually handled by the same caseworker who did the initial assessment especially in small countries like the Caribbean for example, where social service provisions are guided by low budget and inadequate human resources. The overall goal of the on-going caseworker is to provide protection and case management services to an assigned caseload of children and families by establishing a plan of service in conjunction with the family. This can begin with the initial contact of the caseworker and continues through a series of carefully planned steps that help family members identify and make important changes to safely care for their children. These goals can be achieved by providing a variety of services individualized to meet the family's needs

Services that can be utilised include family therapy, budgeting, marital counselling, individual counselling, parenting education and group counselling. They are also responsible for monitoring the child's safety on an ongoing basis by providing a service to promote their wellbeing and for providing at minimum, weekly intensive in-home services to the family where child abuse and neglect has been substantiated.

One could argue without doubt, that caseworkers in ongoing intervention play a myriad of roles when they intervene in the lives of children and families. In short, How the caseworker engages, interacts, build rapport and serves families may have greater impact on the outcomes of cases than any other intervention strategy.

When sexual abuse is alleged or suspected, the person to whom the child first confide need to handle that confidence and ask sufficient questions to confirm that there is an allegation of a sexual nature and avoiding any cross-examination or carry out any detailed examination of the child. All allegations of sexual abuse must be investigated without delay and with a carefully thought out plan to include:

1. Establish the facts about the circumstances giving rise to the allegation
2. Decide if there are grounds for concern
3. Identify sources and level of risk
4. Inform the police immediately as they may need to work together to prevent the child from repeating the story twice
5. Decide what protective or other action to be taken in relation to the child and any other children in the home.
6. Notify the Supervisor who will assist in the decision about any further action to be taken, or has been taken.

The investigation worker must be aware that in sexual abuse there are less likely to be physical manifestations therefore the child's account of what has happened assumes a greater importance.

If the child was abused by a family member, he/she may be under great pressure not to tell, and because of the charged emotion that may be present it is not always possible to be as open with the parents initially as one would be when investigating other forms of abuse.

When there is intra-familial sexual abuse, a judgement must be made urgently about the level of risk to the child and any other siblings in the household, bearing in mind that it is possible for the abuser to target only one sibling. In such a situation, the child and the alleged abuser may need to be separated immediately not only to protect the child from further abuse but to ensure that the child is not victimized or threatened. While considering whether the abuser leaves the family the worker can make recommendations to the court for an order of protection which mandates that the abuser leaves the home while the investigation is ongoing rather than remove the child. Depending on the severity of the allegation, the worker has the option of referring the whole family for family therapy sessions dealing firstly with family members individually, then the child, the abuser and the mother then move to family therapy targeting low self esteem, lack of trust, isolation in family relationships and fear of new relationships. This therapeutic intervention is intended to avoid interrupting the family and subsequently the family unit.

When sexual abuse is carried out by someone other than an adult living in the immediate family, or someone not emotionally involved with the family, the initial contact may be with the parent. This can help promote a collaborative relationship with the parents and mobilize them to provide the necessary protection to the child. The abuse should be referred in the same way as abuse committed by an adult living in the home, and should receive the same therapeutic consideration.

Interviewing the Sexually Abused Child

Interviewing a child is considerably different from interviewing an adult. In an attempt to obtain the child's statement, it is important that the interviewer should be armed with as much information as can be obtain. It will be helpful to know the child's name, chronological age, family relationships, name of the child's school, teacher and grades, socio-cultural background, name and address of the abuser, the relationship of the child to the abuser, the duration and extent of the abuse in the case of older children, the name of anyone else having knowledge of the abuse, whether the child has been bribed, threatened and/or physically harmed at any time and the name of any one the child has told in the past and what was the outcome. It is also important to know as much as possible about the circumstances leading up to the disclosure. Keeping in mind at all times that you should not suggest what may have happened nor offer an award for talking, or a threat of some retribution if the child does not talk. Interviewers should be aware that children respond better when they go from the general to the specific and from the less sensitive to the more sensitive areas in a gentle but persistent progression. An important aspect of interviewing a sexually abused child is assessing the child's level of maturity and an understanding of its sexuality and the functions of various body parts in securing pertinent information during the interviewing process.

The following guidelines are considered to be of key importance and have proven both practical and effective when conducting an initial interview with a child where there has been an allegation of sexual abuse with the understanding that each child and each situation will present unique features.

A sexually abused child will likely be highly anxious at the prospect of talking about the details of the abuse. Prolonging the disclosure over more than one interview can increase the anxiety further. The child is likely to talk more spontaneously at the time of the interview; therefore, it should be comprehensive and aim toward gathering all information required.

Preparation for the interview should include:

1. The interviewer's feelings
2. Establishing the purpose of the interview
3. Establishing trust by building a rapport and establishing a relationship with the child
4. The child's feelings
5. Obtaining the child's statement
6. Background information
7. Validating the child's credibility
8. Concluding the interview

The Interviewer's Feelings and Attitude to Child Sexual Abuse

In interviewing a sexually abused child, a number of factors should be considered perhaps among the most important are the knowledge and experience of the interviewer, including an awareness of the attitude and perception brought to the situation, a knowledge of the subject area, i.e. the dynamics of child sexual abuse, stages of child development, an ability to communicate in a non-judgmental, sincere and flexible manner, be willing to work cooperatively with other agencies and professionals, develop special techniques that you can use comfortably when a young child is having difficulty verbalizing the details of the abuse, being clearly aware of the purpose and goals of the interview you are conducting and develop the ability to plan for a successful interview. This can be achieved by:

1. Selecting a good and comfortable location which allows for privacy and avoidance of interruptions are needed since these can divert an already short attention span
2. Deciding who will be present at the interview
3. Choosing a convenient time of day
4. Choosing the length of the interview. A lengthy interview can divert an already short attention span and may produce apprehension on the part of the child
5. Allowing time for telling the child who you are and why you are there
6. Be aware of your own feelings and responses. This is an emotionally demanding work that can cause stress and pressure in your professional as well as your personal life.

Children reporting sexual abuse should be presumed to be telling the truth even in the face of initial denial by the alleged abuser or other individuals, bearing in mind that denial of sexual abuse is more common than false reporting.

When a child begins to disclose about sexual abuse, even experienced social workers may experience a sense of shock, revulsion or outrage at the offender. The child, however, may not be feeling this way at all. Therefore, if the child senses a horrifying response from the interviewer, it communicates to the child that he/she has been involved in something of which he/she should be ashamed. Any negative reaction can have the effect of increasing the trauma the child has already experienced. While it is critical that interviewers should be both self aware and empathetic, they should not convey their own feelings to the child. Instead, they should be encouraging and supportive while maintaining a degree of professional objectivity.

The Purpose of the Interview: Establishing the Child's Trust

Tell the child your name and what your job is. Begin by building a rapport and establishing a relationship with the child by engaging in light discussions about interests and hobbies etc. which will help to ease the tense situation. Ask the child if he/she knows why you are talking to them and what he/she was told by the person accompanying him to the interview. If he does not know, tell the child that your job is to help children who may be having a problem and indicate that you understand that he/she has been having a problem and ask the child to tell you what has happened.

If the child has previously told someone else about the suspected abuse refer to the fact that you are aware that he/she talked to that person about something that happened and ask him/her to tell you what happened. Refer that someone may have done something that wasn't right and ask the child to tell you about that, making every attempt to clearly understand the nature of the abuse. Be alert for any signs of anxiety and reluctance to talk. The interviewer can address these by telling the child that it is important to talk if something happened, and reassure the child that it is ok to talk. Random and general conversational exchanges can usually help to ease the tension and allow the child to articulate the information. Assure the child that he/she is neither guilty nor responsible for what has happened, and state clearly that you will see that every effort will be made to protect him/her from further abuse.

Child's Language in Sexual Abuse Interviews

Allow the child to tell the story in his her own words. Young children may know only words for parts of their body and may be embarrassed to say them. When this happens, interviewers can develop techniques that can be used comfortably when a young child is having difficulty verbalizing details of the abuse by the use of anatomically correct dolls or ordinary rag dolls. They should also be familiar with colloquial dialect the children may use to describe private parts and what was done to them, and ask questions to assure themselves that they and the child understand the same meaning for the words. For example, if an adolescent says "made love", do not assume that he/she means vaginal or anal intercourse. Ask them precisely what happened in terms of placement of hands, penis, vaginal touching, when, where and how often the abuse occurred, and so on. With younger children, it is good to prepare a simple kit containing paper, crayons and pencils. The use of art work and play therapy can also assist the interviewer in getting the child to describe what happened.

When the child talks, listen carefully to the child and be patient. Only after the child has begun talking and is describing an incident should the interviewer press for clarification of details. This must not include asking direct questions, questions that require a response. These must emanate from the child and not the interviewer. Neither should the interview be tape recorded as this violates the child's human rights.

The Child's Feelings during the Interview

When it has just been disclosed that a child has been the victim of sexual abuse, the child experiences a new crisis in his/her life. For example, the molestation which has previously been a secret probably for some time has now come out in the open. This disclosure now creates for the child, feelings of shame, guilt, anxiety, fear and confusion and for the first time is exposed to adults who are outside the abusive relationship and outside the family who may have their own biases. It is worthy of consideration, how the stigma and distress caused by the disclosure can bear heavily on a child when he/she begins to question whether he/she will be believed, if people will be angry, disappointed or rejecting. It is possible that the disclosure was not deliberate. If this is the case, he/she may be reluctant to talk and fearful of the implications. Remember, that it is not uncommon for the child to have been bribed, coerced or threatened into maintaining the secret. It is also common for abusers to tell children that they are responsible for the abuse or the breakup of the family; or, that no one will believe their story.

Validating the Child's Credibility

A useful framework for validating the child's complaint has been developed by Dr. Susan Sgroi 1975 who has found that the presence of certain characteristics tend to enhance the credibility of the child's story, such as:

1. The presence of multiple incidents occurring over time
2. The progression of sexual activity from less intimate to more intimate type of interaction
3. Elements of secrecy
4. Elements of pressure or coercion

When establishing these criteria, the interviewer must review the methodology to be used in the interview, and be satisfied that the methods used were conducive to allowing the child to articulate information relating to the sexual abuse.

Concluding the Interview

A child disclosing sexual abuse has usually revealed his/her deepest, most confusing and frightening thoughts. Professionals should realise that these children need praise, reassurance and protection. They should also realise that their knowledge about sexual abuse can be translated into responsible action that is humane, rational and mature. When the children discloses, the worker must believe the child because children rarely lie about sexual abuse except in other emotional situations. The interviewer may wish to briefly explain to the child that what the person did is against the law and that it is not his/her fault. Also, be sensitive to to the fact that the child has already been traumatized by the assault and may see the interview or examination as yet another assault.

If after the interview and it is decided that the child should be taken into protective custody, he/she should be told that a decision has been made about him/her staying where he/she will be safe, and be reassured that the interviewer will be staying in touch to make sure that he/she will be alright. If it is necessary for the child to be interviewed again by you or a police officer this should be told to the child.

The Physical Examination

The growing recognition of maltreatment to children has brought with it, special problems in determining whether acts of abuse has in fact actually occurred. However, in the case where sexual abuse is alleged, as part of their investigation, the police department is responsible for ensuring that the child has a physical examination. This is to substantiate that sexual abuse took place and not proof of guilt by the alleged perpetrator. It is also the responsibility of the police department to determine if an offence has taken place and by whom. When a physical examination is considered necessary, care should be taken to ensure that the child and parents are made fully aware of the reason for the nature of the examination. At this point, a careful decision should be made regarding who would carry out the examination. In the case of child abuse and neglect, it is generally agreed that a General Practitioner appointed by the Police Department. In all cases the female social worker who conducted the initial interview must be present as she would have already built up a relationship with the child, and is able to further offer the child reassurance and support during the examination.

When sexual abuse is alleged, prior to commencing the examination the examining practitioner should be fully briefed regarding the allegation. He/she should not be expected to prove that a particular individual sexually abused the child but may state that the result of the examination is compatible with sexual abuse, or, that sexual abuse is established beyond a reasonable doubt.

A good beginning is to recognize that sexual abuse is not a medical problem requiring diagnosis, but an event that may have actually taken place.

Research literature has over the years, concluded that professionals working with sexual abuse have had many reservations about the appropriateness of a physical examination for sexually abused children because of its potential to cause further trauma to the child. Today, most of these professionals advocate the use of a physical examination, the perspective being that as a context the child's parents/ caretakers can be assured that he/she was undamaged and intact. The opinion being that any child suspected of being sexually abused should have a physical examination at some point during the investigation since it is highly likely that positive findings will ultimately be used as evidence in the possibility of court proceedings.

Case Conference Criteria

In order to assist the model of one type of case conference, the following criteria are used for calling a case conference:

1. There is suspicion that the circumstances of the child meet the locally agreed definition of child abuse and neglect or for the Register.
2. The appropriateness or continual appropriateness of statutory action, registration and when the overall multi-disciplinary case management plan needs to be reviewed
3. Consideration is to be given to reunification and rehabilitation
4. De-registration is to be considered.

The Child Abuse Case Conference

After the investigation and assessment and there is harm or risk of harm to the child, a child protection case conference shall take place without delay and be regarded as a multi-disciplinary function.

Child abuse case conferences have been an integral part of child abuse and neglect procedures for over three decades. The goals of the case conference is to discuss what has been found out during the enquiry, and to enable professionals involved in the case to assess the relevant information, and plan for the child's welfare and wellbeing. Members of the case conference will hear information about the family and about concerns that have been expressed, discuss whether or not in their professional judgement the child is at risk of significant harm, whether abuse exists or is continuing, whether statutory action was or is appropriate, whether registration should be made, continued or ended, whether the multi-disciplinary co-ordination is functioning effectively, whether the overall case management plan is appropriate or whether a child protection plan should be in place.

It is emphasized that membership of the case conference should be those Senior officers who are in local contact with any individual child and all others who are involved, potentially involved or have relevant information such as teachers, General Practitioners, specialist police officers and other health and legal representatives shall attend as a matter of absolute priority.

Although functions within the case conference are official, it is important that in the face of civil liberties it must be clear that the conference members make only recommendations and not pass judgement on whether abuse has occurred.

Under child abuse procedures there should be only one type of child abuse case conference. Other less formal meetings such as "Case Reviews" or "Case Discussions" should not be tempted into reaching conclusions which are in the province of a formally constituted case conference as they can lead to confusion if written into the child abuse case conference procedures.

Functions of the Case Conference

Child abuse case conferences have several functions within the overall framework of diagnosing abuse and subsequent professional action. These are:

1. Pooling medical, psychological and social information
2. Assessing risks to the child
3. Formulating general treatment plans
4. Recommending to agencies with statutory powers whether statutory action needs to be taken
5. Decisions whether to Register or De-register
6. Nominating the key worker and identifying key personnel
7. Agreeing if and when to reconvene.

Professional Attendants

Attendants should usually be restricted to relevant professionals. However, the police with specialty in child abuse matters should be invited to all child abuse case conferences and not restricted to those involving physical abuse only. It is hoped that this regular participation would lead to greater team work and minimal unilateral action. It is the belief that a senior social worker or Team leader should be present when the key worker is responsible for a case that is being presented even if a senior is chairing the conference. This gives the key worker personal support and takes away some of the burden of resource and allocation decisions while they concentrate on the child and family.

The Child in Attendance At The Case Conference

The child who is the subject of a case conference may attend the meeting if they so wish and if they are old enough to understand what is happening. The key worker and the conference co-ordinator in consultation must be sure that the child's attendance at the conference will not be harmful to the child. If it is felt that the child should not attend the conference, this should be discussed in advance. The nature and purpose of the conference should be explained to the child at a level that is appropriate to their age and level of understanding bearing in mind that the protection of the child must always be the paramount decision.

Parental Participation

If the child's situation is serious enough to warrant a case conference the key worker should inform the parent as a matter of importance and invited to attend all or part of the conference unless in the view of the conference chair their presence will preclude a full and proper consideration of the child's interest. However, the general consensus among social workers involved in child abuse is that parents should not attend entire case conferences which are basically meetings where professionals take information and advice from each other and form recommendations for action, some being related to statutory duties. Furthermore, it is most unlikely that the best interest of the child can remain the objective focus of a case conference if the parent(s) is present. While giving credence to the decision that any parental attendance must be only for part of the meeting it is believed that within a clear structure parents ought to be given the opportunity to put forward their views and have the chance to ask questions as they relate to the process of their child's protection.

The Butler-Sloss Report 1987 of the enquiry into the circumstances surrounding investigation of sexual abuse in Cleveland was particularly critical of parents being left in a situation of isolation and a lack of support by professionals. This included lack of information about what was happening, lack of contact and prolonged separation without adequate explanation.

After the case conference, it is the duty of the family case worker to inform the parent(s) of major conference conclusions. If the decision is to place the child on the child abuse Register where this policy applies the facts of and reasons for this decision should be confirmed to the parent(s) in writing.

The Child Abuse Register

On the basis of recommendations made by the enquiry into the death of Maria Caldwell in 1974 at the hands of her step-father, the research unit of the National Society for the Protection of Cruelty to Children (NSPCC), carried out research to produce a general estimate of the level of child abuse and neglect in England and Wales. As a result of these studies, it was recommended that a register should be established to estimate the level of child abuse and neglect and the percentage of children affected.

The Register known as the Child Abuse Register has the advantage of providing a readily available list of reported cases of child abuse and neglect which has been professionally identified and categorised into types of maltreatment. If managed properly, the Register can guide social workers in assessing risks to children and as a therapeutic tool with particular families. It also allows for cases to be systematically followed up and to identify trends over time.

The child abuse Register should be administered by a manager who is a senior professional social worker with experience in an agency with statutory child protection powers and duties. The manager may be known as the "child abuse co-ordinator" or "child abuse consultant" and must have proper clerical support to ensure that an efficient cohesive system is maintained.

Social workers must always remember that the rights of children are to be considered at all times, therefore a child's name should not be placed on a Register other than through a case conference decision with specific reasons clearly recorded.

Criteria for Registration

Placing a child's name on a child abuse register includes not only children who are physically abused or neglected, but carries a broader use to include any child under the age of seventeen where there is:

1. Definite knowledge or reasonable suspicion that the injury was inflicted other than non-accidental
2. Where the child has been persistently or severely neglected
3. Where the child has been medically diagnosed as suffering from severe non-organic failure to thrive
4. Where social assessments find evidence of persistent or severe neglect or rejection
5. Where there is illegal sexual activity between the caretaker and the child within the family context, or failure to protect the child from other inappropriate sexual activity, or that
6. One of the mentioned criteria might be met such as indication of high risk after medical and social assessment.

Data to be Included in the Register

Before putting a child's name on the abuse register, the following data is required.

The child's full name, known address, sex, date and place of birth, full name and address of parents or caretakers and other adult members in the household with information on their relationship to the child, the name, address and phone number of the child's Doctor, the child's school, day nursery or other person taking care of the child, the nature of the injury, by whom inflicted, reason for the referral and whether the abuse has been substantiated, date of registration, the name of the key worker, other agencies involved, date of next monitoring or review, the legal status of the child, whether the parents or caretakers have been informed when and by whom the registration was instituted, minutes of the case conference which should contain justification for the registration and other correspondence/information about the child which was received by the person in charge of the register.

The decision to remove a child's name from the register is a decision which must be made by the case conference members who in their professional judgement believe that there is no longer a significant risk to the child and where case management under the child abuse procedures is no longer necessary. Here, parents should be told verbally and in writing that their child's name has been removed from the Register and with full significance of this explained.

According to Social Service Department policy, there is no minimum period before a child's name can be removed from the Register provided that careful monitoring and assessment have been carried out.

The Family Case Worker

When a conference decides to place a child's name on the Child Abuse Register, it will also appoint a key worker to co-ordinate the case. This will in most cases be the social worker who is most closely concerned with the case and is responsible for its management. The key worker has a responsibility for facilitating any necessary statutory action and preparing reports in accordance with practices of the social service agency. In addition, the key worker:

Checks that the parents have understood the meaning and purpose of the Child Abuse Register, will be the central focus of communication about the family and will actively seek, collate and disseminate relevant information about the progress of the case, ensure that the wellbeing of the child is being monitored, noting any significant changes in the family's circumstances and functioning, initiate and or undertake any legal action which may be necessary to safeguard the child, maintain regular contact with other professionals involved with the family in order to share information and co-ordinate work including any exchange at the conference, ensure that the agency's records on the family are kept up to date and adhere to the Agency's code of practice for social workers dealing with child abuse.

In order to manage child abuse cases, the key worker should be a qualified and experienced social worker trained in child abuse matters. He/she must be provided with experienced and skilled supervision and be accountable through the line management of the agency which must provide the necessary resources to allow the key worker to effectively work and actively participate in decisions where appropriate rather than leave all responsibility with the key worker. It is possible that there may be other professionals in touch with the family whose work may overlap with that of the key worker but should in no way interfere with the role or responsibility of the key worker. Since the tragedies of the 70's in Great Britain regarding abuse of children and the controversies surrounding the effective management of cases, considerable progress has been made in the quality of work with child abuse cases. Nevertheless, from time to time there are seemingly avoidable tragedies to children who are being supervised by qualified social worker. These incidents provide reminders of the high standard of work which is demanded of those dealing with child abuse and neglect and the difficulties of maintaining standards.

Children at risk of abuse must be supervised by professionally qualified social workers who fulfil the criteria laid down by the values and ethics of social work practice, and with specific training in dealing with child abuse matters. They must have regular supervision from a qualified and experienced senior social worker. They must also recognise the high level of anxiety created by child abuse work and its impact on both themselves and others. They have that responsibility to share this anxiety with their supervisor and to enter regular supervision sessions in a prepared and open way including a rational system of workload management. If the key worker in carrying out her work with high risk families feel unable to further take on that responsibility due to the complexity of the family dynamics such as aggression toward the worker and lack of co-operation by the family because they feel that they are not getting the support or commitment they expect, or concerns about their own personal safety, the supervisor should be informed and the case reassigned to another specialist social worker in child abuse matters after careful discussion of ethical and role conflict between the worker and the parent, and any factors that interfere with delivery of care.

Case Transfer and Closure

Where the family of a child whose name is on the child abuse register moves out of the area to a known address, the key worker must notify the appropriate agency in the new area as soon as this is known initially by telephone and confirmed in writing as soon as possible so that child protection services in that area will be promptly alerted. After consultation with the co-ordinator, the key worker must inform the chairperson and other case conference members and ensure that the referral is followed up as soon as possible with information including a full case history for the use of the new supervising authority unless it is agreed that the whole case file is passes over. It is expected that a Child Protection Case Conference will be convened by the receiving authority and the key worker accompanied where possible by members of the Case Conference from the previous area will be asked to attend.

If the family moves to an unknown address urgent steps will be taken by the key worker to trace the family. If all efforts fail, a senior member of the Social Service Department may seek assistance from the Police Department in tracing the missing family. In the event that the case is recommended for closure by the conference, other agencies previously involved with the family must be informed.

INTERPROFESSIONAL MACHINERY IN CHILD ABUSE MANAGEMENT

Supervisors of Social Workers Dealing With Child Abuse and Neglect

Supervisors in the management of child abuse and neglect must be professionally qualified and experienced with an understanding of the impact child abuse work can have on social work staff. Supervisors must have direct responsibility for supervising social workers who work with child abuse cases along with other management responsibilities while remaining in close liaison with the child abuse co-ordinator. Although supervisors must allow a degree of profession autonomy in their staff, they remain accountable to the agency for the quality of work by social workers. It is therefore necessary to balance their knowledge and skills about child abuse and its supportive functions with a clear managerial function which includes:

1. Acting on behalf of the agency which is ultimately responsible for the services it provides on child abuse

2. Being familiar with the Law relating to child abuse and both inter-agency and multi-disciplinary procedures on child abuse case management

3. Ensuring that social workers within the agency have also seen and understood these guidelines

Supervisors need to recognise the high level of anxiety that can arise by working with abused children and their families, and offer appropriate support, guidance and control. They must ensure that supervision sessions are regular and that child abuse cases are regularly reviewed and discussed, and that standards of report writing are maintained. Similarly, there needs to be a rational system of work load management in order for social workers to give agreed and urgent priority to at risk children and their families with a regular pattern of home visiting.

Not only should supervisors be informed about the progress of a case where abuse had occurred, but their opinion should be sought and information given in the decision to close cases where children have been at risk of abuse.

Responsibilities of The Child Abuse Co-ordinator

According to the organization structure and within a policy framework, the child abuse co-ordinator has a duty to offer professional guidance to both professional social workers and their supervisors involved in the management of child abuse cases. To respond to the challenges which child abuse present, there must be collective responsibilities at administrative level within the agency some of which will rest with the supervisor while others will be in the remit of the co-ordinator up to director level. The child abuse co-ordinator is entrusted with the authority to:

1. Make the most constructive use of available resources and to inform more senior managers or governing bodies where there are shortfalls and how these can impair the service to children at risk of abuse

2. Convey to staff at all levels agency policy on child abuse in order to provide a clear framework within which staff can undertake such stressful work

3. Endeavour to create and maintain a service which enables social workers with child abuse and their supervisors to fulfil the code of practice on child abuse and neglect

4. Encourage a process of evaluation and research into the most effective ways of both protecting children and the prevention and treatment after abuse has happened

5. Recognise the stress involved not only for field workers but for supervisors

6. Ensure that child abuse work is allocated to experienced and trained social workers who will be supervised by appropriately qualified staff

7. Ensure that supervisors have a regular pattern of supervision with social workers carrying child abuse cases

8. Recognise the importance of supporting supervisors and be able to assist them with immediate decisions in child abuse cases

9. ensure that there is a system of internal review of abuse cases on a regular basis which must not be confused with case conference reviews

10. Review training needs of staff dealing with child abuse at all levels, and to work towards an adequate allocation of resources to meet these needs

11. Keep up to date with major developments in child abuse including responsibility for the management of the child abuse register

12. Provide professional support to the whole child abuse management system within the agency.

The child abuse co-ordinator has a duty to enquire into the circumstances of the death or injury of a child under the supervision of their staff and co-operate with such enquiry by making available to the enquiry such records and staff as would assist the process of the enquiry. In representing their agency, they must be equipped with the skills in dealing with the media for themselves and treat with utmost caution any request from them while being careful not to breach confidentiality.

There are a number of different and equally valid perspectives one could assume in an attempt to examine the natural series of changes taking place in social work today. One of these is the interrelationship of knowledge and skills which are processes of investigation, assessment and evaluation in a context of professionalism in which it always takes place.

A child's suffering and that of all those associated with the child tends to bring out a natural sense of sympathy and frustration with the feeling that it should have been prevented. It is the author's view, that those professionals working with children, in their desire to rescue them from the ravages of abuse need to approach the problem in as rational and scientific a way as possible. The range of protection, caring and therapeutic resources needed in child abuse work reflects the range of objectives that these professionals will be trying to achieve with abusing families.

REFERENCES

Ainsworth, M.D.S. and Bell, S.M "Mother Infant Interaction and the Development of Competence": In the Growth of Competence, edited by K. Connolly and J. Bruner. London: Academic Press. 1974

Albert, Vicky, N. and Richard, P. Barth Predicting Growth in Child Abuse and Neglect Reports in Urban, Sub-Urban and Rural Counties. Social Service Review.1966.

Allen, S.M. and Hawkins, A.J. Maternal Gate Keeping: Mothers Beliefs and Behaviours that Inherent Greater Father Involvement in Family Work. Journal of Marriage and Family.1999.

Archer, E.Y. et al. Profile of Teenage Mothers and their Parent's Attitude to Teenage Sexuality and Pregnancy. West Indian Medical Journal. 1990

Astor, R. Children's Moral Reasoning about Family and Peer Violence. The Role of Provocation and Retribution: Child Development. 1994.

Aarne, C. Boudewin and Joan, A. Liem Childhood Sexual Abuse as a Precursor to Depression and Self-Destructive Behaviour in Adulthood: Journal of Traumatic Stress. 1995

Becker, W.C. Consequence of Different Kinds of Parental Discipline: Review of Child Development Research Vol. 1. Russell Sage Foundation. New York. 1964.

Belsky A. Family Analysis of Parental Influence on Infant Exploratory Competence in F.A. Pederson (Ed) The Father Infant Relationship. Observational Studies in a Family Setting. New York: Praeger. 1980.

Brooks-Gunn, J. And Duncan, G.J. The Effects Of Poverty On Children: The Future of Children. 1997

Behlmer, G.K. Child Abuse and Moral Reform in England: 1870-1908 Stanford University Press. 1982.

Bronson, W.C. Mother/Father Interactions: A Perspective on Studying Development of Competence.

Berry Juliet. Social Work with Children: University of Sheffield. Routeledge and Kegan Paul.1972.

Belsky,A.AetiologyofChildMaltreatment:ADevelopmental-Ecological Analysis.1993.

Bakar, D.(1971)

Bell, L and Tooman, P. Mandatory Reporting Law: In International Journal of Law, Policy and the Family Oxford University Press. 1994.

Balky, J. Parental and non-parental Child Care and children's socio-economic Development: A decade in Review: In a Journal of Marriage and Family. 1990.

Bronstein et al Parenting Behaviour and children's social, psychological and academics. In diverse family structures: Family Relations. 1993.

Bowlby, J. Child Care and the Growth of Love 1953.

Brooks-Dunn, J., Schley, S. And Hardy, J. Marriage and the Baby Carriage: Historical change and Intergenerational continuity in early childhood. In I.J. Crockeell and R.K. Siberssusen, (Eds). Negotiating Adolescents in times of social change. New York: Cambridge University Press. 2000.

Browne, A. and Finklehor, D. Impact of child sexual abuse: A review of the Research: Psychological Bulleting. 1986.

Bremmer, J. Gavin et al. Blackwell Hard Book of Infant Development: Oxford, U.K. Blackwell Publishing. 2004.

Bloom, B.L. The Evaluation of Primary Prevention Programmes in Comprehensive Mental Health: The University of Wisconsin Press. 1968.

Bartlett, H.M. The Common Base of Social Work Practice: National Association of Social Work. New York. 1970.

Butler-Sloss, E. Report of the Enquiry into Child Abuse in Cleveland: London H.M.S.O. 1988.

Constantine Larry and Floyd Martinson. Children and Sex: New Findings, New Perspectives, Boston: Little, Brown. 1981.

Caffey, J. Multiple Fractures in the Long Bones of Children Suffering from chronic subdural Haematoma, American Journal of Roentgenology, Colombia University. 1946.

Child Abuse: Breaking the Cycle: Caribbean Regional Conference. Port of Spain, Trinidad and Tobago 1989.

Convention on the Rights of the Child: Declaration of Children's Rights 1959.

Child Abuse and Neglect: State Statue Series Vol. 1. Reporting Laws: National Clearing House on Child Abuse and Neglect Information Washington D.C. 1

Collins et al Contemporary Research in Parenting: The case for nature and nurture. 2000.

Courtois, C. The Incest Experience and Its Aftermath. 1979

Clarke, E. My Mother Who Fathered Me: London. Allan and Unwin 1957

Cohn, A.H. and Daro, D. Is treatment too late? Child Abuse and Neglect, Vol 11. 1987.

De Francis. Protecting the Child Victim of Sex Crimes Committed by an Adult: Final report Denver: American Humane association, Children's Division. 1969.

De Vine. Sexual abuse of children: An overview of the problem. 1977.

De Moise, L. The evolution of childhood.1974.

De Schweinitz and Elizabeth Mc Cord. Can we define Social Casework? 1939.

Eggleton et al. Sexual Attitudes and Behaviour among Young Adolescents in Jamaica: International Family planning perspectives. 1999.

Egeland, B. The Consequences of Physical and Emotional neglect on the development of young children. Child neglect monograph: proceedings from a symposium, Washington D.C. U.S Department of Health and Human Services. 1988.

Epps, K. and Fisher, D. A. Review of the Research Literature on Young People Who Sexually Abuse. In G. O'Riley, W.L. Marshall. A. Carr and R. Beckett, Eds. The Handbook of Clinical Intervention With Young People Who Sexually Abuse. Hove: Brunner. Routeledge 2004.

Elder, G.H. Jr Children of the Great Depression: Social change in life experience. 1974.

Elder, G.H. Jr 1974. ibid

Field, T. Emotional care of the "at risk" infant: early intervention for infants of depressed mothers. 1998.

Fine, R. Freud: a critical re-evaluation of his theories. George Unwin Limited. London. 1962.

Freud Sigmund "Three essays on the theory of sexuality" Standard edition, Vol 3 London: Hogarth. 1905.

Forde, N.M Legal aspects of child abuse in the English Speaking Caribbean. "Breaking the Cycle". Caribbean Regional Conference on Child Abuse and Neglect: Port of Spain, Trinidad and Tobago.1989.

Finklehor, D. Child Sexual Abuse: New Theory and Research. New York. Free Press: In violence in the family. 1985.

Finklehor, D. Sexually Victimized Children. Free Press. N.Y. 1979

Ferstenberg Frank F. "Fathers in the Inner City": In William Marsiglio. Ed. Fatherhood: Contemporary Theory, Research and Social Policy. Thousand Oaks, Sage Publications.1995

Gough, D. The Phenomenon of Child Abuse.1987.

Gelles, R. Child abuse as psychopathology: A sociology critique and reformation: American Journal of Ortho-Psychiatry.1973.

Goldberg, S. Social Competency in Infancy: a need for parent/child interaction. 1977.

Gesell, Arnold. Maturation and Infant Behaviour Patterns: Psychological Review.1929.

Gesell, Arnold ibid.

Grusec, J.E. and Goodnow J.J. The Impact of Parental Discipline Methods on the Child's Internalization of values: A re-conceptionalization of current points of view: Developmental Psychology. 1994.

Giarretto, H. Humanistic Treatment of Father/Daughter Incest: In child abuse and neglect, the family and the community. Edited by Helfer, R.E. and Kempe, C.H. Ballinger, Cambridge, Mass. 1976.

Glaser, Danya. Emotional Abuse and Neglect. Psychological Management. A conceptual framework: Child Abuse and Neglect 2000.

Helfer, Ray. E The theology of child abuse

Hetherington, E.M. et al. Coping with mental transition. Monograph of the society for research in child development.1992.

Hetherington, E. M. Children and Divorce: In R. Henderson (ed.) Parent child interactions. Theory, Research and Prospect. New York. Academic. 1980.

Hamilton Gordon. Theory and Practice of Social Casework: N.Y School of Social Work. Columbia University Press.1947.

Hopps, June and Pauline Collins. Social Work Profession Overview: In Encyclopaedia of social work 19th edition. Edited by Richard Edwards and June Hopps. Washington D.C. N.A.S.W. Press 1995.

Jaffe, P.S, Wilson, S. Wolfe, D. And Zak, L. Family violence and child adjustment: comparative analysis of girls and boys behaviour symptoms: American Journal of Psychiatry. 1986.

Jantz, G.L. healing the scars of emotional abuse: Grand Rapids, M.I. Fleming and H. Ravel. 1995.

Jenkins Richard. Disability and Social Stratification: British Journal of Sociology. 1991.

Katz, S.N. "When Parents Fail". Boston, Beacon Press. 1971.

Katz, S.N ibid

Kempe, C.H., Silverman, F.N. "The Battered Child Syndrome". Journal of the American Medical Association. 1962.

Kempe, H. "The Battered Child Syndrome". 1962.

Kornfein, M., Weisner, T.S. and Martin, J.C. Women into Mothers Experiential Family lifestyles: The legal and economic impact of marriage: Sage Publication.

Koop, Everet.C. Surgeon General: U.S Public Health Service.

Kristen Luker. Dubious Conceptions: The politics of teenage pregnancy, Cambridge: Harvard University Press. 1996.

Kathy Silva and Ingrid Lunt. Child development, a First Course: Blackwell Publishers. Oxford. U.K.1982.

Kathy Silva and Ingrid Lunt ibid

Kelmer Pringle, H. "The Needs of Children":Hutchinson. London.1974.

Lasswell Harold, D. Politics: Who Gets What, When, How. New York, Mc Graw Hill.1936.

Loseke Donaleen, R; Gelles Richard, J; and Cavanagh Mary, M. Current Controversies on Family Violence; Thousand Oaks California. Sage Publications Inc.2005

Lystad, Mary. Interdisciplinary Perspectives on Family Violence: An Overview. Brunner Mazel Publishers. New York. 1986.

Lystad Mary ibid

Leo—Rhynie, E. The Jamaican Family, Continuity and Change: Grace Kennedy Foundation Lecture. Grace Kennedy Foundation, Jamaica. 1993.

Lieberman, E.J. and Ellen Peck. Sex and Birth control: A guide for the young. New York: Thomas, Y. Crowell. 1973.

MacMillan Alistair. Ed The West Indian Illustrated: Historical and Descriptive, Commercial and Industrial facts, figures and Resources. W. H and L. Collingridge, London 1909.

Minturn, Leigh and Williams W. Lambert. Mothers of six cultures: Antecedents of child rearing. New York: John Wiley and Sons. 1964.

Marsden, D. Mothers Alone. Poverty and the Fatherless Family: Penguin Books Ltd. Hardmonsworth, Middlesex, England. 1973.

Beatrice E. Kirton

Marsden, D. ibid.

Mason, M.M. Out of the Shadows: Birth Fathers' Stories. Minesota. O.J. Howard Publishing. 1995.

Mc Adoo, H. Socialization of Black children: Priorities for Research. Ed. L Gary, Washington. D.C. Howard University, Institute for Urban Affluence and Research. 1974.

Messer, D.J. et al. Relation between Mastery Behaviour in Infancy, and Competence in Early Childhood: Developmental Psychology. 1986.

Martinson, Floyd, Constantine and Larry: Children and sex: new findings and new perspectives. Boston: Little, Browne. 1981.

Mintz Sydney, W. and Sally Price. Caribbean Contours: The John Hopkins University Press. 1985.

Mzarek, D.A. and Mzarek, P.B. Psycho-sexual Development within the family: In sexually abused children and their families. Edited by P.B. Mzarek and C.H. Kempe. Elmsworth New York. Pergamon Press. 1981.

Mzarek, P.M. and Kempe, C.H. Sexually Abused Children and Their Families. 1981.

Mc Dowell Zanifer: Elements of Child Law in the Commonwealth Caribbean, University of the West Indies Press, Kingston Jamaica. 2000.

Naylor, A.K. Some Determinants of Parent/Infant Relationships: In What We Can Learn From Children. L. Pitman. Ed. Washington. D.C. 1970.

Naylor, A.K. ibid

Norman, A. Polanski. Prevalent Types of Neglectful Mothers: In Child Neglect, Understanding and Reaching the Parents. 1972.

254

Nightengale, N. and Walker, E. Identification and Reporting of Child Maltreatment by Head Start Personnel: "Attitudes and Experiences": In Child Abuse and Neglect. 1986.

Parker, R.D. and Collmer, C.W. Child Abuse, an Interdisciplinary Analysis: In E.M. Hetherington, Ed. Review of Child development Research: University of Chicago Press. 1975.

Parker, R.D. and Buriel, D. Socialization in the Family: Ethnic and Ecological Perspectives. 1998.

Pringle, M. Kelmer the Needs of Children Hutchinson. London. 1974.

Pringle, M. Kelmer. ibid

Peter, J.J. Child Rape. Defusing a Psychological Time Bomb. Hospital Physician. 1973.

Prilleltensky, I. and Pierson, L. Contributing Factors and Consequences. Promoting Family Wellness and Preventing Child Maltreatment. Fundamentals for Thinking and Action: Ontario, Canada. Wilfred Laurie University. 1999.

Perlman, H.H. Identify Problems, Role and Casework Treatment: In New Development in Casework, ed. E. Young-husband University of Chicago Press. 1966.

Rudd Jane M., Herzberger Sharon D., Brother/Sister Incest; Father/Daughter/Incest: a Comparison of Statistics and Consequences: in Child Abuse and Neglect: Psychology Dept, Trinity College, Hartford. Ct. U.S.A.

Radbill, Samuel, X. A History of Child Abuse and Infanticide: In the Battered Child, Ed. Ray, E. Helfer and C. Henry Kempe, Second Ed. Chicago University Press. 1974.

Reid, J.R. Patterson, G.R. and Loeber, R. The Abused Child: Victim, Instigator or Innocent Bystander? In J. Bernstein Ed. Response, Structure and Organization: Lincoln University. 1982.

Reid, J.R. Patterson, G.R. and Loeber, R. ibid

Regis, H.A: The Theoretical Framework. 1991.

Rutter, M. Stress, Coping and Development: Some Issues and Some Questions: In N. Garmezy and M. Rutter Eds. 1983.

Roche, Jeremy, Rogers, W.S. Child Abuse and Neglect: Facing the Challenge. Better Protection for Children: The Open University. 1992.

Richmond, Mary, E. what is Social Work? N.Y. 1922.

Rogers, Wendy Stainton. Child Abuse and Neglect: Facing the Challenge: The Open University.1992.

Ramkissoon, M. An Investigation of the Physical and Psychological Presence of the Jamaican Father: In Caribbean Childhood: From Research to Action. University of the West Indies. 2003.

Roberts Karen: "Becoming Attached" Warner Books.1994.

Smith, M.G: Culture, Race and Class in the Commonwealth Caribbean. 1984.

Smith, M.D.

Smith, H. and Israel, E. Sibling Incest: a Study of the Dynamics of 25 cases of Child Abuse and Neglect

Shaw, J.A. Child on Child Sexual Abuse: Psychological Perspectives. In Child Abuse and Neglect 2000

Sedlac, A.J. and Broadhurst, D.D. Executive Summary of the Third National Incidence Study of Child Abuse and Neglect. Washington. D.C: U.S. Department of Health and Social Service.1996.

Sedlac, A.J. and Broadhurst, D.D ibid

Sedlac, A.J. and Broadhurst, D.D ibid

Sedlac, A.J and Broadhurst, D.D ibid

Straus, M.A., Gelles, R.J. and Steinmetz. Behind Closed Doors: Violence in the American Family. Garden City. New York. Doubleday. 1980.

Staub, E. Socialization by Parents and Peers and Experiential Learning of Pro-social Behaviour.1979.

Starr, R.H., Jr. Child Abuse. American Psychologist. 1979.

Stevens, D. and Berlinger, L. Harborview Social Work Advocate: Special Techniques for Child Victims 1976

Stuart, A. Separating Together: How Divorce Transforms Families. New York. Guildford Publication.1998.

Sobo, E.J. Abortion Traditions in Rural Jamaica: Social Science and Medicine.1996

Stevens, Joseph, Jr. and Marilyn Matthews. Mother-Child, Father-Child Relationships. Georgia State University.1978.

Sandstrom, C.I. (the Psychology of Childhood and Adolescence. Penguin Books Limited, Harmondsworth, Middlesex, England. 1968.

Sandstrom, C.I. ibid

Schecter, M.D. and Roberge, L. Sexual Exploitation in Child Abuse and Neglect, the Family and the Community. Ed. Helfer, R.E. and Kempe, C.H.Ballinger, Cambridge, Mass. 1976.

Schecter, M.D. and Roberge, L. ibid

Sgroi, S.M. Sexual Molestation of Children: In Children Today. Lexington Mass. Lexington Books. 1975.

Sgroi, S.M. ibid

Stevens, D. And Berlinger, L. Harborview Social Workers Advocate. Special Techniques for Child Victims. 1976.

Salter, A.C. Predators, Rapists and other Sex Offenders. New York. Basic Books. 2003.

Silverman, I.J. International Journal of Offenders Therapy and Comparative Criminology, Vol. 37. 1993.

Stone Carl. Class, Race and Political Behaviour in Urban Jamaica. Kingston: Jamaica Institute of Social and EconomicResearch.1973.

Tanner, J.M. Education and Physical Growth: London University Press. 1961.

Towney, R.H. Equality. 1931.

Timms, N. The Language of Social Casework. Routledge and Kegan Paul. New York. Humanities Press. 1968.

UNICEF in Latin America and the Caribbean 2007

Weber, M. Power and Bureaucracy. Sociological Perspective. Edited by Kenneth Thompson and Jeremy Tunstall. The Open University.1971.

Wolfe, D.A. Child-Abusive Parents. An Empirical Review and Analysis, Psychological Bulleting. 1985.

Wilson, C. and Gellinger, M. Determinants of Child Abuse Reporting among Wisconsin School Psychologists. Professional School of Psychology. 1989.

World Health Organization (WHO) Cost of Caribbean Crime. The Wall Street Journal, May 2007.

Wallace, H. Family Violence. Legal, Medical and Social Perspectives. Needham Heights, MA, Allyn and Bacon. 1966.

Weightman, K. The Department of Health and Social Service Guidelines; Working Together for the Protection of Children from Abuse. "Social Work Today". 1988.

Westneat, D.F. and Sherman, P.W. Parenting and the Evolution of Parental Behaviour; Behavioural Ecology.1993.

Young, L "Wednesday's Child" a Study of Child Abuse and Neglect. New York. Mc Graw-Hill. 1964.

Yegedis, B.L. Family Violence. Contemporary Research Findings and Practice Issues. Community Mental Health Journal. 1992.

Yegedis, B.L. ibid

Zenel, J.A. Failure to Thrive. The General Paediatric Perspective, Paediatric Review. 1997.